THE LIFE AND WORKS OF GLASGOW ARCHITECTS

THE LIFE AND WORKS
OF GLASGOW ARCHITECTS
JAMES MILLER AND JOHN JAMES BURNET

JOHN STEWART

Whittles Publishing

Published by
Whittles Publishing Ltd.,
Dunbeath,
Caithness, KW6 6EG
Scotland, UK
www.whittlespublishing,com

ISBN 978-184995-491-4

Also by the author

Alvar Aalto Architect
Nordic Classicism: Scandinavian Architecture 1910–1930
Twentieth Century Town Halls: Architecture of Democracy
Sir Herbert Baker: Architect to the British Empire

Printed in the UK by Short Run Press

TO MY GRANDSON, WILLIAM MUNRO

CONTENTS

ACKNOWLEDGEMENTS

Researching this book has been a real challenge with neither Burnet nor Miller having a significant archive in any collection. My starting point in both cases has been Professor David Walker's excellent online *Dictionary of Scottish Architects* which has provided both biographical details and listings of projects. This resource has been invaluable. Fortunately, by the 1880's when Burnet and Miller started to build, much of their work was recorded in both the professional and public press and the Royal Institute of British Architects' (RIBA) outstanding collection of architectural publications and photographs in particular, has provided everything from competition entries to published designs and even obituaries, while the British Library has provided me with many hours of background reading.

My original intention was to re-photograph the surviving buildings myself, but unfortunately, this process was rudely interrupted by the global Covid-19 pandemic, which eventually made most travel impossible. I am therefore indebted to numerous photographers who have been kind enough to allow me to use their images in the book. In particular I would like to thank Tom Bastin, David Gray, and Ian Stubbs, who have provided numerous images, and especially Colin Mackenzie, Ian Gilmour and Roger Edwards, who very kindly offered to photograph several Burnet and Miller buildings for me.

Finally, I'd like to thank my wife Sue for her constant encouragement and support, and for checking births, deaths, marriages, newspaper articles, and creating the index, as well as her companionship on numerous building visits.

INTRODUCTION

This is the tale of two Scottish architects – two very different men, from very different backgrounds, who were almost exact contemporaries and thus competitors throughout their professional lives. They were both exceptional architects in an outstanding generation of British architects for whom the wealth of the British Empire created what appeared to be endless opportunities. They both practiced in Glasgow when it was the 'Second City of Empire' and (now somewhat incredibly) one of the most prosperous centres of commerce and industry in the world. This allowed them to pursue and develop their art, and in both cases, to make a substantial contribution to the rich architectural heritage of Britain.

John James Burnet, the son of a successful architect, is simply one of Scotland's greatest artists. During his lifetime he was knighted and received the gold medals of both the RIBA and of the Paris Salon – and yet – there isn't a single publication on his life or work. James Miller is Scotland's most prolific architect – the product of Victorian Glasgow – rising from farmer's son, via the engineers' department of a railway company, to establish and create Scotland's largest architectural practice, designing not only the International Exhibition buildings of 1901 but also Turnberry Hotel, Gleneagles Hotel, Glasgow Central Station, the Institute of Civil Engineers in Westminster and many of Glasgow's city centre banks.

These two outstanding Scottish designers have largely been forgotten by generations of architects and historians who have been indoctrinated into the cult of Modernism. I studied architecture at the Glasgow School of Art and I do not recall any of their buildings being mentioned, studied or visited during my entire course. The few reviews of their work have largely considered it in terms of their contribution to the emergence of Modernism and thus in their *Architecture of Glasgow* Andor Gomme and David Walker identify Burnet's McGeoch's Warehouse in West Campbell Street, as 'a nearly perfect expression of the constructional techniques which Burnet was pioneering'[1] while describing his Glasgow Savings Bank in Ingram Street (one of what I believe to be the finest buildings in Glasgow) as, 'Not a building of charm'[2] while James Miller's buildings are variously described as 'absurdly insignificant'[3] and a 'dreary monster'.[4] Similarly, Audrey Sloan and Gordon Murray's[5] very complimentary though brief book on James Miller, desperately seeks to give his architecture critical weight by similarly characterising him as a pioneer of the Modern movement – suggesting that he disdained ornament and sought to express the function of his buildings above all else, while in reality, Miller's buildings were generally richly decorated and in various traditional styles.

Both men's architecture was highly eclectic and thus perceived to commit the crime of 'lacking consistency' by Modernists, for whom (like the great Victorian Gothic architects) there could be but one true style. They both adopted whatever they believed to be the most relevant architectural style for each building commission – a shared typological eclecticism – and in some cases, such as in Miller's railway stations, even employing contrasting styles for the interior and the exterior of the same building. They both relished, rather than avoided rich sculptural detail and surface ornamentation; indeed, during their early careers their stylistic versatility was particularly highly regarded. Despite making a modest contribution to the development of the Modern movement in Britain in the latter part of their careers they were both extremely capable Victorian eclectics at heart.

The careers of both architects spanned a period of unprecedented architectural change, from the hand-carved stone revivalism of nineteenth-century architecture to the slow emergence of Modernism in Britain in the twentieth century. They were both commercial architects, not individualistic artistic outsiders like Charles Rennie Mackintosh, and their clients were the leading men (and surprisingly often, women) of Glasgow – an elite band of largely self-made individuals who shared directorships of the city's banks, railway companies, and shipyards. It was only natural in this context that they should be just as interested in the architecture of the United States, the emerging industrial capitalist superpower, as they were in the rich architectural heritage and emerging radical trends of old Europe.

Neither architect was ever truly committed to Modernism and while much of their later work certainly moved in that direction (in both cases much influenced by their younger partners) they both returned to Classicism with something like a sense of relief, for their last great buildings – JJ Burnet's 200 St Vincent Street of 1927 and Miller's Commercial Bank in Bothwell Street of 1934–5. Their modest contributions to the emergence of Modern architecture in Britain are among the least of their achievements.

Like most of Glasgow's architecture, their work was built with the proceeds of colonialism. It was deeply symbolic of a laissez-faire entrepreneurial capitalist society and their clients presided over a city that was racked with poverty. They often served but a small, upper strata of the population and yet, even allowing for all this, no-one can deny that their buildings also rank among their country's greatest artistic achievements.

James Miller and JJ Burnet were part of that last great generation of Scottish architects who, along with Mackintosh, Salmon, Campbell, Mitchell, Anderson, Keppie and Leiper, contributed the best of what remains of Glasgow after the loss of so much to post-war planning and comprehensive redevelopment. Burnet is simply one of the best architects that Scotland has ever produced – while Miller is the country's most prolific. Like Charles Rennie Mackintosh, they deserve to be household names in the country of their birth and their buildings celebrated and preserved for future generations to appreciate.

CHAPTER 1: 1857–1877

In 1857, Scotland was one of the wealthiest countries in the world and, as home to almost 40 per cent of the country's citizens, Glasgow was the vast machine that was driving the country forward. Its population had overtaken that of Edinburgh, the country's capital city, a few years earlier in 1851 and at 450,000 residents, Glasgow was considerably larger than both Manchester and Birmingham and thus second only to mighty London, which then had a population of 2.7 million as the capital of the vast British Empire.(1)

Glasgow's industry had expanded dramatically during the previous hundred years, diversifying from trading in tobacco and cotton (both the products of slavery in the United States), to the establishment of an industrial base that itself was now moving away from distilling, soap, glass, and textiles and into heavy engineering and shipbuilding. New foundries fed by local coal brought by rail from the mines of Lanarkshire and Ayrshire were producing iron in vast quantities both for further local manufacture and for export to every corner of the Empire. Glasgow was fast becoming the workshop of the world and its growth and wealth were now inextricably linked to the continuing expansion and extraordinary success of the British Empire.

From the opening of the first Scottish railway from Monkland to Kirkintilloch in 1826, a profusion of private railway companies using various gauges of track sprang up linking towns, cities, and regions, most of which were eventually subsumed within either the North British Railway Company (established in Edinburgh in 1844) or the Caledonian Railway Company (which was founded in Glasgow in 1845). It was the Caledonian that was the first to connect Edinburgh and Glasgow by rail in 1848, the same year that they also linked their network to the English rail system via Carlisle. St Rollox Locomotive Works was founded by the Caledonian Railway Company in Springburn in 1856 and they were soon not only supplying the Caledonian Railway but also, increasingly, railway systems across the Empire, with the people of Glasgow witnessing the almost daily sight of new rolling stock being transported through the city streets to the banks of the Clyde, where the massive Finnieston Crane would lift the locomotives onto the steam ships which would transport them onwards to almost every corner of the world.

While boatbuilding had been carried out on the Clyde for centuries, the first commercial shipyards to build iron steamships were also founded at this time. Denny's shipyard on the River

Leven was founded in 1844, followed by Scott and McGill in Bowling Harbour in 1851. Robert Napier and Sons had been building the fastest steam ship engines in the world since the 1820s and in 1864 Napier founded his own shipbuilding company, Fairfields in Govan on the back of a large Royal Navy contract. John Brown's famous shipyard in Clydebank was opened in 1871 and Lithgow's in Port Glasgow in 1874, and by the end of the century these companies and the others on the Clyde would be responsible for generating a third of the entire world's ships' tonnage.(2)

Fig. 1   A horse-drawn tram heads west down nineteenth–century Sauchiehall Street. Courtesy of Mason Photographic Collection.

Workers flooded to Glasgow from across Scotland and Ireland, soon making it the most over-crowded and one of the unhealthiest cities in Britain, with both cholera and typhoid epidemics regularly breaking out to such an extent that for much of the nineteenth century, life expectancy was on a steep decline from the already low level of 42 years for men and 45 years for women of the 1820s, very largely driven by the appalling levels of child mortality that affected almost every Glaswegian family of all classes. 'Simply living in the city was damaging to health'.(3)

Glasgow was expanding rapidly in all directions as its population soared and soon its old historic centre – the Merchant City – was extended to the west with a new grid of streets which fortuitously, was much enlivened by Glasgow's various minor hills (Fig. 1). The central business district thus swept up from the new George Square onto and over Blythswood Hill and onwards to the West End of the city where the homes of the wealthy were spared the smoke of a thousand furnaces by their exposure to the Atlantic's westerly breezes. While ships packed the busy quays of the Clyde, gas lights shone in the streets and horse-drawn carriages struggled up the cobbled hills and as if in celebration of its new-found wealth, Glasgow's great contribution to the history of civic and commercial architecture had commenced.

In 1857, Alexander 'Greek' Thomson (1817–75) one of Britain's greatest architects, was at the height of his powers. He had just completed the Caledonia Road Church and construction was underway on his St Vincent Street Church, his finest house *Holmwood* and his highly original Walmer Crescent. Charles Wilson (1810-63) led the supporting cast that followed Thomson, with the towers of his recently completed Free Church College on the side of Woodlands Hill dominating the skyline in the west of the city, while perhaps his most famous work, Park Circus, which crowned the very top of the hill, was then under construction. Close on his heels was John Burnet (1814–1901).

The son of a soldier, Burnet had been apprenticed as a carpenter before becoming a clerk of works and eventually, with the Italianate design of the Free Church in Alloa of 1844, a self-taught architect. After completing an almost identical church in Clackmannan, he moved to Glasgow, where he soon established a successful practice. By 1857, he was a highly regarded architect in the city, having completed one of his finest buildings, the mighty Ionic temple which was Elgin Place Church, 'the purest example of the neo-classic in Glasgow,'(4) the previous year (Fig. 2).(5) He had married Elizabeth Hay Bennet, the highly ambitious daughter of a Leith merchant, in 1845 and they and their two sons, George and Lindsay, lived in some style at 97 West Regent Street on Blythswood Hill in the centre of the city, where they were served by a cook, housemaid, nurse, and nursery maid. On 31 May 1857, Elizabeth gave birth to a third son, who was named after his father – John James Burnet. (J. J. Burnet).

Seventy miles north of Glasgow in rural Perthshire, George Miller was working as an inn-keeper and farmer at New Inn Farm, Auchtergaven, where, on 11 July 1860, his wife Betsy gave birth to their first son, James. Soon after James' birth, his father took up a new position as a tenant farmer to the Earl of Kinnoull at Upper Cairnie Farm on his estate at Dupplin Castle near the village of Forteviot. It was a much-improved position that entailed a fine two-storey stone farmhouse for his family and responsibility for the management of a 260-acre arable farm. Soon young James was joined by three sisters and two younger brothers; George was employing six

Fig. 2   John Burnet Snr.'s neo-classical Elgin Place Church, prior to its demolition. Courtesy Wikimedia Commons.

men and a boy on the farm and Betsy had two staff of her own to help run their growing household. James turned out to be a bright boy and was soon walking the two miles each day to the local village school in Forteviot, where he excelled.

Young John Burnet's education was a much more considered affair, as his family were relatively wealthy and the city offered many more options than the countryside. Indeed, the only constraint upon their choice of educational institution for young John was their own strict religious beliefs, as both John Burnet Snr. and Elizabeth were devout Congregationalists. The Congregational Union of Scotland had been formed in 1812 with the twin aims of church aid and home mission, and as strict Calvinists they were thus at the forefront of the local temperance movement. They rejected all forms of church hierarchy and any connection between Church and State, and believed in the complete autonomy of each local congregation to run their own affairs, (including the election of their own minister). Suffice to say, their youngest son was to have the strictest of upbringings, with his education starting at the Collegiate School on Garnethill before a few years at the Western Academy in Kelvinbridge, from where he moved on to commence his secondary education as a boarder at the then highly exclusive Blair Lodge School in Polmont, near Falkirk.(6) Founded in 1841 by the Reverend Robert Cunningham (who had earlier founded Stewart's Melville College in Edinburgh), it advertised its aim as 'religious instruction to make Bible Christians, without reference to denominational peculiarities.'(7) By the time that John Burnet attended, it was already successfully attracting the sons of Scotland's rich and famous, providing the typically Victorian menu of religion, sport, and the type of severe discipline to which his parents entirely subscribed.

James Miller's secondary education was to be at the less fashionable Perth Academy (founded in 1542) who's entrance exam he easily passed and whose fees his now successful tenant farmer father could fortunately afford. The fine Classical main Academy building of 1807 by King's Surveyor Robert Reid (1774–1856) overlooking the North Inch and River Tay, was enough to inspire any schoolboy with more than the slightest interest in architecture, and while his studies were broad, in the Scottish tradition, they had mathematics and science at their core (Fig. 3). He travelled from Forteviot station each day to Perth by the Scottish Central Railway and every week he would pay his teachers their tuition fees directly himself. By the standards of the time, it was an excellent preparation for a life in the service of the Empire, either at home in one of the professions, or abroad, protecting and extending its vast and growing boundaries.

By the start of the 1870s the sons of John Burnet had already decided upon their professions, with the eldest, George, destined for the law, Lindsay already committed to engineering and young John (no doubt with some parental encouragement), opting for architecture. In those days there were no full-time university architecture courses (indeed, the only contemporary Glasgow architect who is known to have attended university was John Honeyman, who originally studied for the Ministry) and the education of an architect was built around a pupillage of three or four years during which he (and back then it was always 'he') would learn from his master while attending evening classes that (depending largely on where he lived) would vary from basic construction and engineering to the fine art of architecture. Once architecture had been decided upon, John Burnet Snr saw no benefit in his son completing his secondary education and he thus left Blair Lodge at the age of fourteen years in the summer of 1871, to join his father's office. It was never however, John Burnet Snr's intention that John James should be his pupil, as he wanted the best possible architectural education available for his son, whom he hoped would become his successor in the family business.

Fig. 3   Robert Reid's Academy building of 1807 on
the North Inch in Perth. Courtesy of Timon Rose.

The level of architectural education available in Glasgow at that time was extremely limited. The Glasgow School of Art had only one lecturer in architecture and much of the extra-office teaching consisting of listening to papers read at the Glasgow Institute of Architects and attending a technical college. John Burnet Snr therefore looked to London for his son's professional education, with the initial idea of securing him a pupillage with one of the city's most fashionable practices, which would allow him to study at either the South Kensington Museum, the Architectural Association or the Royal Academy or, as was becoming increasingly popular, attending all these schools to cover the broadest possible range of relevant subjects. Accordingly, he discussed the best option with Richard Phené Spiers, the master of the Architecture School at the Royal Academy of Arts. To his surprise and consternation, Spiers proposed that if suitable funds were available (and they were), John James should attend Phené Spiers alma mater, the *École Nationale Supérieure des Beaux Arts* in Paris (Fig. 4).

The thought of sending his impressionable young protestant son to Paris was abhorrent to Congregationalist John Burnet. After all, France was a Catholic country and as for nineteenth-century Paris itself – why, it was simply a den of vice and immorality. It was not an option. However, on hearing that the École was the world's best school of architecture, his wife Eliza soon persuaded her husband that they must do what was best for their son regardless of the risk, and so in the autumn of 1872, still filled with trepidation as to his son's future moral wellbeing, John Burnet personally travelled with young John James to 'The City of Light'.

With Phené Spiers advice and assistance, a place in the atelier of Jean Louis Pascal had been procured for young John as a probationer from where he would study at the Ecole, if he were accepted. JJ Burnet later recalled their first meeting:

Fig. 4   The courtyard of the École des Beaux Arts in Paris. Courtesy of KoS.

He had just succeeded Lefuel as Chief Inspector on the building for the completion of the Louvre. I was but a boy, and perhaps even younger than my years, but I will never forget the sight of the short, well-built man, his coat off, and a cigar in his mouth, who rose from his desk and advanced to meet us, as one of his assistants led us up the long and lofty gallery, which formed his office in the new buildings, to present our letter of introduction from his former pupil Phené Spiers. His fine, intellectual head with his rather long black hair and keen though kindly eyes, and his beautiful courtesy as he greeted my father in perfect English as a brother artist, immediately won my admiration, and I felt that he was just the type of man one would expect to create such work as I had seen and delighted in on my arrival in Paris; and one under whom it would be a privilege to study. To me he seemed then, and I still believe he was, the ideal type of architect, eminently sympathetic, breathing efficiency, and prepared to spend himself in understanding the needs of his day and generation, and giving them artistic expression.(8)

It was arranged that John James would board with the family of another student, Henri Paul Nénot, who was four years older and just completing his studies. Then, with the arrangements completed, John Burnet Snr, no doubt racked with doubts, caught the boat train back for London and Glasgow. After a year in Pascal's studio, John James successfully passed the entrance examination for the École and commenced his studies.

John Burnet Snr. had been well advised, as the *École des Beaux Arts* was then the world's undisputed leading school of art. The origins of its architecture school lay in the *Académie Royale d'Architecture*, which was established in 1671 during the reign of Louis XIV with the aim of assuring the highest level of taste for royal buildings. At first, its members met weekly to discuss architectural theory and practice as well as providing public lectures on architectural matters such as geometry, perspective, and stone cutting, but early in the eighteenth century these lectures had coalesced into a two or three-year course of study. By the end of the nineteenth century the Academy's School of Architecture had developed a highly structured design methodology that was built on the atelier system, with each student joining the atelier of a leading architect who also taught at the school. Students were not required to attend lectures but instead, from their first day, were set design projects that were treated as competitions. John James joined as a *nouveau* and as such would be given 'second-class' building types to design – single houses, a small library or school – earning a 'value' or medal, when a jury of professional architects judged that his design proposal had reached an acceptable standard. He progressed quickly to the next stage: '*ancien*', at which point he was set 'first-class' building types to design, such as an opera house, palace or museum. Every project was expected to be developed in the language of Classicism and the study of the great books of Classical architecture such as Vignola's *Five Orders of Architecture*,(9) were essential to the development of an understanding of every aspect of the style.

Even the method of developing a design was prescribed in detail, with students having to quickly produce an '*esquisse*', which was a sketch that was to contain all the key elements of their proposed solution. Once their e*squisse* was accepted, an appropriate Classical order would be selected and the design further developed until it was presented as an '*analytique*', which would be beautifully rendered in monochrome, before finally developing the design fully in plan, section, and elevation, in a coloured *analytique rendu*'. The standards expected were exceptionally high, and beautifully composed drawings with immaculate draftsmanship and perfectly rendered shadows were required of all students if they were to receive medals for their work. It was a methodology that, perhaps unsurprisingly, would stay with Burnet all his life, with a particular emphasis on the *esquisse*, which he continued to use to capture the essence of a design solution quickly and succinctly, while the entire educational process provided him with a solid grounding in the language of Classical architecture, in which he would later excel.

By all accounts, Burnet distinguished himself – as a later wealthy Scottish *nouveau* at the school, Alexander Paterson, confirmed, Burnet left, 'behind him the reputation of a hard working student of equal brilliance in design and construction'.(10) His father's fears that his son would be led astray by the bright lights and temptations of Paris also proved groundless, as his moral rectitude soon earned him the nickname 'Joseph' among his fellow students, while his ruddy Scots complexion prompted the sobriquet '*confiture de groseilles*'. His friendships with both Pascal and Nénot, as well as with several wealthy American fellow students, would last their lifetimes. He obtained his *diplômé par le gouvernement* in Architecture and Engineering in the summer of 1876 and, after working for several months in the Paris office of another architect, François Rolland, he departed upon the type of grand tour which was then regarded as the natural conclusion of one's studies at the École. This was extensive and covered much of France as well as the great Renaissance cities of Italy, before he finally undertook the journey home to a wintry Glasgow in December 1876, in time to spend Christmas with his family, prior to starting work with his father in the new year.

CHAPTER 2: 1877–1889

At the start of 1877, John Burnet Snr's practice was flourishing, and since the death of the pre-eminent Alexander Thomson two years previously he led his profession in Glasgow along with James Sellars and John Honeyman (with Sir Robert Rowand Anderson dominant in Edinburgh). His Glasgow Stock Exchange building was complete and in operation and the economy of the city, like that of the great Empire that it served, was advancing in leaps and bounds, thus providing its architects with a constant flow of opportunities to celebrate both its commercial success, private wealth and, occasionally, public spirit. Burnet's now well-educated and well-travelled son was made a junior partner on his arrival back in the office and, with his new-fangled continental ideas seems to have made an immediate impact on the work of the practice.

Burnet Snr had been commissioned to provide a new façade to the great banking hall of Lanarkshire House on Ingram Street (now the Corinthian Club), which had originally been designed by David Hamilton in 1841. While the complex Baroque façade with its screen of free-standing granite Corinthian columns would have been well developed and under construction by the spring of 1877, its mighty decorated doorway shows a first hint of the work of John Burnet Jr (Fig. 5). Comparing it with his father's earlier Clydesdale Bank in St Vincent Place of 1870, it suggests a freer hand was at work. In the Clydesdale Bank the main entrance is set within a relatively modest recessed arch, albeit lavishly detailed like the rest of the façade. Above, is a broken segmental pediment and this element is repeated on the main entrance in Ingram Street. But in Ingram Street there is a new vigour and boldness to the composition. Here the pediment is supported on heavy carved consoles complete with scrolled shields (which would have looked perfectly at home in contemporary Paris), while the coat of arms of the bank is proudly displayed by two topless maidens who look brazenly down at passers-by. In the Clydesdale Bank the pediment provides a frame for a carved coat of arms, whereas in Ingram Street (where John Burnet Jr. had surely been at work), the architecture and John Mossman's (1817–90) sculpture is completely integrated into a single composition. This doorway and the boldly projecting eaves and balustrade high above can therefore safely be regarded as the first built work of JJ Burnet. On its final completion in 1879 it provoked favourable comments, with

Fig. 5   J. J. Burnet's first built work – the door surround to his
father's Lanarkshire House of 1877. Courtesy of Dauvit Alexander.

The Glasgow Herald regarding 'the new front [as] one of the most striking architectural features
of a neighbourhood particularly rich in fine buildings.'(1)

As well as representing JJ Burnet's first contribution to the architecture of Glasgow, his work
on Lanarkshire House also constituted his first collaboration with the great John Mossman. John
Mossman was the son of William Mossman, who had founded the family firm of J&G Mossman
monumental sculptors, along with John's brother, George. John was the pre-eminent sculptor of
nineteenth-century Glasgow, contributing hugely to the city's architecture, public monuments,
and its famous Necropolis cemetery, and also one of the founders of both the Glasgow School of
Art and the Glasgow Institute of Fine Arts; he had regularly collaborated with Alexander Thomson,
who was a close friend of his. In fact it was Thomson who had designed Mossman's sculpture
studio. For the young JJ Burnet it would have been a privilege to work with this great artist and
master craftsman and without Mossman and what Burnet Jr. learned from him, it is unlikely that

the integration of sculpture and architecture in his early work (which was to become one of his greatest strengths) would have been so successfully achieved.

John Burnet Snr., who was now sixty-four years old, quickly gave his son a leading role in the office. It was certainly nepotism within what he hoped would become a family firm, but he was also discerning enough to recognise that his son's abilities were already rather special. Accordingly, from this point on, John Burnet Jr. had the pick of the work and was also responsible for most of the practice's architectural competition entries, and Burnet Snr did not have to wait long for his son's first success.

On his part, James Miller, having excelled in both art and science at Perth Academy, had also been guided towards a career in architecture. His father secured and paid for a pupillage for him with Andrew Heiton Jr., Perth's most prominent architect, and from July 1877 he continued to travel from Forteviot each day by train, but now to Heiton's office at 72 George Street. Miller was fortunate in his master, as Heiton was a successful and well-connected regional architect as well as a notable historian, with an excellent library and fine collection of antiques, which he displayed in his ancient tower house at Darnick that he had inherited and restored. He was responsible not only for Miller's employment but also for his architectural education, and while his own work was invariably in the Scottish Baronial style, he was in touch with architectural developments in Glasgow (his proposers for a fellowship of the RIBA being no less than John Honeyman, John Baird, and James Salmon Snr). Heiton's practice covered country and suburban houses, railway stations, banks, and churches, and the experience Miller gained in the office was supplemented by evening classes in building science at the local technical college. By the standards of the day, it was a good, solid architectural education.(2)

Glasgow, however, remained the crucible of Scottish architectural development and in 1878 an architectural competition was held for the design of an exhibition building on Sauchiehall Street for the recently formed Glasgow Institute of Fine Arts. To the astonishment of his elders, it was young JJ Burnet's entry that was selected and, with funds already donated, his design proceeded quickly to construction. His proposal offered a Classical response to the competition brief, but it was a style of Classicism that had an academic purity that was entirely new to Glasgow (Fig. 6). It was a typical Beaux Arts *analytique rendu,* but now erected full-size on Sauchiehall Street. Its largely blank façade, containing the top-lit galleries, rose from a sharply rusticated base to a giant Ionic order intertwined with a carved frieze, *Artists at Work by* John Mossman, with the entire composition brought to its climax above its central entrance by a pediment supporting a towering *Athena, Goddess of the Arts,* sculpted by Mossman. And yet, there is something in this untypically horizontal piece of imported scholarship that makes it Glaswegian, too. The entire façade is like a single sandstone wall into which has been carved the architectural detail (much in the style of Thomson's incised decoration), and it thus offers a fascinating insight into the young Burnet's combination of continental architectural education and considerable local knowledge, even at the very start of his career. (Regrettably, like his father's excellent Elgin Place Church, we can no longer enjoy this early work, as like the church, it was demolished after a fire, in this case in 1967).

Fig. 6   J. J. Burnet's first building
design – the Glasgow Institute of Fine
Arts building of 1878. Courtesy of the
Mason Photographic Collection

1878 ended with a commercial disaster for the city, when on 2 October one of the city's most popular and apparently successful banks, the City of Glasgow Bank, refused withdrawals and closed its doors. It was an unlimited company whose dividends of between 9 and 12 per cent had attracted investors from right across the city and beyond; all of whom now found that they were liable for its considerable debts. As J. M. Reid explains in his book on the history of Glasgow, 'Those whose fortunes survived paid up to 2750 per cent. Depression swept over the wintry city. Factories closed, buildings stood half-completed. The directors were tried for fraud and imprisoned.'(3) It was the first check in the city's apparently relentlessly advancing prosperity and had a glacial effect on investment for several years, during which the city's architects, among many others, felt the icy chill. In a show of confidence and civic leadership, the City Council proposed to counter the depression after the bank collapse by announcing that they would build new council chambers on a site on George Square (proposed by City Architect John Carrick), on a scale that would rival any other town hall building in the world. In 1880 an architectural competition was held, with John Burnet's practice among the ninety-eight entrants, but it was George Corson (1829–1910) a Leeds-based Scottish architect, whose design was selected to proceed in July.

James Miller completed his pupillage in Perth that summer, and to broaden his experience he left both Andrew Heiton's practice and his home for the first time, securing a position in Edinburgh with Hippolyte Jean Blanc, who himself had only recently left the government Office of Works to establish his own practice on fashionable George Street in the city centre. Like Heiton, he was much involved with various antiquarian societies, and indeed Miller's master may have provided his pupil with an introduction. Like so many other architects of the period,

Blanc had founded his practice on a competition win – in his case Christ Church Episcopal Church in the salubrious Edinburgh suburb of Morningside. His design was in a particularly muscular and richly modelled Gothic style that soon brought him several further church commissions across the city and beyond. Blanc's work would have provided Miller with an introduction to the Gothic style after several years of a strictly Scottish Baronial diet with Heiton, as well as his first experience of life alone in the capitol, and yet within a year, we find him back in Perth, having accepted a position with the Engineering Department of the Caledonian Railway under the engineer John Morrison Barr. After a number of years in private practice and at such an early stage in his career, it may have seemed an unusual move to join a company where his workload would be limited more or less to a single building type, but the ambitious young man clearly viewed the Caledonian Railway Company as a successful, fast-growing business where he could progress quickly on merit, without the need for family connections or significant personal financial investment.

Based in Glasgow, by the early 1880s the Caledonian Railway had established itself (largely through something of a frenzy of acquisitions of smaller private railway companies) as the main provider of train services from Scotland to England. Its routes also linked Aberdeen to London and Glasgow to Edinburgh, and in 1879 it had opened Glasgow Central Station in the very heart of the city. One of the Caledonian Railway's acquisitions was the Scottish Central Railway, which had been based in Perth and which had built the station there. It was their network, running north of Perth to Dundee and Aberdeen and beyond, and also east to Stirling, on which James Miller would have started to work. Perth station itself was much extended at this time and numerous further, entirely new stations were built as the Caledonian Railway both rationalised its network and continued to compete with its great rival, Edinburgh's North British Railway Company.

With his flying start and on the strength of his diplôme from the École, John Burnet was accepted as an associate of the RIBA on 3 January 1881, having been proposed by John Honeyman, Sir Charles Barry (the architect of the Houses of Parliament) and his father, and that spring he embarked on a second European tour, on this occasion in the company of his advocate brother, George. The following year a second competition was held for the design of the new Glasgow Council Chambers as George Corson's previous winning entry had been rejected by the Council on the grounds of cost, and on this occasion, John Burnet Jr. was entrusted with the design of the firm's entry.

For this second competition, the City Architect, John Carrick laid down strict conditions in terms of the building's height and width, and also added the requirement for a massive central tower (stolen from Corson's previous winning design). JJ Burnet broke almost all the competition rules by offering a superb reworking of *Les Invalides* in Paris, complete with a dome and steeply pitched roofs, all of which were compressed into Carrick's specified dimensions. The dome alone disqualified it, but the exercise (if rather reckless from the firm's perspective) did offer a first version of Burnet Jr.'s *ancien régime* Classicism (which would later reappear in his Charing Cross Mansions of 1891), albeit with a lively vertical rather than traditionally expansive horizontal emphasis. Any disappointment over their failure to secure the vast City Chambers commission (which was won by William Young, 1843–1900) was tempered by JJ Burnet's successful competition entry for the Clyde Navigation Trust building later that same year in 1882. It was an achievement which would earn him a full partnership in the practice and see it proudly renamed John Burnet & Son.

The Clyde Navigation Trust had been formed in 1858, superseding the earlier River Improvement Trust, to enable Glasgow's shipbuilders, merchants, and industrialists jointly to manage the river, its banks, and its trade. The site that they had acquired for their new offices was appropriately on the Broomielaw, which ran along the north bank of the river, with the greater length of the site stretching north up Robertson Street towards the city centre. John James' proposed design offered a pedimented main entrance on Robertson Street (which had strong echoes of the central entrance section of the Fine Arts Institute) from where the building continued down towards the Broomielaw, with a striking square Italianate clock tower marking the corner and providing a landmark for the Trust, which would be seen from up and down their river. It was soon decided that the building should be completed in two phases, starting with the main entrance section along Robertson Street. While this first phase was not completed until 1886, all the principal elements of Burnet's design are there in his 1882 competition entry and after the Classical restraint of his Fine Arts building on Sauchiehall Street, the Clyde Trust building includes many of the elements of his more vigorous mature style (despite his being only twenty-five years old at the time of this design) (Fig. 7). He had clearly already grasped what it took to succeed in the tall sandstone

Fig. 7 J. J. Burnet's Clyde Navigational Trust building of 1882–6. Courtesy of Andrew B.

Fig. 8   Detail of the rich sculptural modelling of the Clyde
Navigational Trust building. Courtesy of Roger Edwards.

canyons of central Glasgow – the need for richly modelled façades with real depth to capture the weak northern light and to provide interest when viewed obliquely from pavement level; the role that sculpture could play in this quest, as an integral part of the design as in Baroque architecture, rather than as a superficial addition; the opportunities for expression that carved sandstone could offer over the mechanical regularity of the cast-iron frame; and the extraordinary vitality that a designer of his ability could still extract from the language of Classicism.

As in the Fine Arts Institute, the *piano nobile* is raised to second-floor level above a crisply rusticated base, where here a Corinthian temple expresses the importance of the principal interior space – the boardroom. Above its pediment sits *Father Clyde*, supported by the sea gods *Poseidon* and *Triton*, brilliantly sculpted once more by John Mossman. But it is within this already impressive framework that Burnet's brilliance and originality is first fully expressed; in the carved prows of the boats that flank the main entrance and project out over the pavement as a symbol of the building's role; in the blank tablets below the first-floor windows that boldly interrupt the keystones of the ground-floor arches, and, most interestingly of all, in the first-floor window aedicules that project right up to second-floor level, where they are transformed into balconies to serve the unusually high windows of the boardroom (Fig. 8). This is the work of a very confident young man who is revelling in bringing a new level of cosmopolitan sophistication

Fig. 9   J. J. Burnet's Drumsheugh Turkish Baths in Edinburgh of 1852. Courtesy of David Gray.

to his home town. The quality of the (very well-preserved) internal spaces is equally high, as Pevsner confirmed: 'the interior, complete with original furnishings, light fittings and mostly heraldic stained glass though splendidly rich, is beautifully controlled, with none of the showy eclecticism of the contemporary City Chambers'.(4)

As if his virtuoso Classical performance on the Clyde Navigation Trust building was not impressive enough, in 1882 he next produced a Moorish design for the Drumsheugh Turkish Baths on a difficult sloping site in Edinburgh (Fig. 9). Here he offered a deeply overhanging entrance roof on great sandstone brackets along with something of the Alhambra in Spain in the interior, which boasted arched masonry colonnades with his own version of carved oriental column capitals, pierced stone friezes and Moghul ironwork. It was a piece of rather ostentatious exhibitionism from an extraordinarily skilled and confident young architect.

J. J. Burnett was already making a name for himself and his next commission for two terraces of houses for Glasgow University teaching staff on what is now University Gardens, would further enhance his growing reputation. The first terrace, which curved gently around what was then called Saughfield Crescent was for numbers 2 to 10, and took the form of three-storey Classical townhouses with deeply channelled rustication to their ground floors and smooth ashlar above (Fig. 10). Their principal feature was a continuous first-floor stone balustraded balcony supported

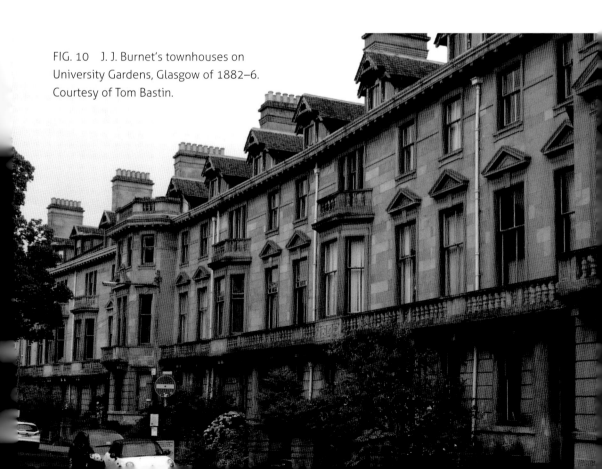

FIG. 10   J. J. Burnet's townhouses on
University Gardens, Glasgow of 1882–6.
Courtesy of Tom Bastin.

on paired stone brackets, which spanned the entire length of the terrace between three full-height canted bay windows on either end, with the balustrade – highly originally – also forming the base of each house's first-floor bay window. A deeply overhanging, continuous, modillioned cornice topped off the ashlar wall plane, which continued around the great canted bays below a stone balustraded parapet. Opposite, on what was Sauchfield Terrace, Burnet built numbers eleven to twenty-five, (of which fifteen to twenty-five were demolished to make way for one of the ugliest concrete buildings in Glasgow, which itself has now, fortunately, been replaced). Here Burnet dispensed with the continuous balcony but retained the first-floor bay windows, which now alternated with shared ground-floor Tuscan Doric entrance porticos. The end of this terrace, where the building turns onto University Avenue, is treated as another full-height canted bay, but here with a delightful composition behind it, in which the blank gable end is extruded to become stone chimneys at roof level, between which a glazed attic floor weaves in and out. The interiors were equally fine, with columned entrance halls, decorated plasterwork and pedimented fireplaces, all of which have survived in numbers two and four. Burnet's starting point was almost certainly Charles Wilson's curved Park Terrace of 1855, but where Wilson's design is very much a curved wall plane with features added, Burnet's design has a sculpted three-dimensional plasticity that makes it much more architecturally convincing and engaging.

The two terraces were built in sections between 1882 and 1886, which otherwise proved to be something of a lean period for the Burnet practice. After the bank crash there were fewer opportunities to pursue, and even worse, the next few years were characterised by a string of competition failures for the firm, including the Glasgow Sick Children's dispensary, Coats Memorial Baptist Church in Paisley, St Andrews Free Church in Edinburgh and the Birmingham Law Courts. The son of a wealthy Glasgow merchant, John Archibald Campbell had joined the practice as a pupil in 1877 and on the advice of John Burnet Snr, had also attended the École des Beaux-Arts in Paris, returning to the practice with his diplôme in 1883. Despite the tough times, he was having some success in bringing in work to the practice and after winning the competition for Shawlands Parish Church on his own account in 1885, he was offered a partnership in the firm, which thus now evolved into John Burnet, Son & Campbell. His appointment seems to have proved a catalyst for the new team and in quick succession they won their first commission from Glasgow University, the first phase of The Athenaeum, opposite Burnet Snr's Stock Exchange building (on what is now Nelson Mandela Place), and the competition for the Edinburgh International Exhibition of Industry, Science and Art to be held in 1886. This massive project for exhibition buildings (while hardly their finest hour architecturally), represented a large and much needed commission and created a substantial workload and income for the firm. The main pavilion was topped, or to be more accurate dwarfed, by a massive 36-metre-high dome which was decorated with the signs of the zodiac, behind which were ranks of vaulted top-lit galleries displaying the latest wares from around Europe, including everything from Glasgow steam engines to Turkish embroidery and Hungarian violins. Without a great deal of competition, the architectural highlight of the exhibition was the recreation of a seventeenth-century Edinburgh street, which was demolished along with everything else when the exhibition closed in autumn 1886. Nevertheless, with 2.5 million visitors, the publicity did its architect's reputation no harm at all.

JJ Burnet's building for Glasgow University – a long, low, rather medieval, Students Union building (now the McIntyre Building) on University Avenue, was much more successful both architecturally and in terms of the practice's establishment of what was to be a long and mutually beneficial relationship with this key city institution. The Glasgow Athenaeum (which was modelled on Sir Charles Barry's earlier building in Manchester), had been founded in 1847 to provide classes on a broad range of subjects aimed at young Glasgow businessmen and professionals (Fig. 11). The new building was to be their base in the city centre and John Burnet Jr. produced another symmetrical composition, albeit with little of the strength or bravura of the Navigational Trust Building (and probably on a small proportion of its budget, too). Perhaps inspired by his friend Henri Paul Nénot's Grand Prix design for an Athenée or John Honeyman's Barony North Church of 1878, a fine rusticated ground floor with flanking entrances gives way to a rather Mannerist main floor in which three arched windows are contained within four engaged Ionic columns, which support four sculpted figures by Mossman. (There are many more impressive examples of this particular treatment, including David Bryce's magnificent British Linen Bank of 1846–51 on St Andrew's Square in Edinburgh).

The new partnership was gaining momentum and in 1886, Burnet and Campbell's joint entry for the competition for Barony Parish Church (now the ceremonial hall of Strathclyde University)

FIG. 11   The first phase of J. J. Burnet's Athenaeum
building in Glasgow of 1886. Courtesy of Tom Bastin.

FIG. 12   Burnet and Campbell's Barony Church of 1886. Courtesy of David Gray.

was selected (Fig. 12). Their design was clearly a development of Campbell's earlier, rather sturdy, Shawlands Old Parish Church, which itself was much influenced by the ancient gothic Dunblane Cathedral, but under Burnet's guiding hand their Barony Church is, to quote Gomme and Walker, 'a much more powerful building, unquestionably the most important Victorian Gothic church in Glasgow, perhaps even in Scotland'.(5) While the exterior has a primitive severity, the great soaring space of the nave manages to combine the feeling of an ancient kirk with a delicacy of Gothic detail below a particularly fine, timber hammer-beam roof. All in all, this was another considerable achievement for two young architects in their late twenties.

There is little doubt that Burnet and Campbell worked closely together on the Barony Church but any thoughts that this might lead to a mutually stimulating artistic collaboration on the design of the practice's future buildings were quickly thwarted as the two architects almost immediately established their own independent teams and workload within the office (even submitting separate entries for the same architectural competition on several occasions). It was a marriage of convenience for both and their characters were very different from each other – Burnet was a devout Calvinist for whom hard work and discipline were central to his faith, and Campbell, who was a tall, quiet, bearded man who enjoyed both golf and a drink or two afterwards. Like almost every other architectural principal of the period, each worked alone in their separate offices supported by leading assistants who managed further assistants and pupils, very much along the lines of the master/pupil relationship of the École. Thomas Tait's recollection of his first meeting with Burnet confirms the philosophy:

> His room in 239 St Vincent Street, Glasgow, with its sculpture work and paintings, had a dignity, charm and order very unusual in an architect's office. After examining my drawings, he allowed me to enter his office because 'I appeared to have the capacity for work'. That was one of the essentials he expected from all who worked under him. 'If you work by the hour' he would say, 'you become a mere labourer.' His office was like a studio, where any evening one would find the men at work, all enthusiastically trying to carry out his ideas. His influence on his assistants was enormous. He had the power of instilling a vital enthusiasm in his men, and even workmen with whom he came into contact.(6)

If Burnet's relationship with Campbell was one of necessity, the other principal relationship in his life at this time, which also developed into a contractual partnership in 1886, was much more genuine. It was with Jean Watt Marwick. From John Burnet's perspective, she must have seemed to offer him everything – 'a classic late Victorian beauty with an enchanting smile',(7) her family were Congregationalists just as devout as his, and what's more, she was the youngest of four daughters of one of the most influential men in Glasgow – Sir James Marwick, who had been the Town Clerk of Edinburgh before he was headhunted by Glasgow Town Council in 1873 to become their Town Clerk, at three times the salary. He had already initiated the construction of the City Chambers and over the next two decades he would go on to occupy a unique place in the municipal, literary, and social life of the city until his eventual retirement in 1904. By many measures their marriage was a success, with Jean proving a wonderful hostess when required, but sadly, she was also disposed to hypochondria and spent much of her time in bed. Even more sadly for them both, there were to be no children of the union.

While the construction of the vast baronial country houses that had entertained his father was largely over, JJ Burnet started to produce a string of more modest country homes for his Glasgow clients. In 1886 he remodelled Auchterarder House and added a little gem of a Queen Anne gatehouse; he designed the rather severe Ledcameroch in Kilwinning for Robert Craig King – a two-storey sandstone villa with single projecting two-storey angled bay window, and the much more interesting Corrienessan on Loch Ard for Hugh Kennedy, a railway contractor. Here, on a slightly raised site overlooking the loch, he produced a low, bull-faced red sandstone villa with half-timbered gables, with a broad (rather 'Prairie style') deep veranda wrapping around the corner of the building. The interior was as rich as any of his Glasgow buildings, with carved timber balusters, richly moulded ceilings, and stone fireplaces, amidst acres of pine panelling, which provided more than a whiff of his father's Scots Baronial.

Major new work in Glasgow was still hard to come by and 1887 was again dominated by further unsuccessful competition entries for the Royal Yacht Club and Hotel in Dunoon, and for the Glasgow International Exhibition, planned for the following year. With his growing reputation in Glasgow and considerable experience of designing the Edinburgh International Exhibition the previous year, Burnet must have submitted his entry with confidence, but the prize was snatched from under his nose by James Sellars. Campbell had more luck in 1888, winning the competition for the Ewing Gilmour Institute for Working Girls in Alexandria (where his wealthy grandfather, William Campbell, lived in Tullichewan Castle), and the same year Burnet won the competition for St Molios Parish Church at Shiskine on the Isle of Arran, which was to be another fascinating design and the prototype for several more Burnet churches (Fig. 13).

St Molios could not have differed much more from Barony Church. It was long and low with a huge, tiled roof and deeply overhanging eaves and, with the exception of the squat pyramid-roofed tower, the emphasis is strongly horizontal. Burnet somehow managed to successfully combine a timber porch based on an English lychgate, a Norman tower, and a vast, almost agricultural barn in a beautifully resolved, entirely sympathetic response to the building's

Fig. 13   J. J. Burnet's St Molios Church at Shiskine on the Isle of Arran of 1887. Courtesy of John Davidson.

remote, windswept location. Like the Barony Church, the interior has an ancient feel, with its exposed scissor-trussed timber roof structure, whitewashed walls, and sandstone dressings, but here the timber-work, which descends to the floor level, gives it a warmth and intimacy as well. From the domed stone pillar of its gate to the excellent detailing of all its timber-work, Burnet and his team never missed a beat. With St Molios he established a successful formula that would be much repeated by Burnet and others (not least because it was cheaper to build and easier to heat than the lofty heights of the Gothic style).

St Molios also became one of the legends of the Burnet office. A couple of years before work started on the church, Alexander Nisbet Paterson, the son of an extremely wealthy Glasgow merchant family, had joined the office following his architectural education at the École *des Beaux-Arts*, making Burnet, Son & Campbell the only office in Britain to have three graduates of the École working in it at the same time.(8) While their expensive education had prepared them for succeeding in a world of architectural competitions, the elder John Burnet was appalled at the French construction techniques that they had brought back from Paris and their apparently almost total disregard for the cost of their proposals. He found himself increasingly having to rein them back and convert their detailed designs into something that could both withstand the Scottish climate and be understood and delivered by Scottish building tradesmen. This conflict came to a head over St Molios, when he discovered that the entire church had been designed with the latest continental-style cavity walls. The drawings were complete and ready for issue when he insisted that they were all scrapped and that Alexander McGibbon and William Kerr, Burnet Jr.'s assistants, redraw the entire project in solid masonry.

The opening of the Glasgow International Exhibition by the Prince and Princess of Wales in bright sunshine on 8 May 1888, was greeted with huge enthusiasm across the city and beyond, with many seeing it as Glasgow's coming of age – thus establishing it, along with London (1851), New York (1853), and Philadelphia (1876), as one of the world's leading manufacturing centres. While trade stands (many the subject of substantial investment), were at the heart of the show, there was also an outstanding art exhibition which, in addition to showcasing the work of local painters and sculptors, also included numerous old masters from the collections of local industrialists and British galleries. The exhibition was sited in Kelvingrove Park in the west of the city, and here Sellars erected an exotic series of onion-domed pavilions (constructed in painted wood), which mixed elements of Byzantine, Moorish, and Indian architecture to create what became known as 'Bagdad by Kelvinside'. The theme was the Orient, into which the mighty British Empire continued to expand, with as one of its most successful exhibits a complete Indian street that was even populated by a number of native Indians who had been especially shipped over, to add further spice. A vast, domed main building addressed the city and led on to pavilions, tea rooms, dining rooms, bandstands and concert venues that were dotted across the park right up to the River Kelvin, which was graced by gondolas for the occasion. At night it was brilliantly lit, offering most visitors their first glimpse of electric lighting and, by all accounts, the paying public got good value – 'sophisticated outsiders were generally quite impressed, country visitors gaped open-mouthed, and Glaswegians simply loved it',(9) with the final seal of royal approval coming on 22 August, when Queen Victoria visited the exhibition en route for Balmoral.(10) By the end of the autumn, the final total number of visitors was 5,748,379, making it the most popular British exhibition so far. Importantly for the merchants, bankers, and shipbuilders who had underwritten it, it made the considerable profit of £43,000. This sum was doubled by public subscription to provide a permanent art gallery and museum for the city on part of the exhibition site. For Sellars, the Exhibition was to be a final hurrah, as he died far too early at only forty-four years of age, on the 9 October that year, robbing Glasgow of one of its finest architects of the Victorian period.

One of the visitors from 'the sticks', who would have marvelled at the spectacle and blinked for the first time at the sparkling electric light, was 28-year-old James Miller, who had recently transferred from Perth to the Caledonian Railway's head office in Glasgow. He had already proved himself to be a capable assistant and been recommended for promotion to the team of George Graham, the company's chief engineer. By 1888 Graham was already a towering figure in his industry. He had been appointed engineer-in-chief in 1853, since when he had overseen the management of the company's estate. In 1880 he was relieved of his responsibility for maintenance and asked to concentrate on the expansion and improvement of the network, with a particular new focus on encouraging leisure travel and providing railway links to the port towns of the steamers that now plied the Firth of Clyde. A widower, he disliked any form of ostentation and was modest almost to the point of shyness, but nevertheless had built an impressive reputation for his integrity, total reliability, and extraordinary memory for every aspect of his business. For Miller it was to be another significant stage in his development, and he made an immediate impact in the Glasgow office, as he had already done in Perth, soon leading almost all the new station design and, within months, working directly with Graham himself. The quality of the architecture of Glasgow had made a huge impact upon him and its sophistication emphasised the shortcomings of his own provincial architectural education, so he now sought to remedy this through further study, attendance at lectures at the Glasgow Institute of Architects (founded 1868), and making his first tour of Europe at his own expense, which took in France, Belgium, and Germany.

Within a year of his arrival, he and Graham were working side by side on Fort Matilda station in Greenock, the massive Gourock Pier railway station and a major new building in Central Glasgow at Bridge Street station. Fort Matilda proved to be a modest but satisfactory first building, with the influence of the the London architects Ernest George and fellow Scotsman, the brilliant Richard Norman Shaw, evident for the first time. The station, which was located on the western edge of Greenock, was a long, single storey seven-bay suburban building with timber framed gables above a red brick base, distinguished by three tall, elegant chimney stacks that contrasted with its great horizontal roof. Gourock Pier railway station was a much more substantial challenge for the 29-year-old Miller. By the 1890s the Glasgow tradition of going 'doon the watter' (on holiday) was well established and the transportation of hundreds of thousands of Glaswegians to the Clyde ports represented a major new line of business for the railway companies. The Caledonian Railway already had a station in Gourock but it was some distance from the pier, where its passengers embarked on their ferries to the Kyles and the Islands, and they were therefore losing much of the holiday trade to the Glasgow and South

Fig. 14   The surviving tower of Wemyss Bay railway station gives
a hint of lost Gourock's splendour. Courtesy of Tom Bastin.

Western Railway Company, whose terminal was adjacent to Prince's Pier. The vast new station which Miller and Graham designed served Gourock pierhead directly (Fig. 14). The architectural language was the same as that used in Fort Matilda, with half-timbered upper floors and gables above a brick base, but here developed on an altogether different scale, with two generous curving platforms to cope with Fair Week crowds, sheltered by seventeen bays of beautifully refined steel and glass canopies, and culminating in a great square corner clock tower. When it opened in June 1889 it was served by twenty-six trains a day from Glasgow – today, nothing of it remains.

Bridge Street Station had been the first central Glasgow railway station south of the river in Tradeston, where it had originally been graced by a bold Doric portico by James Collie. (The demolition of this portico in 1950 was as devastating for Glasgow as the loss of Euston Arch in London). James Miller was required to provide an alternative station entrance with apartments over it in 1889 (Fig. 15). This was a major city centre building and huge step up for the railway station architect from Perth, and young Miller rose to the occasion (albeit with more than a little inspiration from Rowand Anderson's recently completed Central Station Hotel of 1884). His eighteen-bay sandstone façade was built with neither the budget nor the vitality of Burnet's city buildings, but nevertheless it is beautifully proportioned and already exhibits the sharpness of detail which was to become a Miller trademark. The four off-centre arches that provided the entrance to the station are flanked by blank bays, which offer more modest entrances to the

Fig. 15   James Miller's Bridge Street station of 1889. Courtesy of Roger Edwards.

apartments below the coat of arms of the Caledonian Railway. It is a very impressive first city building that has the feel of Edinburgh restraint and refinement rather than typical Glasgow swagger.

With James Miller hitting his stride, JJ Burnet was on the cusp of his greatest work. His father retired at seventy-five years of age in 1889, and freed of his restraining hand, the work of the practice, led by Burnet Jr. and Campbell, was about to become even more adventurous.

CHAPTER 3: 1889–1898

The city's economy was booming once more – the bank crash of 1878 a distant memory. Shipbuilding had rescued Glasgow and the entire region contributed to the trade with coal from Lanarkshire and Ayrshire, steel from Motherwell and Cambuslang, technological refinement from Glasgow's marine engineers and the blood, sweat, and tears of hundreds of thousands of shipyard workers. Fairfield Shipbuilders of Govan alone employed 70,000 men and they struggled to cope with the international demand for passenger and naval steamships. In 1889 twelve mighty ships were under construction in their yard on the Clyde. Robert Napier and Sons built the steam engines that powered the British fleet as well as those of twenty-nine other nations, and the Cunard Line (that Robert Napier had founded with Samuel Cunard in 1839 as the British and North American Royal Steam Packet Company), was in constant competition for the Blue Riband, an informal award for the fastest transatlantic crossing. The city was expanding faster than ever, creating apparently endless opportunities for its architects to celebrate its success in sandstone, steel, and glass. Burnet and Campbell would ride this wave, producing much of their best work during the next decade, and as for James Miller, he would build his own practice on the back of it.

Commissions came flooding into Burnet and Campbell's office in 1889 – two large country houses; Baronald, near Lanark, for Mr Allen Farie, who was relocating from his family estate in Rutherglen where coal had been discovered; Garmoyle House in Dumbarton, on a site overlooking the Clyde for Lieutenant Colonel John F. Denny; a new hotel in Elie (in which Burnet's father was a shareholder) on the coast of the East Neuk of Fife and a massive corner block of shops and apartments at Charing Cross in Glasgow – soon to be named Charing Cross Mansions. These two houses and what became the Marine Hotel in Elie may be addressed together, as all three shared a similar architectural approach. Their authorship within the partnership is unclear, and while they are generally all attributed to Burnet, this seems unlikely, as we know that the enormous contemporary Charing Cross Mansions was Burnet's alone. The houses and hotel all draw on elements of traditional Scottish architecture but in a way that appears to make a more genuine, historically accurate connection with the past than the previous Scottish Baronial efforts of either Burnet's father, William Burn, David Bryce or others, whose large Victorian country houses, complete with *porte-cochères,* had been liberally decorated with corbelled bartizan turrets, conical roofs, battlements, and arrow slits.

This fresh interest in the historical architecture of Scotland was led by Edinburgh architect David MacGibbon (1831–1902) and his assistant Thomas Ross (1839–1930), who had embarked on an ambitious survey of the traditional architecture of their homeland on which they regularly lectured in Edinburgh. MacGibbon's influence could be seen in his friend Rowand Anderson's abandonment of the Gothic style in the 1880s, and particularly in the work of James Marjoribanks MacLaren (1853–90), whose design for Stirling High School, which was won in competition in 1886 and Fortingall Hotel and cottages (which were completed after his death in 1891), had enormous influence on later architects such as Charles Rennie Mackintosh and Sir Robert Lorimer. What started as MacGibbon's personal mission developed into a broad and general interest after the publication with Thomas Ross in 1887 of their *The Castellated and Domestic Architecture of Scotland from the Twelfth to the Eighteenth Century,* two years before the three Burnet and Campbell buildings referred to above.

The three designs were all picturesque asymmetrical compositions inspired by ancient Scottish tower houses, with the Marine Hotel and Garmoyle taking their cue from Neidpath and Elphinstone castles, while Baronald is essentially two linked tower houses of different heights at right angles to each other, such as at Leven Castle or the Bishop's House at Elgin

Fig. 16   J. J. Burnet's Baronald House of 1889. Courtesy of Hugh P. Gray.

(Fig. 16). Sadly, the Hotel lasted only until the night of 6 April 1904, when it was gutted by fire, though it was later rebuilt by Burnet in Queen Anne style (and then finally burnt to the ground in 1983). It originally shared the language of Baronald and Garmoyle, (both of which, though facing an uncertain future, still survive) with their snecked sandstone rubble walls with ashlar dressings to doors and windows, crow-stepped gables, generous canted bay windows, occasional balustraded parapets, half-round pedimented stone dormer windows and the occasional armorial panel, cat-slide roof or circular corbelled tourette (Baronald's defensive character was somewhat undermined by their client Mr Farie's demand for a large conservatory adjacent to the main entrance). The interiors were suitably Jacobean with great carved stone chimneypieces and wainscoting throughout the public rooms below geometrically ribbed plaster ceilings. (Like Lutyens's slightly later country houses, they implied that their nouveau riche clients enjoyed a long lineage). They made delightful homes and while their architectural language became common during the next ten years, in each of these cases it was carried off with typical Burnet and Campbell panache. It was a language that would find itself combined

Fig. 17 J. J. Burnet's great swashbuckling Charing Cross Mansions of 1889. Courtesy of Tom Bastin.

with French High Renaissance architecture in their other new commission of 1889 – Burnet's brilliant, swashbuckling, Charing Cross Mansions.

The site for this large apartment block and shops (it is so fine that it would be wrong to describe it as a tenement), was on the corner of Sauchiehall Street and St George's Road where free of the city centre's grid plan, Burnet was able to provide a great curved façade that swept around the corner from Sauchiehall Street, before running along St George's Road and finally turning the corner into Renfrew Street (Fig. 17). This articulated sandstone wall was composed as a short straight bay on Sauchiehall Street with a balustrade at second-floor level, stopped by a vertical tower, followed by a great symmetrical curved bay with an arched attic floor and balustrade at third-floor level that turned the corner to St George's Road, which in turn, is stopped by a broad tower with bay windows, followed by another straight section with a balustrade at second floor level, facing St George's Road. This concludes with another narrow tower before the final flourish on the corner to Renfrew Street where the third-floor attic balcony and arched screen is resumed and the corner turned with a great cylindrical drum. In the centre of the

Fig. 18   Detail of the great clock and sculpture of
Charing Cross Mansions. Courtesy of Ian Stubbs.

sweeping symmetrical curve, double bay windows and an armorial shield with Glasgow's coat of arms and sculpted patron saint Saint Mungo frame a vast clock, itself flanked by caryatids and sheltered by a stone arch on which sit the sculptures *Night* and *Day* (Fig. 18). This central vertical accent is then further developed with a balcony above, with 'Charing Cross Mansions' carved on a solid section of its balustrade below a steeply pitched tower that concludes in a domed lantern. This is merely one of the many eruptions at roof level, with each of the vertical towers of the façade concluded in a series of steeply pitched roofs, with or without cast-iron balustrades, amidst a series of soaring chimney stacks and the great dome of the Renfield Street corner drum. The central curved section also sports stone dormer windows with alternating round and pediment heads, decorated with carved panels and ball finials.

Burnet's sources were once more Charles Wilson's great curved façade on the outside of Park Circus (1854–5), with its double-height bay windows, balustrades, and steeply pitched French Renaissance roof with stone dormers; the eaves gallery pioneered by Alexander Thomson as shown in his Grecian Building a little further along Sauchiehall Street (1865), MacGibbon and Ross's recently published glossary of traditional Scottish details, and with a final dash of the *Pavillon de l'Horloge* at the Louvre. Not many architects could bring all this together and pull it off but JJ Burnet did, by his finely judged balance between the horizontals of the single line of eaves, the balustrades and shop fronts, and the vertical accents of towers, chimneys, and windows. Strongly supported by the sculptor William Birnie Rhind (following the death of the great John Mossman in 1890) Burnet gave Glasgow a superbly confident, rich and vigorous, red sandstone *Gesamtkunstwerk*, which perfectly captured the spirit of the booming city.

In his Clyde Navigation Trust building, the architecture and sculpture were complementary, but in Charing Cross Mansions for the first time, they are integral to this single work of art, as first achieved by the great Baroque architects 400 years before. There was certainly nothing quite like it being produced in London or elsewhere in Britain at the time and it predates the work by at least ten years of several Arts and Crafts architects such as Charles Harrison Townsend or Charles Rennie Mackintosh, who achieved a similar synthesis. Other contemporary attempts to integrate sculpture and architecture, such as 82 Mortimer Street in London by the highly regarded Arthur Beresford Pite, which has a pair of sleeping figures who look as if they have been salvaged from another building before being dropped onto his façade – look amateurish by comparison. Burnet had succeeded in integrating architecture with sculpture, the traditional architecture of France with that of Glasgow and the great Classical tradition with the Scottish vernacular in a design that was both original and yet beautifully resolved. Pevsner's *Guide* sums it up perfectly as 'ebullient', while Glaswegians would perhaps offer the equally appropriate 'gallus'.(1,2) If Charing Cross Mansions impressed his competitors in the city and beyond, his next commission – another building for the Athenaeum – would put clear water between Burnet and the following pack.

The new building was to provide a school of music and drama, including a training theatre, a restaurant, a billiard room and gymnasium for the growing number of students who were by then attending the Athenaeum (Fig. 19). The site was incredibly complex as, rather than being on St George's Place next to his earlier building, it was almost landlocked behind his existing

Fig. 19 The dramatic Buchanan Street elevation of J. J. Burnet's second phase of the Athenaeum of 1891. Courtesy David Gray.

building with just a narrow frontage to Buchanan Street around the corner. To complicate matters, Buchanan Street slopes steeply upwards at this point, making the street level of the slot two floors above street level in St George's Place. Burnet's entirely rational response was to use the vertical slot on Buchanan Street almost entirely for circulation – horizontally, to provide direct access from Buchanan Street to the auditorium, and vertically – with circular stairs and a lift, serving all the upper and lower levels of the new building. The auditorium itself was entered from the street at the level of the circle, with most of the audience who were seated in the stalls (contrary to expectations), descending to their seats. The seating for 790 was arranged in a traditional horseshoe format that extended down either side of the stage while the stage itself was provided with a full fly tower that rose up amidst the accommodation of the upper floors of the building, with a scene dock cleverly accessed from the lane behind. It was an exemplar of architectural planning in three dimensions that was at least the equal of its famous façade on Buchanan Street which for generations of Glaswegians was all they ever experienced of the Athenaeum, and yet quite sufficient for the building to gain their affection and esteem.

As with the best architecture, this elevation works on many levels. It is firstly a very clear expression of the activities that lie behind it and that it lights – on the left, the foyers of the theatre with offices above, while on the right, the thrusting verticality of the stairs and lift. The left-hand plane (which projects slightly, giving its internal spaces priority over the functional stairs to its right) rises from a sharply rusticated base through a triple-height bay window, the first two levels of which are glazed, with the four-storey-high void in the façade concluding in a great arched window below a steep gable with an aedicule, which is finally topped off with a split, round pediment framing a rocketing pylon. The right plane offers a broad entrance (almost identical to those on St George's Place), below another glazed aedicule (which appears from the entrance door surround in a rather knowingly Mannerist way) before shooting skyward with stepped slit windows marking the stair. The stair drives through a fourth-floor window (perhaps symbolising the lift car within) before being blocked by a stone frieze, which is once more flanked by octagonal piers below an octagonal tower, dome, and finial. Unlike all Burnet's previous Glasgow work, the entire composition is, in the words of Walker and Gomme, 'insistently, wilfully, asymmetrical.'(3) The asymmetry, combined with its soaring verticality and the richness of Burnet's architectural articulation, gives this little city-centre tower house an extraordinary feeling of energy, movement and confidence. It is indeed 'a school of drama' from which his contemporaries learned much, and this building and Charing Cross Mansions laid the foundations for the Glasgow Free style(4) of the next two decades.

As in Charing Cross Mansions, Burnet's French Classical education is but a subtext to the lessons he had learnt subsequently, with the Athenaeum referencing an eclectic range of sources, from Alexander Thomson's Bucks Head Building of 1863 in the great double-height cast-iron-framed glazed bay window; Rowand Anderson's Central Station Hotel of 1884, in the arched conclusion of the great vertical thrust of the bay(5) and Richard Norman Shaw's New Scotland Yard of 1887, in the split curved pediment with pylon that concludes the great gable. As in Charing Cross Mansions, few architects could successfully pull off the fusion achieved in the school of music and drama with aplomb, but Burnet did so with total confidence, producing a piece of architecture that combined energy and dignity in equal measures. It was a performance he rarely bettered during the rest of his long career. With no Mossman, it fell to William Kellock Brown (1856–1934) – yet another student of the École, to provide the (relatively restrained) sculpture on this occasion, and Burnet's partner John Campbell must surely be allowed some of the glory (although we do know he was also busy on the *Tulliechewan Arms* in Balloch at this time).

It was another time for the changing of the guard among Glasgow's architectural elite. After Sellars death, his chief draughtsman John Keppie (1862–1945) left to form a new partnership with John Honeyman and in the same year – 1889 – a young assistant, Charles Rennie Mackintosh, joined their firm, later becoming a partner in 1904 on Honeyman's retirement. John Gaff Gillespie, who had shared the Glasgow Institute of Architects' prize with Mackintosh in 1889, joined the office of William Forrest Salmon (who already represented the second generation of the Salmon firm), soon taking over much of their design work before being joined in 1895 by the third generation James Salmon Jr., with whom Gillespie would collaborate to bring Art Nouveau to Glasgow. William Leiper (1839–1916) had completed his much loved Carpet Factory on Glasgow Green in 1889, the same year that Frank Burnet (1846–1923 – no relation) took his assistant William James Boston (1861–1937) into partnership, to create one of the city's most prolific practices of the late 1990s and early twentieth century. Almost all these practices competed unsuccessfully for the commission to build the new art gallery and museum in Kelvingrove Park in 1892, with this plum being picked, to their horror, by the London architect John William Simpson, (in partnership with Edmund John Milner Allen). A small consolation was that at least it wasn't lost to an architect from Edinburgh.

Amidst this stellar cast, James Miller continued his progress with, in 1890, his first significant private commission, Dunloskin in Dumbreck, a house for the railway engineer William Melville, who had been George Graham's assistant at the Caledonian Railway Company before leaving to take over as Chief Engineer of the Glasgow and South Western Railway Company. The contrast between his and Burnet's contemporary domestic work was considerable, Dunloskin being much more a suburban villa than a Scottish tower house, but it was entirely consistent with Miller's railway work to that date, with half-timbered gables, bay windows with balconies over and tall sandstone chimneys, still very much in the Old English style of Shaw. This was quickly followed by the commission for Craiguchty Terrace in Aberfoyle – a speculative development of six houses for Hugh Kennedy, a railway contractor and Ardtornish in Pollokshields, for building contractor William Anderson. Both were similar in style but looked rather racy among their heavy sandstone neighbours (Fig. 20). Troon station, built for the Caledonian Railway Company, with half-timbered eaves over roughcast walls, is also from this period. But the direction of Miller's career was about to change and the catalyst came in 1892 when his entry for an architectural competition for Belmont Parish Church in Hillhead (later Lilybank Church and now converted to apartments) was selected. With an assurance from George Graham that he would continue to use him for Caledonian Railway projects, Miller finally established his own practice at 223 West George Street, just two streets away from Burnet and Campbell's office.

Fig. 20   Ardtornish by James Miller of 1892 – an excellent
example of his sub-Shaw style. Courtesy of Peter Gillespie, Savills.

Dunblane Cathedral is the source once more for the cruciform plan Gothic Belmont Parish Church, but it was further distilled via Burnet's earlier Barony Church, right down to the three lancet windows with vertical apex window above in the gable (Fig. 21). It is a delightful little church and a very competent first venture into the Gothic style by Miller. His practice thus established, the next few years would bring similar fare – railway stations for George Graham, houses for engineers and contractors met through his building work, and competition entries – both successful and, more usually, unsuccessful. His next station was to be the Botanic Gardens station and park entrance gates in the West End – once more in his Old English Shavian style but here, as befitted this part of town, a rather grand affair with twin towers sporting a clock and the Caledonian Railway's monogram below bulbous domes. (After the closure of the railway station it served as a tearoom for the park for many years, before, like so many fine Glasgow buildings, being destroyed by fire, in this case in 1970) (Fig. 22). Unsuccessful competition entries for the Clydebank Union Church and Falkirk Free Church were followed in 1893 with a win, and his largest commission to that date, for Clydebank municipal buildings. His proposal offered a new town hall and municipal offices in a Scottish Baronial style, which was a rather watered-down version of Charles Wilson's earlier Rutherglen Town Hall of 1862. Miller received the commission for the entire project but, with the astonishing growth of shipbuilding in Clydebank and its then

Fig. 21   James Miller's competition-winning design for
Belmont Parish Church of 1892. Courtesy of Roger Edwards.

Fig. 22   Although much of Miller's Botanic Gardens station building of 1894–5 survived a major fire, the decision was taken to demolish it in 1970. Courtesy of Ben Brooksbank.

Fig. 23   Miller's Bridge of Orchy station of 1893–1904 was typical of his work for the Caledonian on their West Highland Line. Courtesy of Nigel Walls.

ever-increasing wealth and citizenry, his initial project was soon regarded as too small and abandoned. Fortunately, having gained the Council's confidence, he was retained to work with them on the development of new proposals. These grew grander by the year and by the end of the century, without a sod cut, the original Town Hall commission had acquired two public halls, a court room, police station, fire station, and swimming baths, which were finally officially opened in 1902. (These are discussed in detail near the start of Chapter 4). While this was on the back burner, George Graham stepped in with a substantial commission for all the stations on the West Highland Railway Line and while each of these was modest, it was a very long line that included Arrochar, Tarbet, Bridge of Orchy, Craigendoran, Crianlarich, Garelochhead, Inverlair, and almost all points west (Fig. 23).

His new practice was stable and growing steadily, and while the inner circle of Glasgow's shipbuilders, bankers, and merchants remained the hunting ground of the architectural establishment led by JJ Burnet, he had a solid base workload from George Graham and the Caledonian Railway and domestic commissions on top of that, along with the very real prospect of more large work via architectural competitions. While the few recollections of Miller that exist describe a quiet, serious, self-effacing man (much in the mould of his former employer and client, George Graham), contemporary photographs from this period show a rather dapper boulevardier, with starched wing collar, a full moustache, and thick, black hair curled off his face in a stylish quiff (Fig. 24). His days as an eligible bachelor about town were not to last however, as he married Emelina Henrietta Crichton, a daughter of the manse, who was eight years his junior, just before Christmas in 1894, and the newly-weds set up home in a tenement flat at 3 Windsor Street in Maryhill. His progress so far had been remarkable, but it would soon be meteoric.

As James Miller's future became more and more focused on Glasgow, John Burnet's practice was becoming geographically more diverse with each year. The early 1890s brought three new church commissions in Arbroath (1893), Glenboig (1893), and Grangemouth (1894). The parish church of Arbroath had been all but destroyed by fire, and only architect John Henderson's early Gothic tower survived. Burnet rebuilt the body of the church as another variant of Dunblane Cathedral, complete with the three lancet windows to the new entrance gable. His Dundas Memorial Church in Grangemouth and Free Church in Glenboig are both delightful variants on St Molios on Arran – long and low below vast sheltering roofs with square towers topped by pyramidal roofs and the same lychgate entrance porch. (Grangemouth is now a funeral home).

Fig. 24   As young, successful and debonair as he was determined – James Miller in the 1890s. Courtesy of HES.

Fig. 25   J. J. Burnet's delightful Hamilton Terrace in Lamlash
on the Isle of Arran of 1893. Courtesy of Peter Roberts

There were also the first of a series of buildings on the Isle of Arran and in distant Campbeltown on the Mull of Kintyre. Burnet's client on Arran was William, the twelfth Duke of Hamilton and Earl of Arran, while his various Campbeltown clients were almost all connected through shipping to Glasgow. On Arran his buildings included Hamilton Terrace (1893) which looks out to sea in Lamlash – a long and very elegant terrace of twenty-seven single-storey houses with attics, sloping dormers, and bay windows, arranged in pairs,with one pair sharing entrance doors and the next particularly tall chimneys that offer both a sense of rhythm and a series of vertical incidents in contrast to the long horizontal mass of the block (Fig. 25). (Remarkably, they have been preserved almost intact barring the now ubiquitous plastic replacement windows). His Lordship also paid for the design and construction of a new village hall for Brodick ('an Arts and Crafts delight' of 1894)(6) and a small hotel in Lochranza (1894 – now the youth hostel) with all these buildings on Arran in a similar style of blue slate over roughcast white walls with red sandstone dressings – as one would expect of Burnet – a most attractive combination of materials. In Cambeltown, his first commission was for a new cottage hospital (1894) that was jointly funded by the local doctor John Cunningham and a Mrs McKinnon of Ronachan (whose family owned the British India Shipping Line). In Alloa in Clackmannanshire the public baths and gymnasium (completed 1895 as a gift to the town from the local millowner John Thomson Paton), were also from this period but they were carried out in such an exuberant Scottish Renaissance style that one wonders if they are perhaps Campbell's rather than Burnet's.

Back in town there were new railway stations at Kirklee (1894, demolished) and Glasgow Cross (1895, demolished) for the Glasgow Central Railway. Both stations were in red sandstone in

Scottish Renaissance style. Kirklee station was a charming little building with stone balustraded parapets and tall stone chimneys, as befitted its location in the West End, while the Glasgow Cross Station was octagonal in plan with alternating arched bays and columns supporting a glazed dome above. Burnet's Pathology Building (1894) for the Western Infirmary is also from this period and in a similar style. His personal involvement in many of these buildings is unclear, as his and Campbell's practice was incredibly busy throughout the 1890s and it would have made sense for the principals to focus on their most important commissions and competitions. One of these of 1894, which we can be absolutely certain is from the hand of John James Burnet is the addition of a new, domed single-storey banking hall to his father's Glasgow Savings Bank headquarters building in Ingram Street. It is probably the finest building that Burnet ever produced (Fig. 26).

With few practical constraints (all the supporting administrative spaces are located in the adjacent bank building by his father) Burnet was able to concentrate fully on form and space, resulting in an exquisite little gem. The entire body of this small building is wrapped in deeply channelled rustication above a grey granite base with only the dentiled cornice and frieze above

Fig. 26   J. J. Burnet's exquisite Savings Bank Hall of 1894 –
one of his greatest works. Courtesy of David Gray.

in smooth ashlar. The main entrance, its flanking windows and the large side windows that light the banking hall are all surmounted with elegant, shallow, curved segmental pediments enclosing cartouches and, in the case of the main entrance, the Glasgow coat of arms below a sculpture of its patron Saint Mungo within an aedicule, framed by twisted columns below his own triangular pediment. On either side of the main entrance two great Doric columns hold back the rusticated skin, within which two granite Ionic columns, aided by two crouching figures, support the mighty pediment above with the scrolls, while the twisted columns (from San Pietro in Vincoli) give Saint Mungo a distinctly Roman feel. The tripartite gable windows are similarly treated, but in lieu of the Saint, the gap in the pediment frames the view of the great glazed copper skylight above the banking hall. This is as exquisitely detailed as the rest of the building, with studded panels between the glazing arching up towards its crowning cupola; the whole ensemble providing an uplifting vertical accent that contrasts with the horizontal emphasis of the stonework (Fig. 27).

Fig. 27   Burnet's architecture and George Frampton's sculpture combine in one of Glasgow's finest buildings. Courtesy of Ian Stubbs.

Like each window and the doorway, the corners of this tiny building are intricate masterpieces in themselves. The dentiled cornices on either elevation stop short of the corner, allowing a curved rusticated wall to continue up past them to the full height of the main parapet, which here steps up slightly to frame the elevations and create space for sculpted panels. Breaking the cornice line and stopping the ashlar frieze short of the corners also has the effect of dividing the elevations into three separate planes, each of which can then be appreciated as separate compositions in themselves. The sculpture, which here has an elegant restraint, is superbly integrated – a partnership between designer George Frampton (later Sir George) and local sculptor William Shirreffs (1846–1902). Overall, it is an incredibly sophisticated, even magisterial, composition, carried off brilliantly by Burnet and one only has to wander fifty yards down Ingram Street to compare the quality of this mature work with the (very fine) doorway of his father's bank from almost twenty years before, to appreciate his development over the intervening years.

Internally, the banking hall almost equals the drama of the exterior. Not only does the dome flood the space with ever-changing natural light but it also marks the shift from the entrance axis to the strong cross axis along what was the serving counter, concluding in the great side windows. Burnet, through the mastery of his craft, has invested this tiny building, which in scale is entirely dwarfed by its neighbours, with a dignity and a sense of grandeur that they can only envy, while at the same time somehow also conjuring up the same vigorous energy of the Athenaeum within an entirely symmetrical building. It is the very embodiment of a confident Glasgow at its zenith.

At the age of thirty-eight Burnet was at the peak of his powers, and while history tends to celebrate his later contribution to the development of modern architecture, viewed outside the myopic lens of Modernism, his Glasgow Baroque masterpieces remain his greatest achievement. He (and to a lesser degree Campbell) were the pathfinders not of modern British architecture but of the exuberant Glasgow Free Style that would dominate the city's architecture until the outbreak of the First World War. Burnet had little interest in the emerging Arts and Crafts movement – he was a Classicist to his very core – and while the few Arts and Crafts buildings of Glasgow such as James Salmon Jr.'s Hatrack (1899) or Mackintosh's Glasgow School of Art (1907) are now more highly regarded (and, in the case of Mackintosh's work, world famous), for the next twenty years it was Burnet – not Mackintosh – who dominated the Glasgow architectural scene (Fig. 28).

To celebrate his achievements, in 1895, the Burnets embarked on an extensive study tour of Germany and Italy. Theodore Fyfe, one of his assistants, recalled that during his travels he 'wrote long letters to his partner, Mr Campbell, with the fresh delight of a debutante about her first ball.'(7) The two architects still shared their love of architecture but their day-to-day working relationship was deteriorating fast. On Burnet's return they separately entered the competition for the North British Hotel in Edinburgh but without success, and again in 1896, both separately entered the architectural competition for the new Glasgow School of Art, and both were unsuccessful once more, as we know, as the competition was ostensibly won by Honeyman and Keppie, though in reality their entry was the design of their young assistant, Charles Rennie

Fig. 28 J. J. Burnet. Courtesy of the Royal Incorporation of Architects in Scotland.

Mackintosh. The days of Burnet and Campbell's partnership were now numbered. Campbell had grown closer to John Keppie, whose bachelor lifestyle he shared, and rumours suggested that Campbell's increasing consumption of alcohol had become too much for Burnet, the strict Calvinist, to bear, while on his part Campbell was unhappy that the firm's profits were being constantly eroded by Burnet's painstaking, time-consuming, and costly search for perfection. In the end, they finally parted in 1897, dividing their then current workload and Campbell quickly established his own successful practice in the city.

Shortly before this parting of the ways, the Burnets had followed up their European tour with their first trip to the United States. With his contacts from the École, which was as popular with wealthy American students as with Scottish ones, introductions were easy. Charles Follen McKim (1847–1909) who dominated his fellow New York architects at this time, was a fellow alumnus, and saw to it that Burnet was soon admitted to the American Cosmos Club of Beaux-Arts and made a corresponding member of the American Institute of Architects. Jean, too, had family contacts, as her younger brother George Marwick had moved to New York where, as an accountant, he had founded his own firm and would eventually become the 'M' in KPMG. While one of the reasons for the visit had been to investigate the latest hospital design (for which Burnet was accompanied by Dr Donald Mackintosh of the Western Infirmary), the impact of the latest American architecture had a lasting (and almost entirely negative) impact on Burnet's architecture. He would have been well aware of many of the developments in American architecture via architectural magazines (*The Builder* was first published in 1843 and the US *Architectural Forum* in 1892), but seeing high-rise commercial buildings and the treatment of their soaring façades in three dimensions for the first time clearly made a huge impression on him. He had delighted in the glory of the past in Italy the year before, but New York in the 1890s offered him a vision not of the past but of the future, and from this point onwards, there is a growing American influence on his work that resulted in the increasing simplification of his architecture.

With the volume of work now being undertaken by his practice, it seems extraordinary that Burnet had time for both these extended visits, and we must conclude that his assistants were taking more and more responsibility for much of the work of the office. His churches from this period, while very fine, offer surprisingly little innovation, with the McLaren Memorial Church in Larbert (1897) and the Gardner Memorial Church in Brechin (1896) being simply variations on the Dundas Memorial Church of 1894, which itself owes almost everything to St Molios (Fig. 29).

Fig. 29   J. J. Burnet's McLaren Memorial Church in Larbert of 1897 was another variant on St Molios. Courtesy of David Gray.

Fig. 30   In Kelvinside Station of 1897, Burnet gave his client, the
Caledonian Railway Company, exactly the kind of opulence that they
sought for this West End location. Courtesy of Colin MacKenzie.

With James Miller overloaded with work on the West Highland Line, Burnet was commissioned
by the Caledonian Railway to design the stations at Anderson Cross, Clydebank Riverside, and
Kelvinside, with the latter's location on the Great Western Road meriting an increased budget
and thus Burnet's significant involvement, as confirmed by its beautiful detailing and elegance
(now restored as a bar and restaurant, after having also being gutted by fire) (Fig. 30). Of his
houses from this period, *Carronvale* in Larbert (1896) is an Italianate villa below an unusual red-
tiled roof (that survives as a Boys Brigade centre). Others were The Towans in Prestwick (1897),
with an untypical Arts and Crafts feel under deeply overhanging eaves, and a beautiful sculpted
sandstone panel over its main entrance (it was destroyed by fire in 1986 after years of neglect)
and Rothmar in Campbeltown (1897), another elegant Italianate villa, which has survived. He
remodelled Finlaystone House in Langbank (1898) in a Scottish Baronial style and in Craigdhu
Mansions, also in Campbeltown (1897) he produced one final Scottish stone townhouse,
complete with turret and crow-stepped gables.

Another of this little clutch of Burnet buildings in Campbeltown is one that deserves to be
much better known – his small library and museum of 1897 (Fig. 31). Funded by local man, James
Macalister Hall, the founder of the British Steam Navigation Company, it was constructed on a
site gifted to the town by the Duke of Argyll. St Molios is the model once more for this long,
low public building but, like his Savings Bank Hall (and numerous Glaswegians over the years), it

Fig. 31   Burnet's Campbeltown library and museum of 1897 brought a little of Victorian Glasgow's sophistication to its remote site on the Mull of Kintyre. Courtesy of Maureen Lussey.

may be small, but it packs quite a punch. Three generous bays topped with balustrades enliven the street elevation and light the lending room while the museum walls are blank, with a long skylight in its vaulted ceiling illuminating the room. The main entrance doorway is marked by a gable and flanked by engaged Doric columns supporting entablatures and urns, with a beautifully carved panel over the door and an aedicule window with a scrolled pediment. The cross axis from the side entry to the long reading room is marked by an elegant lantern cupola which lights the entrance hall. It is Burnet Scots Renaissance architecture, but in response to its provincial location, the rustication is replaced by snecked rubble, the fine sculpted panels of local trades are relatively restrained and contained within plain sandstone piers, and the interior has a dignified simplicity.

Back in Glasgow there was a new domed corner drum to be added to R W Forsyth's department store and his excellent Albany Chambers (1896), also for Robert Simpson & Sons (who had been his clients for Charing Cross Mansions) which abuts Charing Cross Mansions and continues its great sweep onto Sauchiehall Street (Fig. 32). Albany Chambers is another asymmetrical composition in which the canted sandstone bays dominate. An offset entrance at

Fig. 32 Burnet's Albany Chambers
on Sauchiehall Street of 1896 adjoins
his earlier Charing Cross Mansions.
Courtesy of Stinglehammer.

ground floor with a fine split, scrolled pediment divides the two principal bays of the building, rather in the style of the Athenaeum. To the left, double bay windows shoot up to a gable that culminates in an aedicule with a sculpted figure, as in Buchanan Street. To the right of the entrance, the balcony to the second floor of Charing Cross Mansions is picked up with a central bay linking the first and second floors, while flanking bays link the second and third, with their great vertical thrust stopped dead by a deep cornice that forms a broad balcony to the three gabled windows of the fourth floor. It is another beautifully judged composition that has a warmth, richness and suave elegance which almost makes you weep when you compare it to its dreary grid-paper modern neighbours.

By 1896, James Miller was emerging from beneath the deluge of George Graham's station projects. The stations for the West Highland Railway line were complete or under construction and his extensive buildings for Greenock Princes Pier railway station for its competitor, the Glasgow and South Western Railway, were well underway. Architecturally, these were unremarkable, in the same sub-Shaw style as his previous stations, albeit adorned by tall towers that could be seen from across the water by the crowds on the approaching steamers. He had successfully established himself as the go-to architect for railway stations in the west of Scotland and while JJ Burnet might pick up the odd one or two or be selected for a particularly upmarket location, for anything more technically complex, Miller was your man. It was natural, therefore, that the newly formed Glasgow District Subway Company should commission Miller to design their office and first station in central Glasgow.

This was to be an advert for their new subway system and they could not have found a more prominent site than in the centre of St Enoch's Square, below what was then the towering wall of the St Enoch Station Hotel, terminating the long axis of Buchanan Street to its south ('or did until the dreadful entrances to the remodelled underground got in the way').(8) (Fig. 33). Miller's little station building was (and fortunately, still is) a delightful Flemish Renaissance pepperpot, complete with turrets, heavily bracketed balconies, bay windows, and steep gables with sculpted acroterion. There was also a certain air of the Arts and Crafts movement in his swept roofs and ironwork, and a definite nod to Burnet's Glasgow Cross station which then stood at the other end of Argyle Street. Considering the quality of most of his railway stations and the restraint of his only previous city centre building in Bridge Street, St Enoch underground station shows both a new-found confidence and probably, to many of his contemporaries, an unexpected level of skill. If his self-esteem was growing, it would have been further boosted that same year in 1896 by his entry for the architectural competition for the massive new Belfast city hall being placed third, ahead of the only other Glasgow entrant, Honeyman and Keppie. The Caledonian Railway Company had already commissioned him to design Kelvinbridge railway station (a rather neat little sandstone number – destroyed by fire in 1968) and, having bought a site that was rather larger than they needed for the station, they decided to build an annexe to their Central Station Hotel to front its boundary on the Great Western Road, giving Miller this job as well. Although it was connected to Central Station by rail (via the adjacent Kelvinbridge station), the link was tenuous and the annexe unpopular, soon afterwards being converted into the Caledonian Mansions that we know today (Fig. 34).

Fig. 33   Miller's delightful St Enoch subway station of 1896 has fortunately survived, unlike the adjacent railway station and hotel. Courtesy of Tom Bastin.

A four-storey apartment block, Caledonian Mansions is an extremely competent early example of Burnet and Campbell's Glasgow Free Style. Miller's starting point was a tight, regularly fenestrated sandstone wall very similar to his earlier Bridge Street apartments, but here enlivened with projecting, bracketed, rectangular bays, stone pedimented dormers and two very elegant corner towers, which emerged fully at roof level, where they concluded in deeply overhanging ogee roofs with finials. The rear elevation overlooking the tracks and the river is equally interesting. A boldly bracketed, continuous balustraded stone balcony on the

Fig. 34   James Miller's very impressive Caledonian Mansions
on Great Western Road of 1896. Courtesy of Tom Bastin.

second floor serves the upper flats, stopped at either end by two rectangular sandstone towers – one concluding with a balcony, while the other has a pitched roof and curved pediment. On the southern elevation two great vertical sandstone chimneys rise (from a slightly awkward arcaded ground floor) to frame a double-height bay window above a stone balustrade (much like Burnet's earlier gable to Saughfield Crescent), while Miller's attempt to combine a sculpted bracket, bay window, and pediment in the centre of the principle Great Western Road elevation just serves to show the gap between Burnet and his followers. Nevertheless, in terms of Miller's development as an architect, Caledonian Mansions represents both a large stride forward and something of a turning point.(9) Pevsner's *Guide* is suitably enthusiastic about the building, describing 'a façade full of surprises, breaking forward and back with a restless variety of window designs, oriels and dormers among them. This originality extends to all the façades; at the rear, the first-floor access balcony adds particular verve.'(10) To that date, much of his output had been frankly unremarkable, but Caledonian Mansions provided evidence of an architectural ability that over the next few years would take him far beyond his straight Gothic revival churches and sub-Shaw stations to an architecture of considerable quality.

While the Caledonian Railway Company still provided his base workload, he was able to continue to diversify his practice with another church commission for St Columba's Episcopal Church in Bridgeton in 1898 (since demolished), which was a larger version of his Gothic, Belmont Church; Arduaine House in Argyll (1898) for J. Arthur Campbell – a sprawling, white rendered, slate-roofed hunting lodge overlooking Loch Fyne (now the Loch Melfort Hotel) and a very crisp little Georgian sandstone townhouse at 2 Lancaster Crescent in the West End.

In the summer of 1898, *The Builder* magazine examined the vibrant Glasgow architectural scene. Interestingly, this was not in recognition of the quality of Glasgow's contemporary architecture – on the contrary – it was merely one of a series of articles on 'The Architecture of our Large Provincial Towns' and, further emphasising Glasgow's relative insignificance to the London psyche, it was the sixteenth article in the series.(11) The reviewer appears to have been somewhat shocked to find that, far from Glasgow being the 'dirty manufacturing town' that he expected, to his astonishment, he found, 'broad straight streets, laid out with great regularity, and bordered by handsome buildings, in the production of which neither architectural skill nor money have been lacking.' Burnet's work was well covered, along with most of his leading contemporaries, but Miller failed to get a mention.

Glasgow's new great red sandstone art gallery and museum was then under construction in Kelvingrove Park, and after the laying of its foundation stone the previous year in 1897, it was decided that Glasgow should host another great exhibition both to celebrate the completion of the gallery and the start of the new millennium. In May 1898, an architectural competition was announced for the design of the main exhibition building, which was to be adjacent to the art gallery and museum at the far west end of Sauchiehall Street, as well as for the layout of the exhibition grounds and buildings in the park. 'Monochrome drawings on a scale of 1 inch to 16 feet' were to be submitted by 15 August, 'including longitudinal and transverse sections and a perspective'.(12) The opportunity caused quite a stir within the profession and in the end, fourteen sets of plans were submitted and were arranged in Burnet's Fine Art Institute on Sauchiehall Street to be judged. In addition to the submission by Glasgow's leading architect JJ Burnet, entries were submitted by Charles Rennie Mackintosh (under the names of Honeyman and Keppie) as well as separate entries by John Honeyman and John Keppie, William Leiper, Burnet's former partner John Campbell, Alexander McGibbon, James Salmon and Son, and Burnet's former assistant, Alexander Paterson. On 12 September the judging panel's recommendations were confirmed, with Alexander Paterson and John Campbell in the second and third places, respectively and, to everyone's utter astonishment, with James Miller announced as the winner.

CHAPTER 4: 1898–1902

Miller's win has long been resented, as it deprived Glasgow of several more buildings by Charles Rennie Mackintosh, but it was Miller more than any other competitor who really understood what was required for the exhibition buildings. He produced a Ruritanian utopia in Kelvingrove, which gave another generation of Glaswegians the opportunity to escape their ordinary lives for at least a few summer nights of fantasy, in a way that Mackintosh's comparatively drab Art Nouveau offering would never have done.(1) Miller's main building, the Industrial Hall, which acted as the exhibition's main entrance, was a reworking of Sellars's hall of 1888 with twin towers flanking a vast dome off which the exhibition halls extended to the east and west. But there was much more to Miller's design than this basic *parti pris* (Fig. 35). To the north of the hall, facing the park and framing the visitors' first view of the pavilions beyond, Miller created a vast piazza enclosed on both its sides and opening onto the park through a double colonnade with central pedimented arch. His twin towers dominated this space to the south and provided lifts to a high-level open arcade that provided visitors with a (then quite astonishing) bird's eye view of the entire showground. The architecture in white and gold evoked an exotic mid-European sophistication – the vast golden dome of the Industrial Hall topped by a golden angel that shimmered, even under the darkest Glasgow skies – with the entire structure coming alive at night when lit again by sparkling electric light.

Miller's buildings have been described as everything from 'Spanish Renaissance' to 'Pure Confectionary' but his source was the buildings of the incredibly successful and widely publicised World's Columbian Exposition of 1893 in Chicago, which was visited by Glaswegian travel writer James Fullarton Muirhead, who worked for the Baedeker publishing house and who wrote that 'since 1893, Chicago ought never to be mentioned as 'Porkopolis' without a simultaneous reference to the fact that it was also the creator of the White City, with its Court of Honor, perhaps the most flawless and fairy-like creation, on a large scale, of man's invention'.(2) But despite the precedent of Sellars's work and the inspiration of Chicago, there is also something distinctly continental about Miller's buildings, as they have more than a hint of contemporary Vienna and consistently struck a very satisfactory balance between plain white surfaces and exuberant decorative detail.

Fig. 35   The main exhibition buildings of the Ruritanian fantasy that Miller
created for Glasgow's Great Exhibition of 1901. Courtesy of Neil Baxter.

His achievement is all the more remarkable when one considers that most of the buildings were constructed from prefabricated panels of plaster on a sacking base, which were formed in moulds and finished once in place on site. The exhibition halls themselves were much more utilitarian, with exposed steel trusses under glass, for which his railway station experience proved perfect. A separate competition was held for the 3000-seat temporary concert hall within the park, and Miller beat both Mackintosh and the other members of the following pack once more to secure that commission as well. His circular design featured a double-height arched arcade that supported a continuous balcony at first floor, while externally, the language was a watered-down version of the Industrial Hall, with twin decorated Venetian towers either side of an arched main entrance. The Exhibition buildings were a massive and highly prestigious commission for Miller. It both announced his arrival as a new competitor for major projects within the city and also, much more significantly in terms of his career, gave him a new public profile among the city's bankers and industrialists, many of whom had either organised, provided financial backing for, or were participating in, the exhibition. Unsurprisingly, as well as turbo-charging his career, the exhibition also significantly boosted his self-confidence as a designer and evidence of this began to come thick and fast in the new commissions that were now flooding into his office.

Much of the credit for what was to be a change of direction and increase in quality in this new work has been given to the many new assistants who joined Miller's office around this time but, with the exception of James Carruthers Walker (1874–1954) who was soon to become his chief assistant, most only stayed for a year or two and indeed, Walker himself did not join the office until 1900, by which time much of this great wave of new commissions had already been designed. Miller also firmly believed that, as he later stated, the 'profession of architecture is largely a personal one. The personal element is essential in preserving that distinctive originality which should mark the architect's creation'.(3) He maintained this personal involvement in the design of everything that was completed under his name until very late in his career. The constant driving force, both commercially and in terms of architectural approach, was and continued to be James Miller himself, and this could be clearly seen in the changes made to his design of the much-delayed municipal buildings in Clydebank on which construction had also finally commenced in 1900 (Fig. 36).

His Scottish Baronial competition-winning design of 1893 had been entirely remodelled in a very competent Glasgow Free Style and while he managed to include a vast array of Burnet

Fig. 36   Miller's new-found confidence was displayed in his revised design for Clydebank Town Hall of 1900–2. Courtesy of Andrew Henderson.

motifs, from carved ship's prows to split pediments with pylons, nevertheless there is a clarity and sharpness to his design that is distinctly Miller in character. He was not afraid to offer great, smooth planes of stone against which the richer details of door and window surrounds are contrasted, as the great Alexander Thomson had taught his successors so effectively. The mighty corner tower, which dominates the composition, for example, rises in smooth banded ashlar from the simplest of bases to the sharply cut dentils of its cornice high above, in turn supporting

Fig 37   Miller abandoned the Gothic in his Linthouse Church of 1899, producing instead a highly original Glasgow Free Style composition. Credit Roger Edwards.

a colonnaded cupola. The entrance to the civic hall around the corner is a particularly well-balanced arrangement, with smooth flanking towers either side of a recessed entrance, into which openings are sharply punched and carving sparingly added. There is a certain Calvinist ascetism here for the first time in Miller's work (in total contrast to his Exhibition buildings), which was to become a key theme in his future development.

His design of Linthouse United Free Church in Govan from 1899 is contemporaneous with the design of the Clydebank municipal buildings and is again in complete contrast to his earlier Gothic ecclesiastical efforts. Its main entrance elevation to the street was a variation on the entrance to his civic hall in Clydebank, with flanking towers and a high-level band of glazing below a half-round window in the gable (Fig. 37). But here, the towers are extended into engaged corner piers and topped with colonnaded cupolas, making it one of the most original church designs in Glasgow of the 1890s. His competition-winning design of Lintwhite School in Bridge of Weir from the same year extends these themes even further. Here, squat, two-storey towers provide boys and girls entrances either side of a broad single-storey curved bay, above which runs another horizontal band of glazing, this time contained by two tall, very elegant red sandstone chimneys, which conclude in rectangular flat-topped caps. In his detailing, the language of Classicism has been reduced to a minimum and we see instead the first appearance in his work of the sinuous lines of Art Nouveau.

In the midst of this success, 1899 also brought the sad news of the death of Miller's mentor and benefactor, George Graham, but fate continued to favour Miller as Graham was succeeded as Chief Engineer to the Caledonian Railway by Donald Alexander Matheson, who had been one of Miller's school friends at the Perth Academy. Matheson soon confirmed that it would be business as usual, with commissions for new stations at West Kilbride, Glenfinnan, and Mallaig. Miller was also picking up further work on the exhibition site as a result of his role as master planner, including the Sunlight Model Workers Cottages for Lord Leverhulme (the only surviving buildings from the exhibition) and the large Canadian Pavilion, as well as two private houses for exhibitors – Coupar Grange House in Coupar Angus for James Duncan, and Rowallan in Troon for Sir Alexander Walker the whisky distiller, both of which are rather unremarkable in white render below red tiled roofs (Coupar Grange, however, has a particularly good Jacobean interior, most of which has survived). Miller and his new team were overwhelmed with work but he had no intention of resting on his newly-won laurels.

Another major architectural competition was announced in 1900 for the complete replacement of Robert and John Adams' Glasgow Royal Infirmary building adjacent to the city's Cathedral. As with the Exhibition, it attracted entries from most of the leading practices in Glasgow, but such was the scale of the opportunity that it also hit the radar of major practices far beyond the city. JJ Burnet must have felt confident once more, having already designed a building for the Western Infirmary and also recently studied the latest hospital design during his visit to the United States. He was one of the many Glasgow entrants who again included John Campbell and William Leiper, but the scale of this opportunity also attracted Miller's old employer, Hippolyte Jean Blanc, from Edinburgh as well as London architects John Simpson (whose art gallery and museum was nearing completion, and with whom Burnet had become a close friend) and even the great Goth, Alfred Waterhouse himself – the architect of Manchester Town Hall, the Natural History Museum in London and Liverpool Royal Infirmary. The selection committee were to be advised by Rowand Anderson (the architect of Glasgow Central Station Hotel) and they provided the entrants with indicative plans as to their preferred layouts. Anderson advised the committee that, based both on his submitted designs and his hospital design experience, John Burnet's former pupil Henry Edward Clifford (who had already designed the Campbeltown and Kintyre District Combination Hospital which was then under construction), should be appointed. Controversially, the committee rejected Anderson's advice by a majority of one, and instead appointed James Miller who, in deference to the adjacent cathedral, had returned to the Scots Baronial style for his competition entry. Rowand Anderson was outraged to see his recommendation overturned and never forgave either Miller or the committee, and his ire was soon shared by the Glasgow Institute of Architects, who formally protested. The controversy raged for several months in the architectural press but the committee was unmoved and their favoured man – Miller – the upstart railway architect – was duly appointed.

It was another bitter blow for Burnet. He had already lost the Exhibition to Miller despite having already completed the Edinburgh Exhibition of 1886 and now he had lost the Royal Infirmary commission to the same architect, who had no previous hospital design experience whatsoever, and having failed the previous year to gain even a place in the competition for the design of the National Bank of Scotland, must have begun to feel either jinxed or entirely taken for granted in his hometown. He was in an extraordinary position – still the dominant force in his profession north of the border and yet still having to enter architectural competitions to secure the most prominent public commissions. Moreover, even in his commercial and domestic work, few of his clients were willing to pay him the premium that his painstaking and laborious efforts on their behalf deserved.

It is a widely held misconception that architects of outstanding ability can simply dash off a sketch on a tablecloth or napkin that instantly provides an inspired and original solution to any problem that has been set to them. The reality is that behind almost every great artist (and there is no doubt that JJ Burnet was a great artist), lie great piles of discarded attempts to get every proportion, technical solution, and element of detailed design perfect. The sheer hard work involved in this highly labour-intensive process means both that they spend many more hours in achieving their own high standards than their competitors and that the time thus spent involved inevitably erodes the profits of their firm. One of Burnet's assistants, Theodore Fyfe, gave us an insight into life in his office at this time:

> Mr. Burnet rarely worked at a drawing board except in his house. His spruce and perfectly turned out figure, and his active springy step could be seen passing through the office occasionally, though prevailing custom made the senior draughtsmen take sheaves of drawings and tracings into the principal's room. This was seeing 'Johnny' (as he was familiarly called), sometimes a matter of trepidation.... On the comparatively rare occasions when he sat down at some draughtsman's desk he

usually sketched out isometric diagrams with a soft pencil on tracing paper, and after he had left the junior staff crowded round and reverently regarded these masterpieces, as such they generally were of their kind.... I have never known anyone who could touch John James Burnet – he was in a class by himself. He was a master in the art of designing on tracing paper, which means that his fastidious taste was never satisfied till he had gone through a process of trial and error that to his draughtsmen seemed inexhaustible.... It was a commonplace that he would not look at a scheme (he would say 'I can't see it') unless it was presented to him in every possible aspect and drawn to 'the millionth of an inch' in exactness ... He was an autocrat who demanded a great deal from his assistants; but he was just as hard on himself, and his assistants knew it.(4)

In addition to leading the firm's design projects, the principals were of course also responsible for the education of their pupils, who paid their masters for the privilege, and in Burnet's case he took his role as patron extremely seriously, modelling his office on Pascal's Parisienne atelier and teaching his pupils personally. He had acquired his father's considerable architectural library, to which he was constantly adding, and it was used by all the office, with Burnet directing his pupils as to their studies. All this he now had to manage as sole partner with Campbell having left and his father retired, and there is no doubt that as the years went by, the pressures upon him grew ever greater and financial crises soon became unavoidable.

Competition failures were soon put in perspective, however. Burnet's brother Lindsay (the engineer) had died in 1895 at only forty years of age and on 15 January 1901, his father John Burnet passed away. Tragically, this was followed just over two weeks later by the death of his brother George in a cycling accident on 31 January 1901. He had risen to become sheriff-substitute of Aberdeen, Kincardine, and Banff, and now left a wife and three young children, and so with no children of their own, John and Jean Burnet undertook the education of George's son and two daughters. Fortunately, despite the competition losses, Burnet still had enough loyal Glasgow clients to keep him and his team busy through this difficult and stressful period.

Burnet was still the favoured architect for Glasgow University. Sir George Gilbert Scott had already provided their main buildings on Gilmorehill in Gothic style and almost all Burnet's buildings for the University harked back to the medieval architecture of the Old College, which had been located on the High Street before its move west in 1870. He was now commissioned for both the Engineering Building (now the John Watt Building) in 1898 and the Anatomy and Botany Building (now the Thomson Building) in 1899, both of which he delivered in the Scottish Renaissance style that he had already adopted for his earlier Students Union building (Macintyre) and the adjacent main gates. Of the two, the Engineering Building is the more exuberant, complete with turrets, carved shields, and richly decorated chimneys.

With James Miller so busy, the Caledonian Railway Company turned to Burnet for a new tenement on Saltmarket. This is so plain that only the steep conical corner turrets give a hint of its author. He also won commissions for two further churches; Broomhill Congregational, which is another variant on St Molios, and Rutherglen Old Parish Church (the fourth on the site) which is a variant on Dunblane Cathedral, complete with the now familiar three lancet windows in its gable. Unusually, it also has a notable side entrance from Queen Street, sporting a shallow-gabled porch in Early English Gothic style – no doubt in deference to its ancient history.

Considering Burnet's beliefs, extraordinary skills and creativity, it seems strange that there was so little development in his ecclesiastic architecture throughout this important stage of his career. We have two basic models – the Dunblane Barony and St Molios – which he replicated with minor variations for over twenty years, depending on their location and the historical associations of the site. There is no denying the quality of both, nor indeed the originality of the St Molios model, which he made his own and which proved so popular with the congregations of the smaller churches for whom he built, and so one can only speculate that, despite being such a devout Christian, his principle architectural interests appear to have lain in the commercial heart of the city where the budgets were most generous and the architectural competition was most fierce. It seems certain also that, like many successful architects before and since, he had to prioritise his own project involvement within an overall workload, which was far beyond the capability of a single designer. Thus much of the ecclesiastical, minor domestic, and university work was under his guiding hand and only a small minority of projects benefited from his intense personal involvement. Fortunately for us, almost all his own design projects have survived and in the late 1890s he added two further exceptional buildings to his portfolio – Atlantic Chambers in Hope Street (1899) and Waterloo Chambers just around the corner in Waterloo Street (1899). Both buildings rose to what was then a staggering seven storeys in height, made possible by the enhanced electricity supply from the recently completed Port Dundas power station of 1897, which powered their lifts.

While both develop the themes and share architectural elements of the earlier Charing Cross Mansions and Albany Chambers, they offer further refinement without any loss of vitality. Unlike Albany Chambers, both are symmetrical, and Waterloo Chambers provides a much wider elevation to the street. Both have dumbbell plans with central lift and stairs (and Waterloo Chambers originally had a galleried central atrium). In Waterloo Chambers, although the central section rose through three floors to introduce a certain vertical thrust, the emphasis is much more horizontal, with bracketed balconies at the second and third floors below a strong cornice at the wings and a strongly horizontal attic floor to the central section (Fig. 38). Each floor above the shops merits study. On the third floor, a central Diocletian window provides brackets for the balcony above and is flanked by two bay windows and beyond them, two aediculed windows with broken pediments. On the fourth floor the central section becomes a third bay window with its own aedicule and broken pediment, while between the three bay windows, two-storey Ionic columns shoot up to support the massive stone eaves gallery above. The gallery is much deeper than the one at Charing Cross Mansions, where Burnet first used it, and it provides a very satisfying stop to the verticality of the central section. (Interestingly, the eaves of the gallery itself are decorated with Greek acroteria – perhaps in acknowledgement of its source in Alexander Thomson's work). It is another brilliant Burnet composition in red sandstone that becomes ever more dramatic as it climbs higher and higher above the street. With such an

Fig. 38   The extraordinary depth and rich modelling of Burnet's façade of Waterloo Chambers of 1899. Courtesy of Tom Bastin.

expanse of street elevation, Burnet's strong horizontal emphasis achieves a majestic grandeur, whereas around the corner in Hope Street, the much smaller plot has resulted in a strongly vertical composition of quite a different character.

In *Atlantic Chambers,* Burnet's elevation is more restrained and calmer. The bays are simplified and shallower, while the unadorned windows are simply punched into the smooth ashlar façade, giving it a certain spartan dignity and poise (Fig. 39). Here the central section, rather than

Fig. 39   Every horizontal and vertical element is perfectly in balance
in Burnet's Atlantic Chambers of 1899. Courtesy of Ian Stubbs.

expanding above the second-floor balcony, actually contracts, with two vertical channels in the sandstone shooting straight up to the fifth floor. Here they are briefly checked by a recessed arch with a curved pediment before continuing their upward thrust, breaking straight through the sixth-floor gallery to conclude as a bold central chimney. This rocketing verticality is echoed in the two bays that rise through three floors and contrast with the strong second-floor balcony and the very fine top gallery, with its doubled Tuscan Doric columns supporting timber beams and a cornice with dentils so bold that they really do look like the beams of the temple from which the detail was originally derived. As if to sign off his work, the maestro completed it with an elegant Burnet flourish above the entrance. The entrance includes a frieze inscribed 'Atlantic Chambers', flanked by seated figures (*Europe* and *America*) and supporting an aedicule with carved ship between Tuscan Doric columns whose pediment is broken by a decorated bracket supporting a sculpted winged figure. (The excellent sculptures for both the Waterloo and Atlantic Chambers were by Robert Alexander McGilvray and Richard Ferris). When it came to building in Central Glasgow's grid, as Theodore Fyfe suggested, Burnet 'was in a class by himself.'(5)

While Burnet was still clearly Glasgow's professionally pre-eminent architect, James Miller was now clearly its busiest and he was under immense pressure to deliver both the International Exhibition and the Royal Infirmary while recruiting and building a team to assist him in the task at the same time. Of all his new appointments, James Carruthers Walker was to be the most significant and he soon found him to be both a strong designer and an efficient organiser, quickly promoting him to chief assistant. Despite their workload, Miller was able to convince the Caledonian Railway that he still had the capacity to undertake further work for them, and was given his largest commission to date from the company for the rebuilding of much of Glasgow Central Station, including a large extension to the Central Station Hotel on Hope Street (opposite Burnet's Atlantic Chambers) and a massive new commercial building – Caledonian Chambers – which stretched from 75 to 97 Union Street, thus forming a new eastern boundary to the entire station complex. It was another large and extremely complex commission, both architecturally and in terms of construction, with the station and hotel needing to stay open throughout the many phases, with its final phase – the extension of the hotel – not opening until 15 April 1907. Miller personally worked closely on the development of the design with Donald Matheson the Caledonian Railway's Chief Engineer, who himself designed the new railway bridge over the Clyde, as part of the redevelopment.

All the platforms were lengthened during the remodelling of the station, requiring a new bridge over Argyle Street ('the Hielanman's Umbrella'). Four additional platforms were added west of the existing ones. Donald Matheson visited the United States in 1903 on behalf of the Caledonian Railway to study the latest American railway station designs and was much impressed by their use of curved buildings on concourses. These aided the movement of great numbers of travellers during rush hours, likening the crowds to flowing water that naturally finds the line of least resistance. It was an idea that he and Miller would use for the first time in Glasgow Central and their various curved, wood-panelled pavilions under their great glass roof have fortunately survived almost intact to the present day (Fig. 40). These included a two-storey ticket hall that displayed arrivals and departures at first-floor level and a curved extension to the hotel to provide a new entrance directly from the concourse at ground-floor level below an elegant, top-lit bar on the first floor (which has recently been painstakingly restored to its former glory as the hotel's 'Champagne Bar'). Their new concourse soon became a much-loved space and has been a meeting place and the scene of emotional arrivals and departures for Glaswegians for long over a century now. Pevsner's *Guide* described it as, 'one of the most

Fig. 40   The sweeping curves of Miller's Glasgow Central Station
of 1901–7 below his great glass roof. Courtesy of Peter Brooks.

atmospheric in Britain'(6) while Simon Jenkins in his *Britain's 100 Best Railway Stations* even
went so far as to describe the space as the 'custodian of the city's soul'.(7)

Miller's extension to the main hotel building down much of the length of Hope Street
repeated Rowand Anderson's grand ground-floor arches, while injecting some greater interest
above, with a first-floor balcony with pairs of arched windows, a strong dentiled cornice at
third-floor level and another at fifth-floor level, above which a variety of stone dormers echoed
Anderson's lively roofscape. On the other side of the station to the east, on Union Street Miller
designed his palatial Caledonian Chambers – a seven-storey block of offices for the railway
company, with shops at ground level (Fig. 41).

The scale of this block would have challenged any architect, and, in this context, Miller
coped pretty well. The main central section (which is over four times as wide as Burnet's nearby
Atlantic Chambers) has bay windows to the first and second floors, which are stopped by a long
horizontal balcony that is interrupted only by a rather fine Free Style main entrance. Above this,
the fourth floor has paired windows below shared curved pediments that form a base for the
giant Ionic columns spanning the next two floors and supporting a deeply overhanging cornice.
While it is a good attempt to break up a massive wall of sandstone, it has little of the vitality of
Burnet's best work. The other problem is that with a façade that is over a hundred feet long and
seven storeys high, much of the detail that Miller has used to enrich the façade is high above
street level and rarely appreciated. Almost lost, as they are dwarfed by the vast central section,
are two very fine towers that act as book-ends. These extend to the building's full seven-storey

Fig. 41   One of the exceptionally fine bookends to James Miller's
enormous Caledonian Chambers of 1901–3. Courtesy of Roger Edwards.

height and are clearly reworkings of Burnet's Buchanan Street façade of the Athenaeum, with some fine sculpture by Albert Hodge (1875–1918), double-height bays framed by double Ionic columns, supporting (yet another) broken pediment, with this long vertical slot in the wall of stone concluding in an arch and then finally topped with a short gallery (as in Waterloo and Atlantic Chambers). Though it may lack Burnet's brilliance, it remains an impressive building in the city centre, and perhaps even Burnet would have been challenged by the design of an office building on this scale.

In the midst of this avalanche of work, Miller and his team also delivered a small new station for West Kilbride, (currently a tapas bar), a three-storey Glasgow board school, Sir John Neilson Cuthbertson School in Pollokshields, (which conformed exactly to the already well- established Glasgow pattern of classrooms around a central atrium hall, though with a dramatic, largely glazed wall to one end of the atrium), and the much more interesting 10 Lowther Terrace, in the West End for Sir John Traill Cargill, the Burma Scottish Oil magnate (Fig. 42). This is a piece of architecture of considerable sophistication that would not have looked out of place among the townhouses of Ernest George, Charles Ashbee or Charles Voysey in London. It is a beautifully resolved asymmetrical composition in polished ashlar. It has an unusual, two-storey canted bay with parapet to the right and a fine main entrance to the left – with an arched window between – whose projecting keystone forms a bracket to the first-floor balcony above. Two full-height windows at this level are matched on the floor above and paired with two more over the bay to form the lower floor of a beautifully proportioned scrolled Dutch gable. For once, Miller, rather than needing to provide utilitarian office space, had the brief and budget to produce an interior of a quality that fully lives up to the high expectations created by his exterior and he seems to have revelled in the opportunity. The barrel-vaulted entrance hall leads to a beautifully lit open stairwell (with stained glass by Oscar Paterson) which ascends to the exquisite first-floor panelled Baroque Revival drawing room and further equally fine rooms above. Throughout, all the details are executed with Miller's razor-sharp precision, from the fireplaces below the richly moulded plaster ceilings to the Ionic columns of the stairwell and the cross-beamed timber ceilings of the ground-floor rooms (Fig. 43). Finally completed early in 1901, though relatively small, this is one of Miller's best buildings and certainly his greatest architectural achievement to that date. (Incredibly, this Category A-listed gem has survived lying derelict for many years and only recently been saved by conversion into apartments).

Miller was able to pause briefly and celebrate his success at the opening, in brilliant sunshine, of his International Exhibition on Thursday 2 May 1901. With the death of Queen Victoria in January, the exhibition now heralded both a new century and a new age for Great Britain and it was hoped that the new King would perform the opening ceremony. However, in a huge blow to the city's pride, he declined, and it was left to Princess Louise, the Duchess of Fife (on her first ever visit to Glasgow) to do the honours for both the exhibition and the official opening of the adjacent new art gallery and museum on the same day. Both Miller's Industrial Hall and Concert Hall were hugely popular and the exhibition as a whole once more provided the perfect setting for a summer of festivities. In contrast to current opinion, his Industrial Hall was seen at the time as 'a perfect masterpiece of design, marked by a grace

Fig. 42   Miller's work achieved a new level of sophistication in
his 10 Lowther Terrace of 1900–1. Courtesy of Roger Edwards.

Fig. 43   One of the exquisite interiors of James Miller's 10 Lowther Terrace. Courtesy of HES.

and dignity that make the neighbouring Art Galleries ... seem trumpery by comparison',(8) and there were numerous calls for it to be retained after the end of the exhibition, however, Miller's sacking and plaster would not have survived their first Glasgow winter and so all the buildings, with the exception of his Sunlight Cottages (that can still be seen in the park today), were demolished. The exhibition was a huge success however, attracting 11,497,220 paying visitors from throughout Britain and Europe who had marvelled at the city's extraordinary engineering and artistic achievements, helped to generate a healthy financial surplus (that was donated to the city's Art Purchase Fund) and given a phenomenal boost to the reputation of its architect.

The following year he, his wife Emileana, and their young daughter Muriel (whose birth the year before had made 1901 a year of even greater celebration), now moved from their tenement flat to an impressive, double-fronted sandstone villa in the West End at 19 Hillhead Street, and Miller moved his office from West George Street to much larger and smarter premises at 15 Blythswood Square (much smarter, indeed, than the Burnet establishment nearby in St Vincent Street). He joined the Conservative Club and the Glasgow Arts Club, and in April 1902 he was admitted as a Fellow of the RIBA (supported by William Leiper, William Forrest Salmon, and John Slater of London). Officially and unofficially, he had arrived – although his appointment for the Royal Infirmary project against the advice of Rowand Anderson still rankled with his fellow Glasgow architects and this position as something of a professional outsider only grew with his comparative success. James Walker, his chief assistant, gives us a contemporary portrait of Miller, now aged forty-one:

> Very reserved by nature, he did not enter much into public life and was well content to let others talk architecture while he was doing the job. Quick tempered, he could also be very sympathetic and understanding when the occasion demanded. He was also a hard task-master, but few of the men who passed through his hands will deny that they benefitted to a remarkable degree from being employed by Mr Miller, and many of them, now successful architects on their own account later wrote to him to this effect.(9)

Miller's domestic move to the West End also brought him within a few hundred yards of Burnet's home at 70 University Avenue, which he was then in the process of extending. He and his practice may have lost out on several massive opportunities to Miller, but fortunately there was still sufficient work for his team. In 1903, he appointed a promising young architecture student, Thomas Smith Tait (1882–1954) as his personal assistant, thus allowing Tait access to the inner sanctum of the practice and the opportunity to develop a particular understanding of his master's character and working methods, of which Tait later recalled:

> His charm of manner and his strength of character enabled him to overcome successfully those many difficulties an architect is called upon to meet during his varied career. He was meticulously careful in all business transactions, and

endeavoured to be impartial alike to his contractors as to his clients. He kept careful minutes of all interviews and meetings with clients and visits to jobs, a copy of which was handed to each draughtsman concerned with that particular building. All personal letters he wrote by hand, considering it more courteous than to send one typewritten. But his handwriting had the same quality of ordered beauty and clarity.(10)

Burnet's new relationship with young Tait was one that would last his lifetime.

These first years of the new century were unusual for Burnet in that most of his new projects lay outside Glasgow's city centre. There was a chapel for the Glasgow Royal Asylum for Lunatics (now the Calman Cancer Support Centre) and a church – St Gerardine's – in Lossiemouth in the north of Scotland, both in the style of St Molios, with low roofs and covered porches and, in Lossiemouth a square tower, but also unusually, both finished in white roughcast below red-tiled roofs. He designed a tenement in Helensburgh down the Clyde from Glasgow, from whose site he must have strolled up the hill to see Mackintosh's Hill House, which was then under construction. He also designed workers housing for the Harland Engineering Company in Alloa and two very fine buildings in Govan that were endowed by Isabella Elder, the widow of John Elder – one of the founders of what had become the Fairfields Shipbuilding and Engineering Company in Govan – one of the city's most successful yards. These two buildings mark a small, but quite significant, change in Burnet's style.

The first – a cottage hospital in Drumoyne Drive opposite Elder Park (another gift from Isabella Elder) is in a distinctly English Renaissance style with two storeys of honey-coloured ashlar below a deeply overhanging slate roof with dormers (Fig. 44). The traditional window pattern of *piano rustico* and *piano nobile* is cleverly used here to light offices on the ground floor and the higher wards on the first. The entrance elevation (which is at ninety degrees to the park) again has typically English advancing wings that flank the main central entrance, suggesting a traditional H plan (in reality it was a much more solid block arranged around a graceful, top-lit central stair). Only in the entrance, amidst this model of cool Anglican restraint, does Burnet allow himself any real self-expression with a stunning canopy to the front door. Stone Doric columns support carved timber consoles below the shallow vault of the canopy itself and once the viewer is under its shelter, the elaborately sculpted architrave to the door, complete with monogrammed cartouche, can be fully appreciated. It is a bold combination of a very masculine Doric entrance to Mrs Elder's rather genteel, feminine building.

The other building, which is even better, is the Elder Park Library, which sits in the corner of the park itself with its main entrance diagonally opposite Langlands Road (Fig. 45). This is another little pavilion building much in the spirit of his Baroque Savings Bank Hall in Ingram Street, but here he is able to break out of the confines of the city centre grid with a beautiful curved, paired Doric entrance colonnade that swells out from the main entrance to draw readers in. The rear is organised as two wings, each concluding in a gable and bay window either side of an almost entirely plain central section with three high oculi. The interiors (which have fared rather well) originally provided a newsroom, reference libraries for men and women, a small museum, a

Fig. 44   Burnet at his most restrained in his Elder
Cottage Hospital of 1902. Courtesy of Scott Ferguson.

Fig. 45   Full-blown Burnet Baroque in the entrance
to his Elder Library of 1903. Courtesy of Paul Climie.

juveniles' room, a librarian's room and a lending library, all of which were well lit from the tall side windows and the beautiful domed skylight (which again echoes his Savings Bank Hall). The barrel-vaulted side bays conclude in elegantly decorated gables above the bay windows to the park. Its slate roofs are largely hidden by a cornice, which takes the form of a balustrade with decorated urns to each corner, a cartouche over the entrance colonnade, and rusticated chimney stacks on either side of the domed skylight, making a subtle transition from building to sky in this open parkland site. And yet, despite all the similarities with the Savings Bank Hall, there is a new spirit here, as in the cottage hospital – still something of the same Baroque swagger at the entrance, but otherwise, something more genteel – more English Georgian, less Scottish Renaissance.

His other major building from this period – a department store for the Professional and Civil Service Supply Association (a cooperative formed by a group of civil servants) in George Street in central Edinburgh, has a similar vibe (Fig. 46). Its antecedents are clearly his Glasgow offices,

Fig. 46   The first appearance of Burnet's proscenium entrance on the sublime George Street elevation of his Professional and Civil Service Association building of 1903–7 in Edinburgh. Courtesy of David Gray.

and like them it is divided into a central section with flanking wings and a giant Ionic order to the third and fourth floors below a fifth-floor gallery (on this occasion divided by caryatids), split pediments, domes, and balconies. However, there is a new calmness here – perhaps in response to the more urbane Edinburgh rather than the bustling, hustling Glasgow. The composition is perfectly balanced; there are no soaring verticals that need to somehow be contained; no Baroque eruptions combining architecture and sculpture – it is all the very model of good taste and achieves the vitality of his Glasgow buildings only above cornice level, with its fine gallery and the conclusion of its towers. Its one unusual feature is the highly original treatment of the entrance, which sits behind double-height marble and bronze columns flanked by double-height bay windows that double back from the street before forming a screen above the recessed entrance doors. This is a brilliant solution to the problem of providing a largely glazed ground floor within a tall masonry building, with the scale of the two mighty columns seeming to be more than capable of visually supporting everything above them. I can find no precedent for this treatment and it predates Lutyens similar design for 42 Kingsway in London by three years, and Adolf Loos' design for his Looshaus in Vienna by eight. It is a stroke of genius and would come to be known as a 'Burnet proscenium entrance'. (11)

Burnet was still by far the most cosmopolitan architect in Glasgow. He had maintained his friendships with Richard Phené Spiers (who had been one of the proposers for his RIBA Fellowship in 1897 along with John Honeyman and Campbell Douglas), Jean Louis Pascal, Henri Paul Nénot, John Simpson, Charles Follen McKim, and several other fellow students from his time at the École. He had been exhibiting at the Royal Academy's Summer Exhibition in London since 1882, when his drawing, *Centre Portion of the Institute of Fine Arts* had been shown, and he was one of the very few Scots who regularly attended the Academy's exhibitions. He visited London frequently and when friends or their acquaintants were in Scotland, he and Jean were the perfect hosts. Consequently, he was therefore also one of the few Glasgow architects who had achieved a reputation in the capital of the Empire and whose work was thus wider known. He had very occasionally submitted an entry to English architectural competitions (but without success) and so it must have come as something of a surprise to find that the President of the RIBA had submitted his name, along with six others, as possible designers of a major extension to Robert Smirke's British Museum in London. The brief was for the reconstruction of the north library, new galleries, and a lecture theatre, and for the further development of Museum Avenue. Rather than holding a competition, the Office of Public Works and the Trustees of the Museum asked the architects to submit folios of photographs of their executed work. In May 1904, to the astonishment of the shortlisted London architects, it was to be Burnet who on this occasion, was to play the role of winning outsider. It was a triumph, that would take his career and eventually his architecture, in a completely different direction.

CHAPTER 5: 1902–1905

The cult of Modernism has so polluted architectural education and the popular psyche that most people's perception of Glasgow's architecture of this period is completely dominated by the few buildings of Charles Rennie Mackintosh along with James Salmon Jr.'s Hatrack and Lion Chambers, which are regarded as being the innovative precursors of modern British architecture. The reality, however, is that these two friends, along with the other members of Mackintosh's Spook School, were operating largely outside the mainstream of their profession and thus contributed relatively little to the sum of the city's architecture. Artistically, (in addition to Mackintosh and Salmon), John Campbell, William Leiper, Alexander Paterson, James and Robert Thomson, and Burnet and Boston were all making significant contributions, with Burnet and Boston's St George's Mansions (between Woodlands and St George's roads), being the stand-out building of Glasgow in 1900. Fortunately, it too has survived, but now stares in disbelief across the crude cutting of the M8 at Burnet's elegant and equally civilised Charing Cross Mansions on the other side of the concrete chasm. For all these architects, Burnet's success in London merely reinforced his status as the city's architectural leader, with most of his peers enjoying a small degree of reflected glory from his achievement 'Down South'. For the previous decade, Burnet had also been first on the list for many of the city's major clients, but with the dawning of the twentieth century, while he still maintained his role as artistic and professional leader, James Miller now became much more favoured in several client circles. With his success in winning the Royal Infirmary commission in 1900 and the huge publicity generated by his International Exhibition in 1901, he had cast off the mantle of 'railway architect' and was established among the many company directors, bankers, shipbuilders, and shipping line magnates (most of whom had been connected to his Exhibition), as their architect of choice. Suddenly, everyone wanted to commission James Miller.

Lord Inverclyde, who was a director of both the Cunard Shipping Line and the Clydesdale Bank, hired him to extend and alter his home at Cove and his family's rambling mansion at Castle Wemyss; John Christie, the chairman of the United Turkey Red Textile Company commissioned him to lay out a park in his name in Alexandria, complete with lodge and memorial gates; John Wilson, a successful accountant, commissioned 8 Lowther Terrace, two doors down from his earlier No. 10, and was provided with another Dutch-gabled townhouse (though without the fine interiors of No. 10), while Sir John Traill Cargill at No. 10, commissioned the addition of a barrel-vaulted billiard room and conservatory; Surgeon and Professor Walker Downie from the Royal Infirmary commissioned the half-timbered Noddsdale House near Largs, and John Lamb Esq., adaptations and extensions to Glentress House near Peebles.

In the centre of the city he was invited to design Olympic House (1903), a large speculative office development on the corner of George Square and Queen Street (Fig. 47). This is a disappointing effort for such a prominent site, with priority given to the longer Queen Street elevation rather than the more important George Square one, where it towers above its earlier

Fig. 47 James Miller's rather lacklustre Olympic House of 1903 on George Square in Glasgow. Courtesy of Tom Bastin.

neighbour (by John Burnet Snr). This rather stark elevation is a very straightforward affair of a central bay with flanking towers concluding in an unusual (and not particularly effective) arched screen at roof level. The elevation to Queen Street is both richer and more successful, with a long balustrade at fourth-floor level, above which a grand seven-bay Doric colonnade supports a strongly projecting cornice with a gallery above. It is all rather formulaic and certainly not his finest work. One might conclude that with so much work, his architectural standards were slipping, but his other contemporary work denies this and I think we can assume that, like Burnet before him, he was having to prioritise his own time and rely on his assistants more and more.

Between 1902 and 1904, he was commissioned to design three new Glasgow churches; Macgregor Memorial Church (1902) in Govan; St Andrew's East Church (1903) on Alexandra Parade and Jordanhill Parish Church (1904). Of these, the Macgregor Memorial and Jordanhill Parish were both in Gothic style, with square towers and large gable windows, rather than his previous lancets. Macgregor Memorial was much the more interesting of the two, with its stepped buttresses, Art Nouveau details and fine presbytery and hall (demolished to make way for a car park in 1994). St Andrew's East, is in quite a different league and of all Miller's churches it is certainly both the finest and the most original (Fig. 48). With James Salmon Jr.'s adjacent (equally fine) earlier church hall, this little pair of buildings ought to be much better known, both in the context of Glasgow's architectural heritage and of Great Britain's Art Nouveau movement. The interior is very plain (and even plainer now that the pews have been removed) with a shallow barrel-vaulted ceiling and gallery around three sides. Similarly, the side elevations simply reflect the galleried space within, with two rows of windows between razor-sharp buttresses. It is the entrance façade that is the little east end architectural tour-de-force.

This is unlike anything that Miller or any other of his Glasgow contemporaries had previously produced and is much more radical than Mackintosh's famous Queens Cross Church of 1897. Here two square twin towers shoot up almost to ridge level linked only by a lower parapet, below which is a giant stone arch that frames the great gable window and twin entrance doors. The towers themselves are topped with bay windows that appear to have been carved from the solid mass of the stone (much like those in Lutyens's later Castle Drogo), and above all this, an elegant stone and timber bell tower with a swooping, projecting canopy continues the vertical thrust in the attenuated proportions of Art Nouveau. It is a stunning composition that seems to draw on the ordering devices of his previous buildings, with their book-end towers, to provide something truly original in an ecclesiastic context. But there is much more to this little building than just its originality: this is architecture of a high order, finely conceived and executed, in which planes advance and recede, verticals soar, horizontals steady, light is used dramatically, and detail is perfectly balanced with blank planes. St Andrews East thus represent a whole new level of architectural achievement for Miller and his team.

Not to be forgotten amongst his scrum of new clients was the Caledonian Railway, who commissioned their favoured son with design of all the stations on their new West Highland Railway, including Ballachulish, Duror, Glenfinnan, and North Appin, as well as a major new station at Wemyss Bay to serve their new fleet of Clyde steamers (the Caledonian Steam Packet Company). The Glasgow and South Western Railway commissioned him to design a vast new

Fig. 48   Miller's St Andrew's East – his finest church and one of
the best small churches in Glasgow. Courtesy of Roger Edwards.

Fig. 49 Glenfinnan is typical of James Miller's many small Highland railway stations. Courtesy of Andy Grant.

100-bedroom resort hotel at Turnberry on the Ayrshire coast and, having seen his design for Turnberry Hotel exhibited, the Hydropathic Company commissioned him to design a replacement for their Peebles Hydro Hotel, which had recently burnt to the ground.

While the West Highland stations were modest though charming timber affairs (Simon Jenkins having described Glenfinnan as 'peculiarly handsome, with overhanging eaves, bay windows and glazed wind screens'),(1) (Fig. 49). the new station at Wemyss Bay was much more substantial as it had to cope with vast crowds of Glaswegians as they transferred from train to boat for day trips and holidays. The exterior of the station shows little development from his earlier station at Greenock, with half-timbered gables over a sandstone base and here, three towers that could be seen from the approaching steamers (Fig. 14). But internally, what Miller and Caledonian Railway engineer Donald Matheson produced was quite extraordinary. Building on the theories of passenger movement that had informed their work at Glasgow Central, the interior spaces of Wemyss Bay station flow seamlessly from train to boat without interruption, the architectural highlight being the circular booking office from which light steel arches fan out in all directions like the branches of a tree to support the glass roof above, thus creating an extraordinary architectural space as well as being an astonishing feat of British engineering (Fig. 50). Unusually for one of Miller's buildings, Pevsner's *Guide* is close to ecstatic in its praise, describing the building as offering 'a braver new world of sinuous skeletal geometries. Effulgent with light filtered through filigree roofs of lattice steel trusses and patent glazing, this interior space is as fresh and invigorating as it surely was to those first Edwardian travellers who stepped

Fig. 50   James Miller and Donald Mathieson's stunning steel and glass roof of their Wemyss Bay station of 1905. Courtesy of Tom Bastin.

off the Glasgow train more than a century ago',(2) while Simon Jenkins, who regards it as one of the finest railway stations in Britain, describes Wemyss Bay as 'one of the few stations that, in my opinion, qualify as a coherent work of art'.(3) It is Miller's most exuberant and successful station interior – even better than Glasgow Central – and fortunately it has been beautifully restored, which is no less than this little masterpiece deserves.

Fifty miles further down the coast, perched on a rocky outcrop above the sea, sits Robert Adam's Culzean Castle, then occupied by one Archibald Kennedy, third Marquess of Ailsa, who was keen to develop the coast around his estate and lands. Among his various interests was a directorship with the Glasgow and South Western Railway, whose fellow directors he soon convinced of the benefits of building what became the Maidens and Dunure Light Railway. To attract more visitors (again inspired by the railway companies of the United States), they proposed to construct a new resort hotel with sporting facilities including a golf course at the end of the line, and appointed Miller to create it. The site for the hotel was on the top of a small escarpment below which the golf course was laid out, stretching along the coast to the Turnberry lighthouse (Fig. 51). The hotel's main entrance was from a new railway station on the upper level, from where a covered way led to a delightful entrance courtyard with a central fountain, created by two wings of the hotel. This space is dominated by a very neat, asymmetrical arrangement of stepped tower, great stone-mullioned windows to the main staircase and a balustraded sandstone entrance loggia, which is balanced by a slender hip-roofed tower to its right. Beyond this Scottish Renaissance country house flourish, Miller is obviously in holiday mood, and the

Fig. 51   The great west elevation of James Miller's Turnberry Hotel of 1904–5 looks out over its golf course to Turnberry Lighthouse and Ailsa Craig. Courtesy of Colin Smith.

Fig. 52   Miller's palatial Peebles Hydro Hotel of 1905–7. Courtesy of gable-end photography.

remainder of the complex is in a white rendered Queen Anne style, with a deep dentiled cornice below an orange clay tile roof. Logically, the hotel extends north and south along the ridge from the central entrance providing sea views for most of the guests, with the public rooms on the ground floor opening onto a delightful (and long-gone) covered portico from where guests could look out on the links below. The Classical internal public spaces are excellent (and well preserved), with much coffering, egg and dart, and modillion cornicing, and they continue to offer the hotel's wealthy guests a taste of Edwardian opulence. The railway line and hotel were both opened on 16 May 1906.

His design for the Peebles Hydro (completed 1907) was in a similar style, but its focus on healthy living and the lack of what was to become a world-famous golf course meant that it never enjoyed Turnberry's social profile, even though it was a considerably larger and architecturally grander hotel (Fig. 52). Here, the buildings in Queen Anne style rise to three floors of rendered brick below a rather Parisian steeply pitched roof containing two further floors of bedrooms. Three projecting pavilions provide flanking wings and a main entrance bay that is further enhanced by a square Tuscan Doric glass-domed, *porte-cochère* and a delightful third-floor Tuscan portico with balustraded balcony above. Between the wings spans a segmental arched loggia supporting another covered portico similar to that of Turnberry, where guests could enjoy the scenic views (now, almost inevitably, glazed-in, though many of the fine period interiors, including Miller's dramatic staircase, have survived). As at Turnberry, the hotel sits proudly on its ridge, with a grand flight of steps cascading down from its central bay to its grounds below.

The demand for Miller's talents appeared insatiable and when Queens Park Rangers, Scotland's oldest football team, required a new stadium that would also provide a venue for cup finals and international matches, they too approached James Miller. He worked with fellow architect Archibald Leitch to lay out the new stadium, using the natural slopes of the site in Mount Florida to form the terracing and provided a large stand that spanned the entire south side of the pitch, with a single central pavilion that then contained all the ground's facilities. After a disaster at Glasgow Rangers' Ibrox ground, when twenty-five people were killed, Leitch and Miller developed a new form of strengthened terracing to avoid a similar catastrophe. The five-storey central pavilion was flanked by two semi-circular staircases (to encourage the easy flow of crowds, once again) and topped off with a triangular pediment, with its flat roof spanning the stand to provide a press box high above the ground on the pitch side. This was another massive public building project and an instant success. When it opened on 31 October 1903 with over 100,000 people watching Queens Park Rangers play Celtic, it was the largest football stadium in the world.

With so much work to deliver, Miller was generally leaving architectural competitions to his competitors but when the opportunity arose to get his foot in the door with the key city client, Glasgow University, he entered and won the commission for the Materia Medica, Pharmacology and Physiology Building (Fig. 53). Unlike Burnet's smaller previous buildings for the university, this was a major new extension to Gilbert Scott's original complex. Sited slightly to the west and below Scott's buildings, it provided facilities for a broad range of new scientific and medical courses with general teaching spaces, laboratories, and three new lecture theatres, the largest of which formed a semi-circular two-storey conclusion to the two connected five-storey wings of Miller's building. Like Burnet's previous work for the university, the architecture harks back to the Old College on the High Street, with its cliff-like elevations decorated with turrets, crow-stepped gables, and other by now familiar Scottish Renaissance details. The budget was tight and Miller spent his client's money wisely, focusing most of his efforts on the Jacobean linking

Fig. 53   Miller's Materia Medica Pharmacology and Physiology building for Glasgow University of 1907 dwarfed Burnet's previous work for this key Glasgow client. Courtesy of Roger Edwards.

block that formed the main entrance, where their funds would have maximum impact. The quality of this element is high. Miller's detailing was as crisp as ever and a nice balance was struck between the great plain walls with their punched windows, and the Jacobean decoration to the doorway and staircases. Burnet would win more work for the university in years to come, but never anything on this scale. Miller's new buildings were opened by no less than the Prince and Princess of Wales, on 23 April 1907.

In considering Miller as an architect, most academics just examine his buildings, but the skills required to grow an architectural practice at the rate needed to deliver this range and scale of projects successfully while maintaining control of the quality of the work and a personal involvement in the designs, are just as rare as those of any great designer, and are often those that determine the success or otherwise of a leading architect. Burnet, with his head start and greater artistic sensibility, may still have been Glasgow's most respected architect, but Miller was now, only ten years after founding his practice, by far its most successful.

In winning the British Museum commission, Burnet also had a bull by the horns. With the complexity of the project and the need to spend time with his clients while developing his design, whether he wanted to or not, he had no option but to establish a London office. He went one step further, however, and started a new London practice in the name 'John J. Burnet'. 'John Burnet & Son' continued as a separate entity in Glasgow (though it was still entirely under his ownership and control) with William John Blane who had been his chief assistant since 1896, taking over day-to-day control of the practice and its projects. Burnet rented a grace-and-favour residence from the museum at 1 Montague Place, where he established both a London base for himself and his wife Jean and his London office, taking David Raeside, Theodore Fyfe, Andrew Bryce, and James Henry Wallace from the Glasgow office with him. He had advised Thomas Tait to undertake a tour of France, Belgium, Holland, and Italy in late 1904 as part of his continuing architectural education, and on its conclusion in early 1905 he also joined the new London team in Bloomsbury. Their first task was to develop a master plan for the future expansion of the museum, which it was hoped would eventually be extended on all four sides, with Burnet also proposing a new tree-lined British Museum avenue to its north.

No sooner had Burnet established his new practice in London in 1904, than he received a raft of significant new commissions in Scotland. The Marine Hotel in Elie, which he had designed in 1889, had been gutted by fire and required almost total rebuilding. Interestingly, he abandoned his earlier Scottish Renaissance style, adopting instead what can only be described as a variant of James Miller's 'Railway Hotel Queen Anne,' complete with dentiled gables with Serlian windows over double-height bays, as at Turnberry and Peebles. In distant Lerwick in Shetland, the Union Bank had suffered a similar fire and Burnet was commissioned to design a replacement (Fig. 54). Were it not for its remoteness, this Burnet bank would be much better known. Down the lane that is Commercial Street there is a slight broadening, and facing the tiny square is one of Britain's most elegant bank buildings. The language is very much a development of his Elder buildings in Govan but is both richer and bolder. The two-storey façade is divided into three bays by four of the most exquisite engaged Ionic columns that you are likely to see outside Rome. Each of the side bays is then again subdivided into three by unusual pendentive engaged columns that conclude at the string course, which forms the first-floor window-sills – all below a deeply overhanging dentiled cornice. The central section then breaks forward at ground-floor level with a curved bay interrupted by two single-storey Ionic columns that frame the entrance doors and support cornices and a balustrade, with a pedimented cartouche portraying a Viking ship, in tribute to Shetland's Norse heritage. Above this, the central section of the façade then erupts into a great arched pediment containing French windows and a balcony with swirling decoration on either side above a tripartite central first-floor window. Four curved roof dormers and two fine sandstone chimney stacks continue the vertical emphasis and complete this sublime composition. Like his Savings Bank Hall, this is another relatively small building that has an extraordinary presence and in which he manages to symbolise this commercial Scottish enterprise at the turn of the century – dignified, energetic, and superbly self-confident – I'd certainly transfer my account.

He was appointed in the Borders to design a rather grand, and, as it turned out, utterly delightful, country house for Alexander Roberts, a Selkirk mill owner. Edinburgh-based society architect Robert Lorimer (1864–1929) who was then emerging as a force in Scottish domestic architecture, had previously resigned the commission rather than demolish part of the existing historic house to make way for the new. Burnet, in common with most of his generation, had few qualms about such an action and produced in its place his finest domestic work, Fairnilee House in 1904–6 – which more than justified the demolition (Fig. 55).(4) On one level Fairnilee is simply a reworking of many of the Scottish Renaissance elements and features that had typified Burnet's

Fig. 54   Another of Burnet's more remote buildings – the rather
suave Union Bank in Lerwick of 1904. Courtesy of Tom Bastin.

work to date, but what lifts it above his other houses is both the quality of the design and the dramatic change in building materials, with his favourite red sandstone used only for dressings around doors, windows, and chimneys, while most of the walling is carried out in pale cream harled whinstone. The effect is striking and its combination with the contrasting stone brings some of the extraordinary vitality generated in his city centre commercial designs to a domestic project for the first time. It is a finely conceived composition in which a large Scottish tower house, complete with crow-stepped gables, stone pedimented dormers, and a beautiful, corbelled corner turret, is enlivened with Baroque carved details. His use of the red sandstone is finely judged throughout, continuing the bays in red to the top of their parapets, for example, rather than reintroducing cream. Were white rendered houses at Kilmacolm (1899–1901) and Helensburgh (1902–3) by the younger Mackintosh an influence? Very probably: he had already experimented with combining white render with sandstone dressings in his church in Lossiemouth and in his Glasgow Royal Asylum for Lunatics Chapel in Glasgow, but while there is a severity to Mackintosh's white houses, much loved by Modernists, under Burnet's hands at *Fairnilee* this lighter palette has produced a richer, much more romantic, and yet equally sophisticated Scottish country house.

Fig. 55   Burnet's greatest domestic achievement – Fairnilee
House for Alexander Roberts, a Selkirk mill owner.

Fig. 56   Burnet's great corner drum and dome of the second phase of
the Clyde Navigational Trust building of 1905–8. Courtesy of Tom Bastin.

The other great success of *Fairnilee* is the way in which Burnet also controlled and created the outdoor spaces around the house, linking the new structure with the remains of the old by a high screen wall, interrupted by an elaborate set of cast-iron gates between urn-topped gate piers, with another screen wall dividing the entrance forecourt from the garden and concluding in an ogee-roofed pavilion, thus extending the architecture of the house to the treatment of the landscape. This works both in plan and in the creation of a series of stepped terraces onto which the internal spaces of the house open at different levels. As one might anticipate from the quality of the exterior, the principal rooms are of a similar standard, with a beautiful main staircase, much panelling and several fine Baroque fireplaces. Mr Roberts was a very lucky man indeed and we have all benefitted from Lorimer's principled stance.

Burnet was also back at work in Glasgow again with two major commissions. The first was the extension of his Clyde Navigation Trust building along Robertson Street and then around the corner into the Broomielaw to address the river directly. Within the central Glasgow grid the corners of each block were seen as opportunities for architectural expression in the form of towers, drums, and pavilions, often rising above the blocks themselves to terminate in free-standing elements seen against the sky. It is strange that, whereas most Glasgow architects of the nineteenth and early twentieth centuries had the opportunity to 'turn a corner', almost every one of Burnet's buildings within the grid stood within a block, from the Athenaeum on Buchanan Street to Waterloo Chambers on Waterloo Street and Atlantic Chambers on Hope Street. The extension to the Clyde Trust building (1905–8) therefore presented Burnet with one of his first opportunities to show what he could do (Fig. 56). His only previous corner had been in the remodelling of Black's Warehouse for RW Forsyth, and it is the model of the great Baroque drum that he had used there that he developed further, above the Broomielaw.

The first section of the extension along Robertson Street is simply an extrusion of his earlier building, whose rusticated two-storey base simply wraps around the corner, with arched windows punched into the ground floor. Above this rather uninspiring start, the existing elevational treatment is stopped by one of a pair of blank panels that extend above cornice level with sculpted friezes, which provide a frame for the great drum of the Trust Hall below a glazed dome with crowning cupola. The sculpture, both to the linking block at attic level and on either side of the dome is just outstanding (on this occasion provided by Albert Hodge, 1875–1918) with Thomas Telford, James Watt, and William Murdoch looking down on Robertson Street, while two magnificent groups, *Ceres Leading a Bull* and *Poseidon's Wife, Amphitrite* (driving a pair of sea horses) flank the dome (Fig. 57). Brilliant as this all is, its just rather sad (and most unusual for Burnet) that all this wonderful action takes place so high above the street, with just three uncharacteristically dull arched windows above three bronze grilles providing next to no interest at pavement level. The interior spaces within the drum however, do not disappoint, with the circular Trust Hall with columned bays and much nautical detail occupying the prime *piano nobile* spot, from where the trustees can look down on the river that is their charge.

Having hardly had the opportunity to design one corner block, Burnet now had another on his hands almost instantly, with the site for his commission to design McGeoch's Warehouse

Fig. 57   Sculptor Albert Hodge's Ceres Leading a Bull on the
Clyde Navigational Trust building. Courtesy of Jenny Bann.

(1904–8) on the corner of nearby Cadogan and West Campbell Streets (Fig. 58). This is a key
building in Burnet's portfolio as it represents another – this time quite dramatic – change in the
direction in his architecture. Steel and cast-iron framed buildings were nothing new in Glasgow.
John Baird had not only used a cast-iron frame for his 1856 building, Gardner's Warehouse, in
Jamaica Street but also very clearly expressed it in its almost entirely glazed elevations, while
steel-framed structures (which had been pioneered in the United States) had been creeping
into use behind traditional stone façades for a number of years before Burnet started work on
McGeoch's Warehouse. Burnet had witnessed the new fully steel-framed architecture himself
on his visit to the United States in 1896, and importantly, also the manner in which the internal
framing of these commercial buildings was expressed on their façades. Louis Sullivan's 1894
Prudential (later Guaranty) Building in New York, which Burnet would have seen, was typical of
these, with two floors of shops and entrances expressed as a base, above which ten floors of
offices shot skyward until the final floor, in the form of a curved cornice, capped the composition.
The office window treatment was dominated by continuous vertical fins between each window,
which spanned from the two base floors to the cornice, with the horizontals which marked each
floor deeply recessed, and thus secondary. There was a fundamental logic to this elevational
treatment, which (unfortunately) made perfect sense to the highly rational Burnet.

Fig. 58   Burnet's long-lost McGeoch's Warehouse of 1905, which stood on the corner
of West Campbell Street and Waterloo Street in Glasgow. Courtesy of Douglas Scott.

The fact that his Glasgow commercial architecture was not immediately transformed into a
Sullivan-style building was due in part to his Beaux Arts training and in part to the continuing
strength of the Classical tradition that was still being actively pursued, even in the United States,
by his friend Charles Follen McKim, among others. By 1905, however, Burnet was willing to
experiment and McGeoch's demand for a building that was to be part office, part warehouse,
and part showroom inspired Burnet to develop the tripartite vertical expression of the building's
functions in a language that appeared to be stripped to its most basic elements (certainly, in

comparison with his contemporary work for the Clyde Navigation Trust). While many of its features are familiar, such as the soaring chimneys, aedicules, split pediments, and another brilliant Baroque sculpted doorway, the principal elevational element are the three-storey vertical fins that divide the windows of the showrooms and span from the almost-continuous third floor balcony to the attic floor, which itself is treated as a solid cornice with windows cut into it. The corner itself is utterly confused, with solid masonry rising to the third floor, where a circular two-storey bay window emerges from between the two giant chimney stacks, above which is an angled panel. With the exception of the flanking chimneys and beautiful doorway (with a sculpture by Phyllis Muriel Cowan Archibald 1880–1947), it is all rather bleak, dull, and lacking in the life and movement that we have come to expect from *il maestro*. Indeed, if we compare this rather clunky corner with, for example, the elegant, beautifully resolved corners of his Savings Bank Hall (Fig. 27). his change in direction appears all the more painful.

Other commentators (from a Modernist standpoint), have heaped praise on McGeoch's Warehouse, as to them it appears to represent an early example of both Functionalism and an expressed structural frame. It is astonishing to me that Gomme and Walker say it represents the climax of Burnet's work in Glasgow – 'a nearly perfect expression of the constructional techniques which Burnet was likewise pioneering' and 'an impressive moment of the functional tradition in Britain'.(5) Are they seriously suggesting that McGeoch's Warehouse was superior to the drama of the Athenaeum or Burnet's superbly confident Savings Bank Hall? Only by viewing the architecture of the nineteenth and twentieth centuries purely in terms of its contribution to the emergence of Modernism could one possibly come to this conclusion. It is not even a steel-framed building, being in fact an amalgam of steel, cast-iron, concrete, and sandstone masonry,(6) so even for the most myopic of Modernists its principal achievement is to transport Louis Sullivan's aesthetic from the United States to Scotland and apply it to a red sandstone building in the Glasgow grid.

The truth is much less positive. McGeoch's Warehouse signals the start of the long descent of Glasgow commercial architecture into the banality of its modern form, in which the art that Burnet practiced to perfection was replaced by so many mediocre architects in grids, frames and cladding so thin and uninteresting that it hardly merits the description of architecture.(7) Before the emergence of Modernism, for Burnet and most of his contemporaries and predecessors, architecture was about space, mass, fine materials, the use and control of light, and a language of proportion and expression that had been honed over several millennia (with a building's supporting structure and services never exposed to public view). The great quality of the stone that these artists used was not just its intrinsic natural beauty but also in its ability to provide both structural support and a canvas for architectural expression of the highest order. Indeed, it was Burnet's use of sandstone that was fundamental to his best, richly modelled Baroque style in which the sculpture is wholly integrated within his architecture. Nevertheless, measured against the standard of most twentieth-century Glasgow architecture, McGeoch's Warehouse is a work of high art (and in that context it is still sad that it was demolished in 1974).

Burnet's remodelling of Black's Warehouse for R W Forsyth in Glasgow led in 1905, to a major commission to design a completely new store for them on Edinburgh's Princes Street (Fig. 59). Ironically, this was Burnet's first truly steel-framed building and yet, no doubt influenced by his client, it was another very fine example of his Baroque Free Style. His elevational treatment here is really interesting and builds on his work around the corner on George Street in his Civil Service and Professional Supply Department Store. On the George Street building he treated the ground and first floor as a proscenium arch and this idea is replicated on Princes Street, where the ground and first floors are combined within great double-height frames, with plate-glass windows on the ground floor and recessed bays between Ionic columns on the first. Above this device (which here, visually, does not quite support the vast weight of building above), it is business as usual, with a stunning composition of a boldly rusticated second floor below bracketed balconies and giant Ionic columns to the third and fourth floors, supporting the cantilevered balcony of an eaves gallery at fifth-floor level. The depth of modelling of this façade is quite extraordinary and the eaves gallery, which provides a most elegant conclusion

Fig. 59   Burnet's contribution to Edinburgh's famous Princes Street –
R W Forsyth's department store of 1906–7. Courtesy of David Gray.

to the composition, at one time hosted the finest department store restaurant in Edinburgh, from where diners could look out towards the castle and savour one of the most stunning urban views in Britain. This main elevation concludes in a square corner tower with typical Mannerist aedicules at second floor, which rises to an octagonal cupola with a pyramidal roof crowned by a gilded sphere by Gilbert Bayes. Its rear elevation to the lane – which Modernists love – is of white-glazed brick. Sadly R W Forsyth is no more and while the exterior of Burnet's building survives, the interior has been subdivided, with the lower two floors used for retail and the top two currently hosting a Travelodge hotel.

With all this ongoing work – McGeoch's Warehouse and the extension to the Clyde Naviga-tion Trust building in Glasgow, the Marine Hotel in Elie, the Union Bank in Lerwick, the beautiful Fairnilee in Selkirk and R W Forsyth's in the heart of Edinburgh, as well as his new practice and a nationally important building to design in London, Burnet was suddenly overwhelmed. Somehow (it is almost impossible to imagine quite how), by working day and night, he and his team delivered all these buildings with rarely a hint of lowered architectural standards, but this brought Burnet the dawning realisation that, as the museum extension progressed, and if further London work was won, this level of effort simply could not be sustained in the long term.

And so, we reach one of the most fascinating junctures of our tale, as rumour has had it for many years, that Burnet considered sharing his future work, 'and made a tentative approach with a view to partnership'(8) to none other than James Miller. In many ways this made perfect sense to Burnet, as it seems clear in retrospect that he aimed to use his high-profile appointment in London to pursue his future career there, but building a London practice (where the fight for the best work was at least as fierce as in Glasgow) would demand almost all his considerable energies. And yet, he also knew that his income came from Glasgow clients and that for several years to come it would be required to finance his London operation while he built it (presuming of course that he was successful in doing so, of which there was no guarantee). What better, than to merge John Burnet & Son with Glasgow's most commercially successful architectural firm, while going on to build his new practice, John J. Burnet in London?

Miller could hardly have been more flattered than to be approached by Burnet. The outsider, the railway architect, the 'confectioner' of the Exhibition buildings, the 'thief' who stole the Royal Infirmary commission, offered an equal partnership with the most respected architect in Glasgow! How could he refuse – all his professional sins would be absolved with one simple act of acceptance – and yet he did refuse the great John James Burnet.

Why should James Miller share what he had achieved? If Burnet was bound for London, it meant one less competitor in Glasgow (not that he had much difficulty beating Burnet for work in recent years). He had his own practice, under his own name, and by common acknowledgement, it was now the most successful in the city and his own architecture was achieving new heights. What then had Burnet to offer him beyond a little kudos among his professional peers? Miller accepted Burnet's approach simply as recognition of what he had achieved and, 'after careful consideration, Mr. Miller decided to plough a lone furrow, and this he did most successfully to the end of his days'.(9)

CHAPTER 6: 1905–1911

Miller certainly had no need of the extra workload from Burnet, his team were already fully stretched and having to cope with what had now become a never-ending flow of new commissions. In 1905 two further major opportunities arose, both related to Glasgow's booming shipping industry. The first was another city centre building – new headquarters for the Anchor Shipping Line (Fig. 60). Though it was never quite in the league of Cunard or the P&O, the Anchor Line, founded in 1838, was nevertheless a significant player, first on the transatlantic route to New York (where it had opened its first ticket office in 1865) and then with the opening of the Suez Canal, providing passage to India as well – indeed, it was an Anchor Line ship that was the first merchant vessel through the canal on the day of its opening. Its market positioning was to offer value for money and it played heavily on its Scottish roots, offering, 'Scottish ships and Scottish crews for Scottish passengers'(1) and by 1905 a suitable Scottish headquarters building from which to operate was long overdue. Miller's solution to their brief was a radical one which, quite brilliantly, evoked the spirit of their ships in his architecture.

The pristine sandstone city centre buildings that we see in Glasgow today were not always thus. Prior to the Clean Air acts and the extensive stone cleaning that took place in the 1970s, Glasgow's buildings were almost universally black. Decades of the coal fires that had warmed both homes and offices throughout Britain had cast a funereal pall upon the country's architecture. This pollution was well under way at the start of the twentieth century, when new buildings in the city centre stood out sharply against their neighbours. In an attempt to address this problem, architectural faience, a system of glazed terracotta blocks which did not trap soot and, if soiled, could be simply wiped clean, was developed by the Burmantofts Pottery in Leeds in 1859. The benefits of this new material were quickly understood, and it was adopted for numerous public and private city centre buildings throughout England during the latter half of the nineteenth century. It had been used in the interiors of the City Chambers in Glasgow but never on an exterior elevation in the city until Miller attempted it on his Anchor Line Building in St Vincent Street (1905–7).

His concept was to provide the Anchor Line with a metaphorical steamship, glistening white on its exterior hull and with a series of sumptuous interiors that would offer their customers a

Fig. 60   The shimmering white faience of Miller's Anchor
Line building of 1905–7. Courtesy of David Gray.

hint of the quality of life that awaited them should they book a passage on board one of their ships. It was a bold and very demanding experiment for a busy architect to undertake as the use of faience is an extremely complex process in which every element of the façade has to be designed and then reduced to a series of blocks that can be fired, allowing for the fact that each block shrinks slightly during the process. The finished blocks are then assembled on site like a great child's building kit, and supported by a concealed structural frame. As a first attempt with this new technology, one has to give Miller and his team good marks.

The façade is dominated by a central bay that rises from a second-floor consoled balcony to develop into a triple-floor tetrastyle Ionic portico supporting a very elegant attic floor in which small Ionic columns frame three balustraded central bays below four urns with swags. One cannot help but feel that were this central section just a little further projected, it would have considerably enlivened the composition and consequently, one wonders if this slight flattening of the façade was related to this first attempt in faience. Very cleverly (and in contrast to Burnet's R W Forsyth building in Edinburgh) Miller lavished attention on the first two floors to have the maximum impact upon passers-by. Here, he employed a proscenium arch to span most of the ground floor, with two secondary doorways acting as book-ends. In the centre, the shallow arch of the beautifully decorated main entrance interrupts the proscenium and breaks forward boldly on Ionic columns, while the pediments to the side doors, window keystones and balcony brackets are richly decorated with masques, cartouches, and other sculpture. There is certainly no hint of compromise at this level and Miller's response to the problem of a ground floor with large shop windows in a masonry building is exceptionally good. The interiors were lavish in their design and detail, with fine oak panelling, eighteenth-century style plasterwork with wreaths, modillions, and swagged fruit and several excellent fireplaces which employed the Ionic order once more. If he aimed to give the impression of a luxury liner, he certainly succeeded. Fortunately, much of this decoration survives (despite the building having lain empty for over ten years) and as the building is currently a bar, restaurant, and hotel, it can be fully appreciated by the Scottish public once more.

If Burnet's approach had confirmed Miller's new status within his profession, his next commission confirmed that, as far Glasgow's ruling elite of company directors and owners were concerned, Miller was now their architect of choice.

The Cunard Line had held the Blue Riband for the fastest Atlantic steamship crossing for an almost unbroken three decades, but by the end of the nineteenth century it had fallen behind its rivals; the White Star and the Inman Lines. When both these British lines were taken over by American shipping companies at the turn of the century, it meant that Britain had technically lost the title for the first time. In response, the British government provided Cunard with a substantial loan and a subsidy to build two new superliners that would wrest back the title from the upstart Americans. One (the *Mauretania*) was to be built by Swan Hunter in England and the other, the *Lusitania*, was to be built by John Brown's shipyard in Clydebank. On 16 June 1904, Lord Inverclyde, on behalf of Cunard, hammered home the first rivet in its keel. While its principal aim was to win back the speed title, on its completion the *Lusitania* would also be the world's largest passenger ship and it was intended that her interiors should also set a new standard in ocean-going luxury. Miller had already remodelled the interiors of Lord Inverclyde's own houses at Wemyss Bay and Cove, and on the back of that and on his subsequently enhanced reputation, he was now commissioned to design the interiors of the *Lusitania* by Cunard.

Today, regrettably, the *Lusitania* is famous not for winning back the Blue Riband or for the quality of Miller's interiors, but for having been sunk by a German U-boat on 7 May 1915 off the southern coast of Ireland with the loss of 1,198 passengers' lives – an act that contributed to the United States joining the Allies against Germany in the First World War. Luckily, its completion in June 1906 was accompanied by a crescendo of publicity; to support which, its interiors were comprehensively photographed by Bedford Lemere and Company. What they show is a series of lavish public spaces that fully justify the phrase 'floating palace', with dining rooms opening through circular balconies to stained glass domes; a stained glass barrel-vaulted first class smoking room complete with a fully operational fireplace framed with Ionic columns below an elegantly curved canopy; a circular purser's bureau on the promenade deck (with strong echoes of Wemyss Bay station) (Fig. 61); a grand top-lit staircase that wrapped around the ship's two gilded cage elevators and a veranda café, whose walls could be removed in fine weather. While most of the interiors were in white plaster, the first-class areas had richly moulded ceilings and timber panelling which varied from mahogany in the dining room, to oak in the smoking room and walnut in the ladies' writing and reading rooms. It was all in the best possible taste – more Louis XVI than Glasgow Baroque for the first-class areas, a rather strict Georgian for the second class and even the third class enjoyed some panelling and the odd fluted column in their public areas. On its launch, the photographs of Miller's interiors (on which he had been ably supported by his assistant Alexander McInnes Gardner [1878–1934] and Robert Whyte [1873–1949], an interior designer with John Brown and Company Shipbuilders) were reproduced in the press throughout Britain and the Empire, reminding the public in Scotland that the architect of the International Exhibition was still at the forefront of his profession, as well as introducing him to an even wider audience around the globe.

Fig. 61   The circular purser's bureau on the *SS Lusitania* echoes the sinuous forms of Miller's station buildings.

Having been rebuffed by James Miller, as far as is known Burnet made no further efforts to find a new Scottish partner, leaving William Blain to run the Glasgow office. He appointed Norman Aitken Dick, the son of a wealthy Edinburgh family, who had just returned from Paris to assist Blain in Glasgow in December 1907, believing him (incorrectly) to be a fellow graduate of the École (a pretence that Dick maintained for many years) but nevertheless soon valued his lightning-fast drafting skills, which compensated somewhat for his rather standoffish manner and quick temper. By then, the great rush of work in Glasgow was easing and Burnet committed himself almost fully to London, where Jean was now playing a successful role as hostess to friends, fellow professionals, and potential clients at 1 Montague Place. By now the scope of Burnet's commission for the Museum was reducing month by month, as the Trustees were having little luck in raising the necessary funds for the transformation of the Museum that they had originally envisaged, and it soon became clear that only the new Edward VII Gallery to the north of Smirke's building could proceed at this time (as its funding had already been secured by a bequest made by Baron Rothschild in 1899).

Burnet's design brief for the extension of two new exhibition galleries with a new north library and administrative offices was hardly taxing, and his final plan was quickly developed, with a new central museum entrance with public staircase and lift and galleries over, a new galleried library behind on the first floor and a connecting link to the existing museum building at ground level. Inspired by Robert Smirke's great Ionic portico to the main entrance, Burnet decided to treat his new extension as another vast Ionic colonnade spanning almost the entire length of the new building on Montague Place (Fig. 62). The ground floor, which accommodated offices and stores,

Fig. 62   Burnet's great Ionic colonnade on his new wing of the British Museum of 1904–14. Courtesy of John Stewart.

was treated as a low stone base for the two floors of galleries above, within the colonnade. This was then topped with a mighty stone cornice that, like so many of Burnet's Glasgow buildings, is contained on either end by a full height tower. Professor David Watkin offers French precedents, including Louis Duc's Palais de Justice in Paris(2) for the overall composition, but Burnet may have been influenced at least as much by the contemporary Beaux Arts buildings he had seen in the United States, such as his friend Charles Follen McKim's design for the General Post Office Building (now the James A Farley building) adjacent to Pennsylvania station which, though not completed until 1912, had been part of the master plan that McKim had developed in the early 1900s. While the planning of Burnet's building was straightforward, he and his London team laboured long and late over its proportions, details, and construction, as Theodore Fyfe, who was then in his office, recalled: 'Every aspect of the British Museum extension was the result of exhaustive trial and experiment. The entrance doorway (irksome because it was of necessity so low), though seemingly quiet, is a mass of concerted subtleties and is typical of the entire front, which, except for the use of a Greek order showing great refinement, is quite modern in feeling'. (3) As Fyfe noted, like Lutyens in his later Cenotaph and War Stone, Burnet fully understood the classical principle of *entasis*, in which elements of the composition were slightly curved on extreme radii to ensure that on completion they appeared to be perfectly horizontal or vertical to the eye. Fyfe is right, too, that, despite the giant Ionic order, there is a certain modernity to the stepped massing of the elevation, which is further emphasised by the treatment of the doorway and the flanking pylons that mark the low, curved entrance court. Construction started in 1906 and by June 1907, the basement was complete, allowing the foundation stone to be laid by His Majesty King Edward VII – Burnet's first encounter with his monarch.

With much of the design work on the museum complete, the Burnets embarked on another American tour, both renewing old acquaintances and viewing the latest architecture in New York. Like most British visitors of this period, he was again struck by the dynamism of the city, the scale of its architecture, and in some cases, the fearless expression of the new technologies engaged to construct it. The fourteen-storey New York Evening Post Building (1906–7) by Robert D Kohn would have just been completed, with its tall bays of cast-iron windows within thin limestone piers, which very clearly expressed the structural frame behind the façade carrying the loads, while his friend Charles McKim's immense and magnificent colonnaded Pennsylvania railroad station (1902–10) in a Classical Beaux Arts style, which was then under construction, would have suggested the continuing possibilities of Classicism.(4) Architecture was clearly approaching a crossroads and Burnet would soon need to make a positive decision as to the future direction of his practice's design work.

His return to Britain must have been rather depressing, as with no new work in London and little enough to keep his Glasgow team busy, his finances were getting more and more stretched. William Blain, his chief assistant, was growing into his leading role in Glasgow and also establishing a public profile within his profession, both lecturing in Glasgow, Edinburgh, and Aberdeen and acting as president of the Glasgow Architectural Association from 1906 to 1907. By then the major projects such as R W Forsyth's in Edinburgh, the Marine Hotel in Elie and the extension to the Clyde Navigation Trust building were all on site and thus offered little further design work, while most of the new commissions were merely for alterations or extensions to existing buildings, such as a new entrance to the Grand Hotel in St Andrews and the modest extension of their earlier Student Union building for Glasgow University. The only new building from this period was St Philip's Episcopal Church in Edinburgh (1908) which, with its base of red brick semi-circular arches between battered brick buttresses and a white roughcast upper level below a slate roof, gave no hint of the hand of the brilliant JJ Burnet. Burnet had split his forces, was now struggling on both fronts, and urgently needed cash.

Help came in the form of Norman Dick, who bought a ten-year partnership in John Burnet & Sons in 1909 (the Glasgow practice). As can be imagined, William Blain, who was Dick's elder, the more senior member of the office, and who had been a loyal assistant to Burnet through the glory years since 1892, was more than a little upset. Dick was already unpopular before his promotion and had little to commend him beyond his inherited wealth. Burnet must have been desperate.

His intended, James Miller, had called the dice correctly and was continuing to thrive, with major new commissions coming in as regularly as his great Central Station clock ticked the seconds past. Emelina had proved quite as adept a hostess as Jean Burnet and the Millers now entertained regularly at Hillhead Gardens, where they were assisted by their domestic servants.

To the vast resort hotels, city centre buildings, and ocean liner interiors was added a modest commission for one of the largest fire stations in Glasgow in Partick (1906) for which Miller produced a three-storey L-shaped building wrapped around the street corner. Unusually, it was in red brick, with ashlar reserved for the dressings to the five-bay engine entrances and the main entrance for pedestrians and vehicles on Sandy Road. Like his contemporary hotels, it was in the Queen Anne style, with sash windows and a bold modillion cornice, a style that to that date he had reserved for his buildings outside the city. But compared with his next commission, this could almost be categorised as a minor work.

In 1903, the North British Locomotive Company had been formed by the merger of Sharp, Stewart and Company (Atlas works), Neilson, Reid and Company (Hyde Park works), and Dübs and Company (Queens Park works), thus creating the largest locomotive manufacturing company in Britain, and in 1907 James Miller was appointed to design their new headquarters building in Springburn in Glasgow. As befitted an organisation that was pretty much supplying the British Empire with trains,(5) the company headquarters were appropriately palatial, with a vast, four-storey red sandstone elevation facing Flemington Street, behind which, completing a quadrangle around a central courtyard, were four floors of functional saw-tooth top-lit offices. The main façade spanned the entire city block and was on a similar scale to the immense (and then still extant) Hamilton Palace, and it also shared its Palladian *parti* with a central entrance block and flanking pavilions stepping forward from the main façade. These advanced elements are particularly good, with the entrance section divided into three bays horizontally by fine double-height pilasters that run from its rusticated ground floor to the colonnaded attic sitting above the modillion cornice that spans the entire main elevation (Fig. 63). The main entrance itself is excellent, with granite columns supporting Ionic sandstone capitals below a broken pediment framing what at first appears to be a classical cartouche, but on closer inspection

Fig. 63   Miller's fine entrance to his North British Locomotive Company's office of 1907–8 framed by *Science* and *Speed* and decorated with a charging train, blocks and tackles by sculptor Albert Hodge. Courtesy of Thomas Nugent.

proves to be a rather wittier locomotive, charging forward and decorated with swags of chains, blocks, and tackle. Two flanking figures of *Science* and *Speed* by Albert Hodge, complete this delightful little ensemble. The book-end pavilions are also superb, with double Ionic columns standing without support in front of a double-height cast-iron screen.

The central bay contains the main staircase (to which was later added a fine stained-glass window as a First World War memorial) that leads to an appropriately grand suite of Edwardian Baroque principal offices and the boardroom, all complete with panelling, Ionic fireplaces and deeply modelled plaster ceilings. The internal courtyard is also of interest, as it was clad in patterned grey and white ceramic tiles to reflect light into the surrounding drawing offices. Opened by Lord Roseberry on 10 September 1909, the building served the North British Locomotive Company until its demise in 1962, after which it provided a home to the North Glasgow College for several decades, and now staggers on as serviced offices, being one of the very few buildings to have survived the almost total eradication of Springburn from the face of the earth, in the 1960s and 1970s.

Not content with dominating the Glasgow architectural scene, and perhaps inspired by Burnet's major commission in London, Miller next boldly entered and won the competition for the Prince of Wales Museum of Western India in distant Bombay (now the Chhatrapati Shivaji Maharaj Vastu Sangrahalaya). In second place was George Wittet, who had also been a pupil of Andrew Heiton in Perth, and who had taken up a position in 1904 as assistant to John Begg, the consulting architect to the Government of Bombay. In a reversal of roles from the Glasgow Royal Infirmary competition, Wittet was awarded the commission on the recommendation of his boss John Begg, who was acting as architectural adviser to the selection panel, with Miller this time the bridesmaid. Nevertheless, such a win was a considerable further achievement and Miller's Indo-Saracenic winning design was widely published in the construction and architectural press.

The vast bulk of the Royal Infirmary was now taking shape and so delighted was House Surgeon Dr Duncan McCorkindale with what he saw that he commissioned Miller to design a house for him, Dunholme in Hamilton Avenue, Pollokshields (1909). It is interesting to contrast the quality of Miller's design for Dunholme with his earlier sub-Shaw, half-timbered gabled efforts such as Dunloskin of 1890; as Dunholme is a work of considerable sophistication – an almost flawless two-storey asymmetrical Arts and Crafts villa in honey-coloured sandstone, with gabled bays to the entrance elevation, three great flat-topped stone-mullioned bay windows to the main southern elevation, tall, elegant corniced chimneys and deeply overhanging eaves (Fig. 64). This is clearly a development of his work at Lowther Terrace and also reminds one of Lutyens at his most severe – more the garden elevation of Marshcourt (1901) or Little Thakeham (1902) than the warmth of Deanery Garden (1901), all of which Miller would have known from *Country Life* – or perhaps it was Voysey's *Broadleys* on Windermere of 1898 with its three great bay windows that had offered him a clue. A very dignified Scots Renaissance main doorway leads to an outstanding interior which, with its excellent panelling, open staircase, fireplaces and ceilings, is almost on a par with that of 10 Lowther Terrace. All in all, it is a relatively modest but very impressive piece of domestic architecture.

Fig. 64   Miller's Dunholme of 1909 continues the sophisticated language first developed at 10 Lowther Terrace. Courtesy of Robert Russell.

In this context it seemed all the more surprising that he returned to Shaw's half-timbered gables for his next house commission – Monktonhead House in Ayrshire (1910–11) for Glasgow shipbuilder Kenneth Connal. Perhaps it was his client's wish or, more likely, Miller still retained a belief that, while he could stretch his hard urban style of Lowther Terrace to the Glasgow suburbs for Dunholme, South Ayrshire was a step too far into the countryside for it to be acceptable. Monktonhead is larger than Dunholme and stands within its own grounds, complete with gatehouse. It is dominated by its numerous gables and tall chimneystacks, with render to the ground floor and, unusually for Scotland, clay hung tiles to the upper levels with bay windows, a large staircase window and a sheltered terrace (as in his earlier Coupar Grange). The interior is excellent with another, rather English, shared open-panelled hall and stairwell.

While Miller grappled with his incredible workload, there were at last some glimmers of light for Burnet. Far from achieving his aim of building a practice in London to equal that of his family business in Glasgow, so far, all that he had managed to do was focus his efforts on London with limited success, while the Glasgow business withered, but in 1909 after an unsuccessful entry in the competition for the new Usher Hall in Edinburgh, he finally won major new commissions for both his practices.

He was appointed by Alfred Butt (the London theatre impresario who had managed to raise funding from over 800 local investors in the Glasgow Alhambra Limited to support the development) to design the Alhambra Theatre in Glasgow. It was to be a major new theatre for the city, with a capacity of 2800 and the very latest in technology to support a commercial mix of variety, theatre, opera, ballet, and dance (Fig. 65). Its main façade was pure Burnet in

Fig. 65   Burnet's Alhambra of 1908–10
brought something of the Arabian Nights
to Glasgow's city centre for many years
until its eventual demolition in 1971.
Courtesy of John R. Hume.

composition, with a central proscenium frame below a balcony between flanking towers, with
the horizontals of the entrance canopy, balcony, and the dark shadow below the projecting
eaves perfectly balancing the verticals of the towers (as we would expect). (Fig 65) What is
more unusual is that, in lieu of beautifully sculpted sandstone, the Alhambra was in brick, with
some tiled banding of the towers and proscenium, giving it a distinctly frugal feel, particularly
when compared to his Waterloo Chambers of ten years before just a little further down the
same street. One might suspect the influence of his new Glasgow partner Norman Dick, but it
is clear from contemporary documentation that Dick was essentially the office manager and
that Burnet was still very much involved in the design of their Glasgow buildings. One can
conclude only that the shareholders' budget was limited and that the interior took priority.
The auditorium is interesting in that, with the exception of the proscenium arch and adjacent
boxes, which are in the slightly excessive Louis XVI style expected of the day, there is a distinct
American-streamlined feel to the remainder of the circles and balconies, with the rectangular
geometry of the exterior echoed in a deeply recessed auditorium ceiling. Architecturally, it is
confused and in a rather strange way, symbolic of its architect – slightly strapped for cash and
starting to fluctuate between the new world that he had witnessed emerging on the other side
of the Atlantic and the old world of Europe, and between the Classicism of his previous work

Fig. 66 Burnet's finest building in London, the offices of the General Accident, Fire and Life Insurance Company of 1909 on the Aldwych. Courtesy of John Stewart.

and training and an emerging interest in Modernism. It is certainly far from his greatest work, but it proved a very popular venue from its opening in December 1910 until its demolition in 1971.

In London, at long last, he also had his first commissions in the capital since winning the Museum extension. The first of these was a new office for the General Accident, Fire and Life Insurance Company on a very prominent site in central London on Aldwych Street. The curved shape of the Aldwych was developed to navigate the significant change in level between the Strand and the new Kingsway after the latter had been laid out. Burnet's site was at the junction of Aldwych and the Strand, where he had to cope with the double challenge of the falling road level and the curve of the building line. It was an extremely difficult site but also a great opportunity for an architect of Burnet's ability to showcase his extraordinary talent, and he did not waste it (Fig. 66). His elevation is in essence a skin of Portland stone which is curved – almost stretched – around the corner from the Aldwych to the Strand, with rustication up to the third-floor balcony and a sheer ashlar wall above, which concludes in a boldly dentiled cornice below an attic gallery. A curving two-storey proscenium is then cut into this to provide the main entrance, supported by coupled granite columns with bronze Ionic capitals, with the entrance doors recessed in a glazed angled wall that cuts straight across the curve behind the columns. This angled screen is a work of art in itself, with a minor Doric order dividing the bronze windows and each column topped by crouching figures by the busy Albert Hodge. The granite surround of the proscenium is then extended above the door into a central aedicule window flanked by further figurative sculpture and decorated brackets supporting the balcony above. This central vertical thrust then continues above balcony level with another glazed aedicule flanked by Doric columns below a broken pediment. On either side of the proscenium at ground floor are more exquisite minor entrances, each with broken pediments supporting flanking putti. All in all, it is Burnet at his best, working hand-in-hand with a really good sculptor. It is much more restrained than most his Glasgow buildings, partly because his usual red sandstone is here replaced with smooth white Portland stone, but there is also a greater restraint in the detailing and a greater contrast between rich sculptural form and plain surfaces. The interiors were rightly described as 'ingeniously planned and beautifully detailed', while his exterior treatment was thought to reflect 'his more quizzical Scottish manner'(6) but it is as sophisticated as anything else in Edwardian London and sweeps around a difficult corner with considerable panache.

His other London commission was just a few hundred yards away on Kingsway and could not have been more different. His client was George Eastman of Kodak fame, and his brief was a new office building for the Kodak Company in central London. Eastman was a New Yorker and entirely up-to-date with that city's high-rise architecture, but he was not sure how to project his company's image in London nor what this more conservative city would accept. As a result, Burnet developed a number of alternative designs for him that were then worked up by his various assistants. It was the most modern of all these designs (which Thomas Tait had developed) that Eastman preferred. When one considers that most of the new office buildings in the area, like Burnet's nearby building for General Accident Fire and Life Insurance Company,

Fig. 67   Burnet's radical design for Kodak's London offices of 1909–11. Courtesy of John Stewart.

were still, often despite their steel frames, clad in what appeared to be load-bearing stone, Burnet's Kodak House (1909–11) represented something of a revolution in architectural expression (Fig. 67).

Gone were the great carved stone walls, the integral sculpture, the rich play of light and dark, advance and retreat; the balconies, aedicules, pediments, arches, and towers; the Classical orders and sculpture; the historical language that Burnet had mastered so completely – to be replaced by an expressed steel frame – still clad in stone with an implied *piano rustico* and cornice, but with its elevations dominated by long strips of bronze glazing spanning the main office floors. It may have honestly expressed it structure and the activities that it served, but it was deadly dull compared with Burnet's previous work, which was consistently rich and vibrant. It was almost flat, where his façades had previously been richly modelled; the lower floors were lumpen, simply reflecting the dimensions of the frame behind them rather than being exquisitely proportioned, and the little decoration that remained was insipid, rather than bold and confident.

Like most early Modern architecture, it shocked the public, but was lauded then and since by most architectural critics and historians. They used different adjectives to describe it such as innovative, honest and direct. Nikolaus Pevsner, the high priest of the British Modernist cult, later employed phrases such as, 'a new freshness', 'untried, non-period forms', 'the new sympathy with industrially produced materials', 'the new distrust of ornament' and 'this straightforward expression of steel and concrete construction'.(7) For Modernists, Kodak House was innovative, contributing as it did to the development and acceptance of Modern architecture in Britain with its Historic England listing referring to it as, 'a pioneering work of modern design'.(8) At best it is confused, with a typical Classical *parti* of base, body, and head, but with thin stone cladding, a smattering of Edwardian detail around the main entrance, and a cornice in the then-fashionable curved Egyptian style.

What had led to this? Certainly, Burnet was influenced by the contemporary American architecture that he had seen at first-hand, the first hint of which had appeared in his design for McGeoch's Warehouse in Glasgow. He had also made another trip to New York in 1910 during the construction of Kodak House; his client was American and had his own more radical architectural expectations; Kodak, Eastman's company offered a modern technological product to the world of photography, and he wished this to be expressed in a modern building, and finally, Burnet's team in London were young men – William Blain and James Weddell, with whom Burnet had delivered everything from the Athenaeum to the Elder Library, were back in Glasgow working for Norman Dick. Thomas Tait, whose design was selected by Eastman for Kodak House was only twenty-seven years old, as were David Raeside and James Wallace, while Andrew Bryce was only nineteen, with Theodore Fyfe the eldest, at thirty-four years of age. These men looked to the future, and not the past and to the United States, not Renaissance Europe for their inspiration, and while Burnet's position as the revered fifty-two-year-old master was unchallenged, their enthusiasms had clearly rubbed off. Thomas Tait, Burnet's personal assistant and now an award-winning student, led this group and the selection of his proposal for Kodak House further enhanced his status within it.

While James Miller had no intention of following Burnet to London, as we have seen from his Indian competition entry, he was now looking further afield for major projects and when the Institution of Civil Engineers launched an architectural competition for the design of their new headquarters building on a site in Great George Street in Westminster, Miller decided to enter. As with the extension to the British Museum, most of the entrants were London-based and also, as with the British Museum, it was the invading Scot who won it. Having already supplanted Burnet in Glasgow, Miller was now pursuing him south. Beyond any personal rivalries, what their wins indicated was the quality of Glasgow's architects of this period and their ability to compete successfully on the national stage. Indeed, had there been less work in Glasgow, there may have been an even greater incentive for others to look south as well. Even so, as Alexander Stuart Gray noted in his excellent, *Edwardian Architecture: A Biographical Dictionary*, 'Miller was thus yet another Scotsman to achieve a building in Westminster, where there already stood buildings by Shaw (from Edinburgh), Young (from Paisley), Brydon (from Dunfermline), and Gibson (from Dundee)'(9) with Burnet (from Glasgow) just a little further to the north.

The win was another astonishing achievement for Miller, and as soon as his commission was confirmed he established a London branch office at 1 Victoria Street, Westminster in March, 1910. Unlike Burnet, he had no intention of moving to London and thus jeopardising his valuable Scottish practice and so travelled south for several days each month, rather than north. He built a new team in London led by fellow Scot and former assistant to Burnet, Thomas Stewart Purdie, an experienced architect who, like Miller was fifty years old in 1910. He had managed to lure Purdie away from one of London's most successful architects, Sir Aston Webb, where Purdie had served for seven years as a senior assistant. Around Purdie was then built a small team, mostly of expatriate Scots, which included a number of very talented young architects such as Alexander Thomson Scott (1887–1962), who would later partner Sir Herbert Baker. Miller wisely, strengthened his Glasgow team at the same time with the appointment of Richard Gunn another of Burnet's former assistants.

Miller's design for the Great George Street building was published in *The Builder* and *Building News* in May 1910 and construction commenced before the year was out. The basic composition of this steel-framed, Edwardian Baroque building (1910–13) was the Palladian model of an advanced central entrance and corner pavilions, which he had already employed in the North British Locomotive Company's Offices and Peebles Hydro Hotel, but here with a giant Ionic colonnade to the first floor and the ground floor's rustication carried up the corner pavilions to cornice level (Fig. 68). Miller's now characteristically sharp detailing was here even more pronounced in his use of white Portland stone, rather than his usual sandstone. The main entrance and aedicules in the pavilions are excellent, framed with crisp Ionic columns supporting dentiled cornices below another excellent sculpture by Albert Hodge – with the chained prows of boats in the pavilions (first used on Burnet's Clyde Navigation Trust building) and two cherubs (*Science* and *Engineering*) supporting a shield and helmet over the main entrance. Miller had never had a budget like this to spend before and he made sure that his engineer clients got every bang for their bucks.

Fig. 68   The principal facade of Miller's competition-winning design for the Institution of Civil Engineers in Westminster, London, 1910–13. Courtesy of John Stewart.

While the exterior treatment is among his best work, the interiors were never to be surpassed and approached those of the *Lusitania* in sheer luxury. The detailing of the Baroque decoration is excellent, crisp, and finely judged throughout, but it is the spatial interplay of the main circulation areas that represents the real tour de force of this building with views, up, down, across, and through the central spaces on numerous levels enlivening almost every route throughout the building, with each space layered horizontally and vertically, thus linking all the principal spaces across the central hub of the atrium (Fig. 69). Both the main staircase and atrium are topped with glazed domes that flood these spaces with natural light and pick out Miller's immaculate white stone details in sharply contrasting shadows. Moving out from this central hub, the destinations do not disappoint either. The first-floor great hall above Storey's Gate, which rises from its marble base through gilt Corinthian pediments to an extraordinary gold and painted ceiling, being one of the grandest interior spaces in London, while his double-height barrel-vaulted library with first-floor gallery is one of the most intimate (while also providing a rather eery memory of the first-class lounge of his *Lusitania*). The beautifully panelled council and reading rooms on the ground floor somehow also manage to combine considerable grandeur and dignity with that air of confident relaxation so typical of a gentlemen's club. Indeed, comparisons with those pavilions of power and privilege on Pall Mall place the interiors

Fig. 69   A glimpse of the sumptuous interior of Miller's
Institution of Civil Engineers. Courtesy of John Stewart.

of this building among the best provided there by Barry or Burton. Even Pevsner was forced to admit that '[t]he fine, self-assured interiors have panelling, metalwork and fibrous plasterwork to the highest Edwardian standards'.(10) It was an extraordinarily successful London premiere by yet another extremely talented Scottish artist.

So successful was Miller's Civil Engineers' building that the adjacent Institution of Mechanical Engineers commissioned him to add a series of new meeting rooms to the end of their building on the other side of Storey's Gate. He carried this out for them in a similar style, completing both institution buildings in 1913. Shortly after securing these commissions, Miller moved his family from Glasgow to what was to be his home for the remainder of his life – a small mansion, Randolphfield – an eighteenth-century laird's house – on what was then the edge of Stirling. Here he, Emileana, and their three children, enjoyed a life of considerable luxury (not to mention being safe from the health risks of Glasgow).(11) He laid out the garden and soon became a very keen gardener himself. He added a tennis court and taught his children to play tennis as well as golf, and the whole family enjoyed fishing expeditions to nearby lochs and rivers, as well as regular visits to classical concerts in Stirling, Glasgow, and Edinburgh. To their expanding brigade of household servants, Miller now added a chauffeur nicknamed 'Mustard', who drove him in a series of stately motor cars, which over the years included a Delage and a Hispano-Suiza. All in all, these were remarkable achievements for the Perthshire farmer's son.

CHAPTER 7: 1911–1914

James Miller may have moved to the country but he had no plans to retire or even slow his pace. His practice had never been busier and he intended to keep it that way. In 1911, his senior assistant James Walker decided to leave to establish his own practice, resulting in Richard Gunn being promoted to chief assistant in Glasgow. Miller could have easily kept both busy, as the flow of new commissions was still unrelenting. With the massive Glasgow Royal Infirmary now reaching completion several more closely related commissions came along, including the new central dispensary in Richmond Street, Glasgow, a small house for Dr Robert Fullerton at Bridge of Weir and an invitation to design the new Perth Royal Infirmary. This was on a much smaller scale than his hospital in Glasgow and it had a much-reduced budget and a brief of only 120 beds. He must have thought long and hard as to the most appropriate architectural treatment for what was then a greenfield site on the edge of his home city, before finally opting for a fairly undistinguished two-storey brick Georgian with hipped roofs, tall chimneys, and dormers. As was the fashion at the time, each ward concluded in a covered balcony, which Miller enclosed with square towers topped by small cupolas – the only real hint of the building's authorship.

Shortly after Burnet's Alhambra Theatre opened in December 1910, Miller was commissioned to design two new theatres in Glasgow. The first was the 1600 seat Savoy Music Hall at the top of Hope Street in the city centre, which bore more than a passing resemblance to Burnet's theatre in Waterloo Street, though this was hardly surprising as both architects had been framing their city buildings with book-end towers for two decades by then (Fig. 70). In the Savoy, Miller's stair towers have a less oriental feel than Burnet's Alhambra, concluding in deeply overhanging pyramidal roofs over Ionic loggias and the theatre façade as a whole feels more Italianate. He again used white faience, as he had in his Anchor Line building and, in lieu of Burnet's proscenium device, treated his rather graceful central section as a colonnade, with four tall pilasters reaching up to a cornice with 'Savoy' in large letters below dentiled eaves. The interior was strictly Classical, with marble staircases leading from the foyer to the auditorium, whose stalls, boxes, and two half-moon balconies were decorated in white and gold in the theatrical Louis XVI style of the period, (without even a hint of Burnet's Moderne Alhambra streamlining). It opened in December 1911 but was not a commercial success for Miller's client,

Fig. 70   Miller's Savoy Theatre of 1910–11 shared many elements with Burnet's Alhambra but had more of an Italianate character. Courtesy of cinematreasures.org.

impresario Alfred Moul, and closed just a few years later, being converted into the New Savoy Picture Theatre in 1916. It was demolished in 1972 to make way for the concrete bunker which is the Savoy Centre.

His other theatrical commission, Cranston's Picture House and Tea Rooms, just down the hill at the bottom of Renfield Street, was a much more ambitious and architecturally successful project. Miss Cranston, who had been Charles Rennie Mackintosh's great patron, had gone from strength to strength since opening her first tearoom in 1878. By the time that she commissioned Miller for this, her most ambitious venture, Mackintosh had completed all his major architectural works, left his partnership with John Keppie and was now painting watercolours in Suffolk. Unlike the clients for both Burnet's Alhambra and Miller's Savoy, Miss Cranston had a generous budget for her development, for which Miller, as usual, gave good value (Fig. 71). His elevation to Renfield Street, which fortunately survives, shares the familiar *parti* of twin towers with central entrance and foyers above, but here, using white faience, he produced a richly modelled and successful baroque composition, which is at least on a par with his earlier Anchor Line building.

The ground floors are contained below a strong dentiled cornice supported by four (now two) marble columns with bronze Ionic capitals. Above this, in the central section is a bold first-floor arched Diocletian window below an equally strong bracketed balcony; from here the façade soars up until a series of deeply recessed screens divided by massive decorated brackets

Fig. 71   Miller returned to faience for the façade of Miss
Cranston's Picture House of 1914–16. Courtesy of Tom Bastin.

support an eaves gallery, which is flanked by porticos with recessed Doric columns, before the final flourish of a glazed dome that originally lit a top floor winter garden. After the increasing simplification of his and Burnet's work, this marks a joyful return to the strength and vitality of their best earlier designs (while also demonstrating that this depth and degree of modelling could be achieved in faience). The internal structure was actually that of an earlier building of 1898 by the architects, Thomson and Menzies and the process of cutting and carving the new spaces required for the cinema and tearooms was extremely complex, but Miller and Richard Gunn nevertheless managed to create the cinema over the first and second floors with tearooms above and below it. Within, in contrast to Mackintosh's earlier Art Nouveau interiors for Miss Cranston, here we return to the Louis XVI style of his theatres (on which Miller and his team were assisted by architect and local interior designer John Ednie [1876–1934]). Nothing of these interiors remains, and indeed the entire faience façade was replaced in the 1990s with a glass reinforced concrete replica.

With the success of the *Lusitania* and *Mauretania*, Cunard commissioned a third luxury liner the *RMS Aquitania*, from John Brown in Clydebank and the latter retained James Miller once more to design the interiors, along with their own in-house team. Miller himself commissioned Alexander Gardner, who had worked for him on the *Lusitania* before setting up his own practice, to assist him once more.(1) Their brief was to surpass the previous two ships in terms of opulence and the *Aquitania's* interiors thus displayed little restraint (Fig. 72). The centrepiece of

Fig. 72 One of Miller's luxurious interior spaces on the *RMS Aquitania* – the palladium lounge in the first-class suite. Public domain.

the first-class suite was the Palladium Lounge, which enjoyed a vaulted, panelled, and painted ceiling with punched, half-round and circular clerestory lights along its sides. The first-class dining room was on two levels with a first-floor gallery around all four sides, below another deeply modelled and painted ceiling; the ladies' reading room was topped off with a shallow oval dome with circular clerestory lights; the gentlemen's smoking room was panelled below a rather clubby beamed timber ceiling; the swimming pool and gymnasium were executed in a suitably restrained Tuscan Doric; a theatre was introduced for the first time, and all the circulation spaces in the first-class section had the proportions and panelled elegance of an English country house. It was all totally over the top and exactly what Cunard had hoped for. She made her maiden voyage on 30 May 1914 and soon earned the nickname 'The Ship Beautiful', which she remained until pressed into use as a troop transporter during the Second World War. As with many luxurious hotels and country houses, it was an experience she never recovered from, being retired from service in 1949 and scrapped the following year.

Miller was now commuting to Glasgow from Stirling by train most days and rather coincidentally, shortly after he started to use Stirling station himself, he was commissioned to rebuild it by the Caledonian Railway. The original 1848 building by his old master Andrew Heiton was demolished to make way for Miller's dramatic new building. Like most of his stations there was an almost total mismatch between the traditional exteriors of the building and the innovative glass and steel interior and in Stirling his symmetrical stone Scots Renaissance entrance building,

Fig. 73   Miller's reworking of his Wemyss Bay roof structure at his Stirling station of 1912–15. Courtesy of Stuart Robertson.

complete with crow-stepped gables and crenellations, gives no hint of the sweeping curves within (Fig. 73). As at Wemyss Bay, the circular ticket office takes central stage. Curving around it a series of radial steel trusses support a glazed roof that sweeps passengers from the street to the platform in a single continuous curve. It lacks something of the more expansive drama of Wemyss Bay, which was designed to cope with much bigger crowds transferring from train to boat, but nevertheless must have given Miller and his fellow commuters a considerable lift each morning and evening.

The Caledonian Railway Company was still going strong and continued to expand. Miller's friend, Donald Matheson, its general manager, had taken a number of family holidays in Perthshire and was extremely impressed by the scenery – impressed enough to plan another golf resort hotel along the lines of Turnberry that would this time be reached by the Caledonian Railway. He had in mind a particular spot near Crieff Junction railway station that he thought would be perfect and took the name of a nearby pass through the Ochil Hills – 'Glen Eagles' – as the name for a new station and the nearby resort that he planned, as well as the development company that he formed to oversee it. Miller's appointment was made after a brief limited competition and his team were soon hard at work on their largest hotel commission to date, with Open Champion and leading golf course designer James Braid also appointed to lay out the two new eighteen-hole courses around the hotel.

Miller's site for Gleneagles Hotel was unlike that of either Turnberry or Peebles Hydro which both occupied elevated positions and their main elevations and best rooms were strung along a ridge (Fig. 74). At Gleneagles, the site for the hotel was below the hills and the golf courses, surrounded on all sides by breath-taking scenery and his response was thus to make a more compact building. He designed a U-shaped block that was centred on a generous semi-circular, south-facing dining room from which the buildings stepped back and out towards the back, thus maximising the number of rooms with a view. Miller intended its current grey roughcast finish to be white, with sandstone dressings below a slate roof. The main entrance on the west elevation

Fig. 74 Miller's last great railway hotel – Gleneagles of 1913–24. Courtesy of Roger Katzenberg.

was marked by a tower, as at Turnberry, and was flanked by full-height bay windows with three floors of bedrooms below a steeply pitched roof with dormers, as at the Peebles Hydro Hotel. On the southern elevation, two wings and a central section stepped forward, with the curved pediment of the central section and the entrance tower as the only elements to break through the continuous modillion cornice. The main public spaces, including the dining rooms, bars, and ballroom were all designed in a relatively restrained Edwardian Baroque, with construction commencing in 1913.

By then the Glasgow Royal Infirmary was finally complete, having opened in phases over the previous few years. It has few friends among architectural critics, including Gomme and Walker who described it as a 'dreary monster'(2) but I have always thought it quite an elegant hospital building, albeit in a dour grey Giffnock ashlar. Most of the criticism relates firstly to its scale (dominating the, let's face it, rather modest for a city like Glasgow) Glasgow Cathedral, secondly, to the fact that a building by the Adam brothers was demolished to make way for it (hardly Miller's fault) and thirdly, to the long-held criticism over the appointment of Miller instead of one of Burnet's former assistants.(3) The south elevation, in particular, provides an excellent backdrop to the space in front of the Cathedral (which has recently been much improved) and draws on Robert and John Adam's previous building for inspiration, with a strong central bay between projecting wings (Fig. 75). This central section is quite outstanding, with a beautifully detailed, rusticated, projecting entrance block that acts as a base for a seated bronze statue of Queen Victoria by Albert Hodge. Behind and above her, a rather grand, recessed Ionic portico rises to a strongly projecting modillion cornice below the deep shadows of a colonnaded gallery, above and beyond which is the circular stone base of a very elegant dome. This long wing forms just one arm of the vast U-shaped plan that extends to the north, enclosing an entrance courtyard to the west, dominated by the circular towers and turrets that give the hospital its considerable strength of character. Miller's competition-winning design was in Scottish Baronial style in deference to the Cathedral, but during its development it underwent something of a Classical makeover with crenellations replaced by balustrades and the conical roofs of the towers by delightful Baroque domed pavilions. Unfortunately, the bartizans to the central main entrance tower were retained, giving it something of the appearance of an original castle keep. The circular towers, which are a clever architectural device, break up the huge grey elevations and neatly turn corners, while also serving the practical purpose of grouping highly serviced areas such as toilets and bathrooms outside the wards. The twin towers that conclude the northern wing enclose balconies below a Baroque portico, thus terminating this block with particular verve.

It was a massive, extremely complex project, that engaged Miller's team for many years and while I have focused on its external appearance, it should also be noted that the architect 'who had never designed a hospital' had produced what was regarded at the time as a building that was at the very forefront of British hospital design, on which great efforts had been expended by the design team to ensure both minimum noise and maximum cleanliness. It contained several innovations, such as a roof-top promenade and balconies for convalescing patients, as well as incorporating several state-of-the-art technological developments such as X-ray laboratories and an electrocardiograph system linking each ward to a central monitoring area. In common with

Fig. 75   Miller's magnificent advanced central section of his Royal Infirmary of 1901–15 with *Queen Victoria,* sculpted by Albert Hodge. Courtesy of Ian Stubbs.

most of Miller's clients, the hospital authorities came back to him again and again throughout the next few decades for further new buildings, extensions, and alterations whenever they were required.

The Royal Infirmary had provided a financial bedrock for Miller's practice since his appointment in 1901 upon which he had gone on to build the most successful architectural practice in Scotland. For Burnet's two practices, the British Museum extension had assumed a similar role, but in his case, with very few additional major new commissions. Both the General Accident, Fire and Life Insurance Company and Kodak buildings had been completed in 1911 and there was no further new work in London to replace them. Burnet had made a third visit to the United States late in 1910 at the request of Sir Frederick Kenyon, the new Director of the British Museum, to view the latest museum and gallery design, producing a report in March 1911 that influenced the fitting out of the new building as well as the redesign of several areas within the existing one, and later that year Burnet made another private tour of Germany and Austria, where he would have seen the latest Viennese work by Wagner, Olbrich, Loos, and Hoffman, as well as Peter Behrens' German Industrial Classicism.

For his Glasgow practice, 1911 finally brought new work with the commission for the Royal Hospital for Sick Children at Yorkhill, but although Burnet's client's plans were ambitious (twelve wards, laboratories, two operating theatres, a nurses' home and a pathology block), it soon became apparent that their funds, (which had been entirely raised by public subscription) were very limited. It is hard to believe Burnet played a significant role in designing this building, which ended up as a four-storey H-plan red brick barracks, made all the more severe by plain parapets to the flat-roofed wings, with only the central section having a pitched roof, capped with a modest, domed central ventilator. The glazed canopy to the main entrance and two-storey stone bay windows to the wings did little to relieve this building's rather grim, institutional feel. It was replaced by a no less grim modern children's hospital in the 1960s.

By 1912, as the workload continued to fall, tensions began to rise in the London office. In July it was announced that Thomas Tait and another of Burnet's assistants, James Mitchell Whitelaw, had come second in an unofficial competition run by *The Builder* to complete the rebuilding of the Regent Street Quadrant. Burnet was not impressed, as his assistants had failed to seek his consent before entering the competition, and perhaps more seriously, as their entry was largely based on Burnet's previous designs. He was particularly disappointed in Tait, whom he very much saw as his protégé. (Whitelaw drowned when holidaying at Bournemouth the following summer). Early in 1914, Burnet then discovered that Tait had been working in his evenings for another firm of architects, Trehearne and Norman, to augment his income (having recently married and had his first son). This time, Burnet dismissed him. Tait left for New York and was soon employed as an assistant to Donn Barber, the successful American Beaux Arts architect. It was not long before Burnet regretted his action and contacted Tait in New York to offer him his job back and a promotion to junior partner, but Tait refused this offer and on his return to London later that year took up a full-time position as chief draughtsman with Trehearne and Norman. To add to Burnet's woes, his museum extension, which was finally nearing completion, had developed a serious leak in its roof, the source of which could not be found. It took several frustrating months for client and architect before it was finally traced and rectified, involving considerable remedial work and expense. This rather soured Burnet's relationship with the Office of Works who were responsible for managing the project, and led to his later fee claims (which he now badly needed) being disputed. The pressure on him was growing and began to affect his health, including the return of the eczema that he had occasionally suffered as a child.

There was little good news from Glasgow either, where the major commissions of 1912 for John Burnet, Son & Partners were a new church hall in Kilmacolm – again unrecognisable as a Burnet building, were it not for an elegant carved sandstone plaque in one of the gables, and the execution of a restoration project for Duart Castle on the Isle of Mull, which had already been prepared by MacGibbon and Ross. In 1913, Burnet entered the architectural competition for the new Jordanhill Teacher Training College, which was won by David Barclay, with Burnet being offered the design of the lodge and gates, which he refused, before the Glasgow practice was finally saved from running out of work entirely by his old client, Robert Wallace Forsyth. Forsyth's son William had been researching the latest garment manufacturing facilities in the United States and returned bursting with ideas for a large new model factory in Scotland. Burnet was appointed and worked with him directly on the development of his concept for a modern, steel-framed factory with high levels of natural light in an open-plan interior, as well as a series of social facilities for the workers, which were to include a large dining room that could be used for dances, concerts, and as a cinema, reading, smoking, and rest rooms, as well as changing facilities for an adjoining sports ground. Outside, the sports facilities were to be surrounded by formal gardens with avenues of trees and topiary, for the workers rest and relaxation.

Burnet's design for what was christened the 'Wallace Scott Tailoring Institute' (1913–16) (which Dick and the Glasgow team delivered), was a development of Kodak House but here it constituted a monumental five-storey block around a landscaped central courtyard (Fig. 76). The building's frame was clearly expressed below its flat roof, with brick piers spanning the three

Fig. 76   Burnet's Wallace Scott Tailoring Institute for R W Forsyth's of 1913–16 was a bold social and architectural experiment. Courtesy of Malcolm Roulston.

factory floors and large areas of glazing in between, divided by rather jazzy polychromatic tiles. As in Kodak House, Burnet's expression of the building's structural frame was much lauded, but the detailed design was confused, with a formal central entrance leading to a marble split staircase marked externally by two full-height quasi-classical pilasters. Pevsner loved the expressed structural frame but hated, 'the somewhat objectionable semi-classical semi-Egyptian decoration'.(4) In terms of the development of Modern architecture in Britain it was another pioneering building and compares very well with Wylie, Shanks and Wylie's nearby offices for G. & J. Weir over twenty years later (and Burnet afficionados cannot fault the proportions or help but love his subtly recessed corners). The factory eventually passed into the hands of the South of Scotland Electricity Board in 1957, who slowly converted the gardens and playing fields into a very large car park, before the building itself was (rather ironically) converted into New York style apartments in 2019.

At the age of fifty-six, Burnet was in a strange position. As an architect, he should have been at the peak of his creative powers and yet even he must have realised that his best work might be behind him and that his prospects of further major commissions were declining fast. He had failed to establish himself in London, with the first flurry of commissions that accompanied his high-profile appointment to the British Museum now complete. He enjoyed a new circle of friends and admirers in the capital, but they were mostly other architects rather than potential clients, and he was thus now asked to assess architectural competitions more often than enter them (not that he had had much success through this procurement route in any case in recent years). Due to his absence in London his Glasgow practice was no longer the force that it had been in the city, and worst of all, it was struggling to deliver the profits he needed to maintain his lifestyle. Should he abandon his London practice upon completion of the Museum project and return to Glasgow, having failed to make it in the Empire's capital city? Architecturally, he was equally confused. He was a Classicist at heart – a master of the art of carved stone architecture. His last major Classical building on the Aldwych was one of his best, proving that there had been no diminution in his extraordinary skills, and yet the architecture of the future now appeared to be moving in an entirely different direction, where his rare talents appeared almost superfluous, with contemporary buildings stripped of almost all sculpture and decoration with only bare utility remaining. He had always been at the forefront of his profession and led architectural development and, to a degree he still was. Kodak House and the Tailoring Institute were regarded as highly innovative and were professionally much admired. But was his heart and soul really in this type of work? The new American and German architecture he had seen offered a radical vision of the future, but was it a future that he truly wanted to be part of, help to bring about or live in? Was he still leading his office or were his young assistants now leading him?

In the midst of his confusion, he received the kind of commission that once flooded into his Glasgow office – a new house for doyens of the Glasgow commercial world, Agnes and Margaret Wylie, the owners of the Wylie & Lochhead's department store. This enterprise, which was founded in 1829, had started out as a firm of cabinet-makers and undertakers and expanded to become something of a Glasgow institution with a reputation for fashionable design. They had previously appointed James Sellars to design their magnificent store on Buchanan Street (just

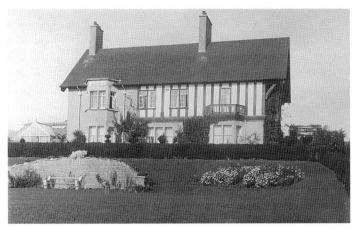

Fig. 77 Burnet's Lethamhill House in Helensburgh exhibits no hint of his London practice's growing interest in Modernism. Courtesy of the Helensburgh Heritage Trust.

surviving as a House of Fraser store) and their pavilions at the various Glasgow exhibitions were always among the most popular. The sisters had acquired a site above Helensburgh just below Mackintosh's Hill House, where Burnet could make his own contribution to a collection of fine villas that already boasted houses by William Leiper and Baillie Scott. Burnet did not realise it then, but Hill House was to be his last house design and in it he rejected entirely the style of Kodak House and the Tailoring Institute.

Lethamhill House, as it was called, is a late Arts and Crafts villa, L-shaped in plan, with roughcast walls and sandstone dressings and mullions below a deeply overhanging red clay tiled roof (Fig. 77). As in the Hill House, the main rooms look south towards the Clyde, with a double-height sandstone bay to one side of the south elevation and a ground-floor bay with balcony over, to the other. A half-timbered first-floor section wraps around the corner of the building from the south side to the entrance courtyard, terminating in a beautiful double-height stepped bay window to the main stair, with the main entrance to its side within a gabled wing. With the exception of the panelled open stairwell and the magnificent stair from which Burnet gives guests the first hint of their first-floor view of the river, the main rooms are understated but delightful. This was Burnet's paean to a fast-disappearing world.

The British Empire, which was so crucial to Glasgow's wealth, was at its peak and while most Britons then still believed that it would last forever (with the 'sun never setting' on it), it was under increasing attack both from within and without. Britain may still have ruled a quarter of the world's population, but by 1913, the United States' share of global gross domestic product was double that of the UK's and Germany had just nudged into second place behind them. Britain and Germany had been locked in a naval arms race since the turn of the century, much to the advantage of Glasgow's shipbuilders, which threatened Britain's control of the seas and thus the effective operation of its Empire. Nationalists from Dublin to Delhi sought independence, or at least local representation. At home, suffragettes fought for the vote for women, Emily Davidson running out in front of the King's horse in the Derby of 1913, and most significantly for Glasgow, organised labour was becoming increasingly militant in its demands for improved working conditions and remuneration, as well as funding its own political representation through their Labour Party. Trade union numbers were swelling year by year and industrial unrest was growing across almost every sector of British industry, with the cities being crucibles of dissent and increasingly – action. In Glasgow four times as many days' work were lost to strikes between 1910 and 1914 compared with 1900 to 1910, and in the five years between 1909 and 1914 the membership of the Scottish Trades Union Congress increased from 129,000 to 230,000. In 1910, there were strikes in the docks, the mines, and on the railways and in 1911, 11,000 workers at the Singer sewing machine factory in Clydebank went on strike in protest against a proposed increase in their workload and decrease in wages. The owners' response was brutal. They threatened to close the factory and move production elsewhere and went on to threaten that none of the strikers would ever work in Glasgow again. The strike was broken and four hundred 'ringleaders' were sacked. 'The shockwaves resonated around the British union movement, emphasising how ruthless they would have to be in the future. In Glasgow the effect was not to intimidate local labour, but to develop the ethos of "Red Clydeside"'.(5)

The government was under pressure and, as the King's private secretary wrote to Prime Minister Herbert Asquith:

> The King is very much disturbed by the present unrest among the working class-
> es and by the possibility, if not probability, of further strikes breaking out at
> any moment. He is afraid that if there were a renewal of recent occurrences, the
> disturbances might lead to political elements being introduced into the conflict
> which might perhaps affect, not the existence, but the position of the Crown.(6)

It was agreed that the King and Queen should play an active role in addressing the issue and consequently, in February 1914 it was announced that they would embark on a series of 'Visits to Industrial Districts'(7) that would include Clydeside and the regional cities of Scotland in July that year. But before then, His Majesty had another duty to perform on the 7 May, that of officially opening the extension to the British Museum, which bore his father's name (Fig. 78).

Largely with the assistance of Theodore Fyfe, Burnet had finally completed the King Edward VII Galleries earlier that year. The exterior was a powerful reworking of Smirke's original, with the central entrance now guarded by two fine stone lions with crossed paws by Sir George Frampton (who had first worked with Burnet on his Savings Bank and since become another of his friends). The interiors were restrained and flawless, with an elegant central staircase, brightly lit first-floor galleries and a beautiful double-height galleried library (which has since fallen victim to a later remodelling of the museum interiors). It opened to general acclaim, with the *Architectural Review* even suggesting that 'The new wing will be counted one of the most important works of English architecture to which the century has, so far, given birth, being a considerable extension of a

Fig. 78   Every detail of Burnet's vast extension to the British Museum of 1904–14 was resolved to perfection. Courtesy of John Stewart.

building that takes rank with Westminster Abbey and St Paul's Cathedral as a unique National Institution'(8) and, while it noted that by introducing three new doorways '[t]he grand rhythm of the columns is thus rudely interrupted,' concludes nevertheless that 'Mr. Burnet is to be congratulated upon having achieved a great architectural triumph, for he has endowed a highly complex structure with the appearance of simplicity.' Burnet was presented to the King in the ground-floor gallery during his tour of the building, and in recognition of his achievement, found out shortly after his royal encounter that he was to be awarded a knighthood for his work on the Museum in the King's Birthday Honours List that June. There was a certain irony that he was to receive this – his highest honour – at one of the lowest points in his career, for a single London building that had none of the verve or originality of his best work.

He would encounter His Majesty again in July during the royal visit to Scotland, which was now designed more to help supress industrial unrest than to celebrate the country's achievements. King George V and Queen Mary were staying in Holyrood Palace in Edinburgh but planned to spend three days in Glasgow starting on 7 July. In an extraordinary coincidence, their first official engagement was to open James Miller's new Royal Infirmary, providing him with his second encounter with their highnesses, followed by lunch at the City Chambers, after which the King renewed his acquaintance with Sir John Burnet in opening his Royal Hospital for Sick Children that afternoon. The royal couple's progress throughout the country was greeted by large cheering crowds (and several protesting suffragettes), and on 10 July they visited Dundee and Perth, meeting James Miller for the second time that week, when opening his new Perth Royal Infirmary. But, despite his many achievements and several royal encounters, there was to be no knighthood for Miller.

With the publicity from the museum official opening and his ennoblement, Burnet picked up a commission – a new building for the Institute of Chemistry of Great Britain and Ireland on a site on Russell Square in Bloomsbury, just around the corner from the museum (Fig. 79). In brown brick with stone dressings, it makes a very polite neighbour to the Georgian buildings of the square, while its main elevation and entrance faces the lane leading through to London University. It is an unusual composition with ground-floor arched windows springing from Doric stone columns and a very fine Burnetesque Mannerist doorway, complete with a split pediment enclosing a sculpture of Sir Joseph Priestly by Gilbert Bayes (1872–1953). Theodore Fyfe assisted and it is interesting that, with Thomas Tait out of the frame, Burnet and Fyfe together produced a very elegant little Classical building that was entirely appropriate to its historical setting. No sooner had they completed the design for the institute than the Clyde Navigation Trust commissioned Burnet to design the third phase of their building along the Broomielaw. Perhaps things were finally looking up?

They certainly weren't on the political front. Following the assassination of the heir to the Austro-Hungarian Empire Archduke Franz Ferdinand by a Serbian terrorist in Sarajevo in June, an international crisis had developed. Desperate diplomatic efforts were made throughout the summer to avoid a descent into war, but to no avail. Through a series of interlocking alliances between the great powers of Europe, what started with a retaliation by Austria-Hungary against Serbia, soon brought first Russia and then Germany into the war. France mobilised in support of

Fig. 79   Burnet's restraint and good manners in his Institute of
Chemistry on Russell Square of 1913–14 was soon overwhelmed by
Charles Holden's later Senate House for the University of London.

Russia, Germany invaded Belgium, and through the Treaty of London of 1839, Britain declared war on Germany in defence of Belgium on 4 August. Soon the world would be at war.

The impact on British architects was immediate, with projects cancelled and valued assistants volunteering to fight for their king and country. Work on the third phase of Burnet's Clyde Navigation Trust building was stopped immediately and construction of Miller's Gleneagles Hotel soon also ground to a halt. Miller had won little new work in London after his success with the Institution of Civil Engineers and, with the outbreak of war, quietly closed his London office. Burnet had settled in the capital and planned to stay, hoping, like most of his compatriots, that the war would not last long and that both his offices would survive it. Little did anyone realise then, that far from 'being all over by Christmas', the war would drag on for four long years, during which much of the wealth and youth of the British Empire would be poured into fighting a long battle of attrition in the mud of France and Belgium; the Russian, Austro-Hungarian, and Ottoman empires would collapse, and the mighty British Empire would be terminally weakened.

CHAPTER 8: 1914–1923

If the First World War was about to hasten the end of the British Empire, few people in Glasgow in late 1914 would have guessed it. The city had never been busier. The demand for warships, coupled with a gradual switch from peacetime production to the manufacture of arms and munitions, resulted in something approaching an economic boom time for almost everyone – the city's architectural profession being one of the exceptions. While non-essential building work could still progress without restriction, the outbreak of hostilities had been preceded by a significant downturn in economic activity during the summer of 1914, which lingered on into the autumn and the winter.

The war came at an unfortunate time for James Miller. He had just completed the Royal Infirmary and while several of his projects, such as Miss Cranston's Picture House, were still under way, with Gleneagles stopped, no prospect of new railway work during hostilities and a large new establishment of his own to maintain at Randolphfield, even he was beginning to feel rather stretched. Richard Gunn, his chief assistant, was soon called up for military service and he was followed, one by one, by most of his more junior staff members. Fortunately, Miller's old client the Anchor Line came to his assistance, along with a number of new clients who apparently still needed country houses, which helped to maintain his much-reduced practice during these first years of the war.

The Anchor Line's commission was very different from the palatial building that he had earlier provided for them in the centre of the city. This opportunity was for a large store near their quay in Yorkhill: 'a three-storey framed building, parallelogram in plan with its acute corners chamfered. The building is entirely functional, its structural grid interrupted only by a lift, two light wells and a corner staircase.... Large windows were articulated by red brick piers with concrete strips at floor level and a continuous band at roof level'.(1) While it has been suggested that its design represented a shift by Miller towards Functionalism, the reality is more prosaic in that it simply expressed hard times. His two country house commissions, however, were much more interesting.

The first was Blanefield House at Kirkoswald in Ayrshire (1913–19) for industrialist and art collector Sir John Ritchie Richmond who, as the first captain of Turnberry Golf Club, would have

Fig. 80   Miller's Blanefield House of 1913–19 for the first Captain of Turnberry Golf Club shares many features with the resort hotel. Courtesy of Paul Graham.

known Miller's work from there. Blanefield represented a final rejection of Shaw's half-timbered Old English vernacular in favour of the more severe Arts and Crafts style that Miller had first developed in the city at Lowther Terrace, then transported to the suburbs with Dunholme in Pollokshields, and now finally adopted in rural Ayrshire (Fig. 80). There is a new restraint in Blanefield (that suggests a continuing interest in Voysey's country houses), with the materials here restricted to sandstone, white roughcast, and slate. The asymmetrical arrangement of the entrance elevation is a modest reworking of Turnberry Hotel's entrance, with one wing of the L-shaped plan providing shelter to the space in front of it. A two-storey balustraded bay projects forward to dominate the courtyard, flanked on one side by a full-height stone gable and on the other by a stone ground-floor wall with white render above. The use of stone reduces incrementally with distance from the main entrance, appearing only as stone mullions by the time we reach the garden elevations. All this is topped with a generous slate roof, pierced by white roughcast chimneys with sandstone cappings, while the panelled interiors and fine staircases are cleverly planned to subtly segregate family, guests, and staff. As Miller would have known from Voysey, the combination of clean, white-rendered walls, warm honey-coloured sandstone and cold grey slate worked superbly well together, and while his sources may have been largely from the south, the final product still achieved a certain Scottish robustness. Further later extensions by Miller to accommodate Sir John's growing art collection detracted somewhat from the simplicity of the original.

The second house was Kildonan, this time at Barrhill in Ayrshire, (1915–23) for Captain David Euan Wallace, who had married Lady Idina Sackville in 1913. Wallace was a Scot (his mother, Janet Wallace of Glassinghall, had largely funded Rowand Anderson's restoration of Dunblane

Cathedral). He had been educated at Harrow and Sandhurst and lived in England. He had earlier inherited around £2,000,000 and the 15,000-acre estate in Barrhill on one condition – that he lived there. He therefore commissioned Miller to build him an enormous country house on the site of a modest predecessor, which he hoped would make life in Ayrshire bearable for himself and his aristocratic wife. It was to be Miller's greatest domestic work and one of Scotland's finest twentieth-century houses, and yet it is hardly known. It is listed Grade 'A' but the only details provided by Historic Environment Scotland are that it is a 'striking modern mansion, circa 1930, by James Miller, architect. Reminiscent of work of Sir Edwin Lutyens'(2) (Fig. 81).

There is certainly more than a hint of Lutyens here, with his Little Thakeham providing the inspiration for a two-storey hexagonal bay window, the internal balcony to the hall, and the tall diagonal chimney stacks, while the great, double-height glazed bay and arched entrance door from Deanery Garden are also re-employed, along with the triple-gabled entrance wing from

Fig. 81   James Miller's vast and very fine Kildonan House for David Euan Wallace is full of references to Lutyens and rather strangely became a home to Lutyens's daughter on its completion in 1923. Courtesy of HES.

Lutyens' Tigbourne Court. There is no hint here of Baronial or Scottish Renaissance architecture, and indeed the entire building could be dropped into Surrey or Sussex, where it would look quite at home. This, of course, was exactly what Miller's Anglo-Scottish client wanted and he was consequently delighted with the effect that Miller achieved.

The site is beautiful – a south-facing, wooded hillside, falling quite steeply down to the River Duisk. A sweeping approach road brings the visitor up to the house, arriving at an east-facing courtyard around which the house is organised in a U-shaped plan. As Pevsner's *Guide* commented, 'The modest lodges and stable court do not prepare the visitor for the vast cream Northumberland stone spectacle that stretches out along the hillside.'(3) On the north side of the courtyard the steep slate roofs are pierced by tall stone chimneys, step up from a single storey, to two and then three storeys, and turning the corner, conclude in a three-storey triple gabled wing that advances towards the visitor – but this is not the entrance. The circular sweep continues around to the south side of the courtyard, where a generous arch is cut in the stonework, finally providing access to the suite of public rooms beyond. These all face due south towards the river and the view, opening out onto a series of terraces, a rose garden, and a lawn, with bedrooms above continuing around the corner to the west. To the left of the main entrance is Mr Wallace's wing, with billiard room and smoking room on the ground floor and his own staircase leading to his bedroom, bathroom, and dressing room on the first floor. To the right of the main entrance is a double-height hall that takes up almost half this side of the house, with its enormous two-storey bay window at one end and the house's main staircase at the other, concealed within a minstrel's gallery (all very much as at Little Thakeham*) (Fig.* 82). The suite of public rooms then continues down the southern side of a courtyard corridor, with a drawing room and then dining room just around the corner on the western side, to catch the setting sun. Beyond this point, all the ground-floor accommodation on both the west and north sides are taken up by room after room of servants' accommodation (all of which, unusually, enjoy both daylight and a view) concluding at the north side of the courtyard with a glazed covered yard serving the gun room, boot room and squash court. (One cannot help but think of Cluedo). The planning of the house is fascinating – not only is it perfectly suited to his client's rather excessive needs but, unlike Lutyens' houses, it is determinedly asymmetrical with no grand axes to order the spaces which flow from corridor to room to room in a much more relaxed manner. The *Architectural Review* agreed, concluding that 'The more one knows of the house and surroundings, the more one appreciated Kildonan as a completely satisfactory expression of plan giving effect to the aims and requirements of the client, and the demands of a somewhat restricted site.'(4)

The house is built in a cream-coloured Northumberland free stone under Caithness silver-grey slates and, as with Miller's best domestic work, benefits greatly from this most restrained of palettes. While Lutyens features abound, the exterior still has the sharpness and precision of detail that we have come to expect from Miller himself at his best. His balancing of both solid and void and the verticals of bays and chimneys with his long low roofs is particularly well judged and were it not that the style invites comparisons with Lutyens' genius, it would be even more impressive. The *Architectural Review* suggested that Kildonan 'bears the impress of close co-operation and mutual understanding between architect and client', and to some extent that

Fig. 82   The interiors of Kildonan have a certain spartan elegance
that entirely suit this remote country retreat. Courtesy of HES.

was true, in that Miller very successfully responded to his client's needs and fully exploited the beautiful site, but the reality was that, despite spending £73,500 on his new home, Euan Wallace's heart was never really in it. Almost as soon as Miller had been commissioned, he was off to war, serving with the 2nd Regiment of Life Guards with whom he was injured four times, mentioned in despatches and awarded the Military Cross. He divorced his first wife Idina Sackville in 1919 (who went on to enjoy four further marriages and fame as the 'Bolter' in Nancy Mitford's books and infamy in 'Happy Valley' in Kenya), and who never took up residence in Kildonan. In 1920, he married (rather bizarrely, considering his architectural sources) Barbara, the daughter of Sir Edwin Lutyens, with whom he finally moved into a partially complete Kildonan in 1923. The interiors were never fully finished as originally planned, with only the hall being part panelled and most rooms plastered and painted white with soft-grey stained woodwork. In 1924 Wallace was elected MP for Hornsey in north London, a constituency he held until his death in 1941, and then used Kildonan as a country home to which they would decamp with their society friends and a retinue of servants for the shooting season. In 1925, the great Gertrude Jekyll designed the gardens, of which just the terraces now survive. Wallace finally gave up Kildonan in 1937 for Lavington Park in West Sussex. It has since been a convent school run by the Sisters of St Joseph of Cluny, a hotel and self-catering apartments and, having changed hands several times, this outstanding twentieth-century Scottish house has now been officially listed as a building at risk.

Despite the scale of Kildonan and his other more modest commissions, Miller was soon seeking new work and almost certainly inspired two of his whiskey-baron friends to help. In Troon, Alexander Walker (Johnny Walker's grandson), Miller's previous client for Rowallan in the town, proposed that a series of municipal buildings should be built including new council offices, a concert hall and library and as chairman of the building committee, Walker brought Miller in to advise. Miller developed a master plan and completed initial designs for the buildings in 1915, but although Walker gifted the town a site, he would have to wait another fifteen years before funding was provided to let construction commence.

His old school friend from Perth Academy, John Alexander Dewar (whose father had founded Dewar's Scotch Whisky) was now chairman of Dewar's, a director of the Distillers Company and MP for Inverness-shire (becoming the first Baron Forteviot in 1917) and he commissioned Miller to reconstruct Forteviot as a model village, to include new housing, a village hall, a smithy, and a carpenter's shop. This provided Miller and his team with a little work but, as with Troon municipal buildings, construction was delayed until after the war.

Miller was searching valiantly for opportunities and managed to obtain commissions through his various personal and hotel connections for alterations and extensions to the Imperial Hydropathic at Grange over Sands, the Hotel Majestic in St Annes on Sea, and the Southport Hydropathic, all in distant Lancashire, where he and his family had holidayed before the war, before finally securing a substantial commission from the Ministry of Munitions for a Scottish filling factory building in Houston, west of Glasgow. This was one of four shell-filling factories to be built around Britain in response to the shell crisis of 1915 (which eventually brought about the fall of Asquith's Liberal Government and its replacement by a new coalition government led by David Lloyd George). Fortunately for James Miller, Lloyd George had appointed William Weir (later First Viscount Weir) as Director of Munitions in Scotland. Miller knew Weir well, having added a large Ionic porch and barrel-vaulted conservatory to Weir's Palladian Skeldon House, in Ayrshire, in 1908.

Although this was one of Miller's least interesting projects architecturally, once secured it saw his reduced practice right through the war and he was able to draw on all his experience of industrial buildings, from railway stations to exhibition halls, to produce a design in record time. The factory required a series of ammunition assembly rooms and filling areas as well as more workshops, a hydro-electric power station, offices, canteens, shifting houses, staff accommodation, and a railway station to transport its many (mostly female) workers west from Glasgow, and its shells and cartridges east to the docks on the Clyde. Construction of the steel-framed buildings started in September 1915 and production commenced the following January, with the first two hundred women assembling cartridges. By the end of June 1916, the workforce had grown to over 3000.(5) The buildings were unremarkable reworkings of his exhibition halls from 1901, with largely glazed roofs and sheet-clad walls above brickwork. As demand for munitions grew, a second factory was commissioned and constructed, along with its support facilities, which included another railway station. By 1918 the vast complex covered an astonishing 200 hectares of land, the facility employed over 11,000 workers and its continual development had seen Miller's practice through the icy cold of this architectural winter.(6)

Sir John Burnet had not fared so well. After the completion of the Institute of Chemistry building, he had no further work in London. Theodore Fyfe, who had assisted on it, found a position in the Ministry of Health that provided him with an income during the war years, while the thoughts he had harboured of a partnership with Burnet slowly receded. David Raeside, Burnet's London office manager, had joined the Royal Engineers (and would be one of the few members of Burnet's London office to return after the war). In Glasgow, Dick had enlisted shortly after the outbreak of hostilities and been commissioned as a lieutenant in the Royal Scots. Many, such as Charles Harvey from Burnet's Glasgow office, who joined the Argyll and Sutherland Highlanders, would never return, in his case dying of wounds in France on 3 April 1916. There was little work in London and many architects with better London connections than Burnet were able to hoover up the crumbs.

In terms of the life of a great artist (and there is no doubt that Burnet was a great artist), the war was four, long, wasted years. In terms of the life of a self-employed professional, it was four years with next to no income, and the Burnets's struggle to maintain first their lifestyle and soon their existence, became more acute as the years wore on. Soon, their only option was to start selling their possessions, and it was the sale of his art collection and that of his father that got them through those four war years. Their prized collection of tapestries that they had built up during their travels at auctions and salerooms throughout Europe, was the last to go – a necessity that they regretted for the rest of their lives.

With little work, Burnet threw himself into professional affairs and became an influential figure in the RIBA. He helped to steer the RIBA's gold medals to his old master Jean Louis Pascal in 1914, his friend Rowand Anderson in 1916, and his old Paris fellow-lodger, Henri Paul Nénot in 1917, and finally the presidency of the Institute to his close friend, John Simpson (architect of Glasgow's art gallery and museum) in 1919. He and Simpson forged new links between the RIBA and its fellow European and American institutions, while Burnet also had a leading role in the establishment of what became the Royal Incorporation of Architects in Scotland (RIAS). Having brought together the institutes of the various Scottish cities into a single body, with Rowand

Anderson as its first president and Burnet its second, the Institute of Scottish Architects was granted a Royal Charter in 1922 and another charter granting it the title, the 'Royal Incorporation of Architects in Scotland', in 1929.

By 1915, Burnet's relationship with Thomas Tait had been repaired and with Tait working in the drawing office of the Woolwich Arsenal throughout the war, they collaborated occasionally when any work was available. That was a rare event, however, and in four years Burnet designed little more than one or two domestic interiors; a new ward block for Kilmarnock Infirmary; outline designs for the Second Church of the Christ Scientist in Notting Hill; a new chapel for Balliol College, Oxford (for which there was no funding); and a memorial tablet for Glasgow University. With air raids in London, food rationing and a victory over Germany being highly uncertain until late 1918, they were indeed trying times for Jean and John Burnet. By the end of the war Burnet was in his early sixties and unwell. His increasingly serious eczema was beginning to impact on his ability to draw, as his hands were badly affected, his team in London was gone and there was little for Norman Dick to do in Glasgow when he finally returned from the front.

But then, out of a clear blue sky, he was gifted an extraordinary opportunity. An American, Harry Gordon Selfridge, had been surprised when visiting London in 1906, at just how comparatively out of date the major London department stores were compared with those of New York and Chicago. Sensing an opportunity, and with the courage and resources to back his hunch, he invested £400,000 in building his own store in London on what was then the unfashionable end of Oxford Street. He hired the American architect Daniel Burnham (1846–1912), who had led the design of the World Columbian Exhibition in Chicago of 1893 (that had inspired James Miller's Glasgow Exhibition), and who had already designed Marshall Field's main store in Chicago, as well as other stores in New York and Philadelphia, to design his new London store. Burnham's design was based on a huge, Ionic colonnade that spanned from a ground floor base with large shop windows to a vast fourth-floor glazed frieze. English architect Robert Frank Atkinson (1869–1923), who had completed Waring and Gillow's department store in 1906 in London, was appointed as local executive architect. He was assisted by Canadian architect Francis Samuel Swales (1878–1962) who had been trained at the École under Jean Louis Pascal. The first phase of the nine bays from Duke Street was completed in 1909 and was an immediate commercial success for Selfridge, but construction of the following phases was delayed by the First World War. By 1919, when Harry Selfridge was finally able to proceed with the completion of Burnham's design, both Burnham and Atkinson had died, and Swales had moved home to Canada. When Swales was consulted about carrying out the work, he recommended another of Pascal's pupils who was based in London – John James Burnet. Selfridge quickly established that Burnet had just completed a major London building, which included a giant Ionic colonnade, and that he had considerable previous retail experience with R W Forsyth. Burnet was thus back in business.

With his friendship with Thomas Tait rekindled and David Raeside having returned safe from active service, Burnet made them both the offer of junior partnerships and renamed his London practice, Sir John Burnet and Partners. At this stage, Burnet was still clearly the leader in all matters, while Raeside managed the office and Tait assisted Burnet on design and project management, but as Burnet's health continued to decline, Tait took on more and more responsibility for design, soon leading several of their major commissions. Andrew Bryce and James Wallace also returned from military service and as the massive commission for the completion of Selfridge's department store got underway, they were soon joined by further new recruits.

The Selfridge's commission was quickly followed by further new work and by projects that had been previously cancelled, such as the Second Church of Christ Scientist, which was resurrected. Burnet's client from the British Museum, its director Frederick Kenyon, had also been appointed as the Imperial War Graves Commission's (IWGC's) artistic adviser by Fabian Ware, the founder and vice-chairman of the Commission. Before Kenyon's appointment, Ware had already involved London's leading architects; Sir Edwin Lutyens, Sir Herbert Baker, and Sir Reginald Blomfield in his vast project to commemorate the one million Empire war dead, and they had been assigned the design of all the major cemeteries and monuments in Europe. But, despite the focus on the Western Front, the war had been waged around the globe, and after his appointment as artistic director Kenyon secured commissions for Scottish architects Sir John Burnet and Sir Robert Lorimer for the more far-flung memorials. Burnet was thus assigned Palestine and Gallipoli and Lorimer was offered Italy, Macedonia, and Egypt. Each of these principal architects was then supported by one or more assistants, who were also commissioned by the IWGC, and Burnet managed to secure an appointment for David Raeside as his assistant to work on the memorials and cemeteries. These appointments by the IWGC attracted numerous further commissions for all these principal architects for city, town, company, and family memorials, throughout the 1920s.

In Glasgow, there was work again as well – a similar mix of previously cancelled projects and new commissions. Burnet's new chapel for Glasgow University, which he had designed before the war, now proceeded as a war memorial chapel and extensions were required for the Wallace Scott factory and the Sick Children's hospital. His problem in Glasgow was now resources, and he had to lobby hard to get Norman Dick demobilised from the Royal Scots, before the practice could be rebuilt.

He also had another family complication to deal with. Since his brother's early death in 1901 he had unwaveringly supported his brother's three children throughout his own financial struggles. His niece Edith (1888–1971) had been educated at the Sorbonne in Paris, followed by periods of study in Dresden and Florence before enrolling in Gray's School of Art in Aberdeen in 1911, where she planned to study garden design but soon switched to architecture. There she had met Thomas Harold Hughes (1887–1949) who was one of her tutors and through the next few years they had worked together on competition entries and secured a few commissions, while supporting themselves by lecturing. They married in September 1918, after which Edith informed her uncle that they would like to join his practice in London and that her new husband ought to be made a partner. Sir John (who had benefitted considerably from a similar act of nepotism himself) was committed to helping and proposed to Thomas Tait that the newly-weds should join them with Thomas Hughes as one more junior partner. Tait, unsurprisingly, was uncooperative and put up every argument that he could think of against the proposal (even suggesting at one point that there was no ladies' toilet at Montague Street for Edith). Having fallen out with Tait once already, Burnet could not afford to risk losing him again, and so proposed that Edith and Thomas should instead join the Glasgow practice, where Thomas could become a junior partner to Norman Dick. Dick accepted the proposal but the relationship never really got off the ground and within a year Edith left to start her own practice. Hughes, meanwhile, was so unpopular that he was made to work alone in a small first-floor room on his own. Then in 1920, Mr Duncan, the Glasgow office's chief clerk disapeared, along with a substantial sum of money that the firm had been holding in trust for payment to contractors (not an unusual event – Lutyens had previously suffered the same fate). To avoid damage to their reputation, Burnet and Dick did not involve the police but they had to make good the loss. To do so, Dick repurchased his ten-year partnership but agreed to do so only on condition that Thomas Hughes' services were dispensed with. Burnet acquiesced and Hughes left to take up a teaching position at Glasgow School of Art. For Burnet, it had been another highly stressful conflict of unhappy family, personal, and professional relationships which took its toll on his already poor health, resulting in his eczema being so severe that he now had to wear gloves almost constantly, as well as a (rather distinguishing) skull cap.

James Miller was also rebuilding his office and, having abandoned London at the outbreak of the war, he had no intention of dividing his resources again. Richard Gunn had been badly gassed during his war service, a condition he never fully recovered from, but he returned in 1918 to take up the role of chief assistant. James Walker, Miller's former chief assistant who had left to form his own practice, also returned after the war to provide further reinforcements, and was now to stay with Miller throughout the remainder of his career. In Glasgow work was slower to recover than in London, and the bells that rang out from the city's churches to celebrate the end of the war also unknowingly signalled the start of the city's long and painful economic decline. World demand for steel, coal, steam engines, ships, and trains reduced dramatically after the war, as the major European states sought to recover from their self-inflicted near annihilation, and many of Britain's far-flung export markets in Latin America and the Far East had been taken over by Japan and the United States during the conflict. Britain never regained its pre-1914 export volumes and by 1929, exports were still only 80 per cent of what they had been in 1913.(7) The United States, aided by their valuable war loans and long neutrality, now achieved a position of unchallenged economic leadership. Britain, which had been the great creditor nation of the nineteenth century, was now an international debtor and many of its Empire's subjects now sought independence as a reward for their loyal military service and human loss. Growth for the remainder of the decade became erratic, with brief periods of stagnation constantly interrupting progress. Major extensions to Glasgow City's boundary apparently boosted its population, but in reality, merely masked its underlying decline. While no-one at the time could foresee that the decline would be inexorable, Miller was quick to recognise that the world post-war world would be very different from the one that had gone before and that he and his fellow architects would have to adapt or perish.

In November 1920, he was invited to present a paper to the Glasgow Institute of Architects and chose the 'business side of architecture' as his topic. His fellow professionals would have been only too happy to take notes from their most successful competitor and such was the paper's impact that it was republished in full in the *RIBA Journal* the following year. Miller told his audience that '[t]he high costs of labour and material now prevailing, and so far as we can see, likely to prevail for an indefinite period, are such as will prevent what has been termed for lack of a better name the "luxury" type of building being carried out on any great scale for an indefinite period.' While this was regrettable, he still saw limitless opportunities and potentially a return to growth 'as long as it is not throttled by labour.' In a thinly veiled attack on Burnet, he went on to suggest that '[w]e frequently find that where the art faculty is largely developed, the business faculty is lacking' and further, that '[i]t is common knowledge that certain professions, our own among them, look with indifference – if not with contempt – towards anything pertaining to commercial matters.... This prejudice, it is supposed, had its origin in the superior qualities of mind and character possessed by the professional classes, as distinguished from the general body of the population,' and with an admiring look across the Atlantic to the best architects in the United States, he observed that 'It would have been impossible for them to have acquired such extensive practices, and to carry them on so successfully, without possessing great business talent in addition to high architectural skill.'(8)

He freely shared what he believed to be the keys to his commercial success with his audience; client satisfaction as the principle goal; clients always having access to the principal of the practice; employing 'tact' in all his business relationships, with clients, staff, and contractors; always delivering within budget; never accepting or seeking work if one's own resources are already stretched; never feeling satisfied with his work or his achievements and last of all – persevering. It was both an admonishment of the values of his fellow professionals and a frank and open sharing of his knowledge and experience, (which would be just as relevant to his profession today). However, even more importantly, at the age of sixty-one, he showed no nostalgia for life before the war, merely a steely determination to make the best of whatever circumstances he might find himself in and a constant, optimistic search for future opportunities without backward glances, nostalgia or regrets.

For Miller, there was to be no Selfridges to restore his practice immediately to pre-war levels, and worse, his major pre-war commission that had been abandoned when hostilities broke out – Gleneagles Hotel – was given to the engineering office of the Caledonian Railway Company to keep them in work with the only crumb he received from his old client being the commission for the new Gleneagles railway station. It was going to be a long climb back to rebuild his practice, resolutely, step by step.

Perhaps Burnet's gamble to move to London had finally paid off. It had certainly won him a knighthood that he was very unlikely to have been given in Glasgow and Selfridges alone would feed his team for almost a decade. Any lingering doubts about this were soon quashed by a mini-boom in London that resulted from pent-up demand during the war and delivered two further major commissions, for Adelaide House on the north bank of the Thames by London Bridge (which, on its completion would be the tallest building in the City) and for Vigo House in Regent Street, which was to be the new London department store for R W Forsyth. He was busy again, but frustratingly limited in terms of what he could contribute personally as a result of his declining health. Despite this, I think we can be certain that the magnificent central entrance to Selfridges was pure Burnet alone, with another proscenium arch enclosing clocks and a sculpture, the *Queen of Time* (by Gilbert Bayes [1872–1953]) in front of a triple-height cast-iron glazed screen (Fig. 83). He also personally designed a great tower for the store, which, along with an underground link to Bond Street station (which would have been renamed 'Selfridge's'), was never constructed.

In Adelaide House we see Tait's influence growing, although the basic organisation of the office block is classic Burnet, with flanking stair towers, a central proscenium entrance supported on four massive black marble columns and a strong vertical emphasis blocked by a high, horizontal eaves gallery – all as in McGeoch's Warehouse (Fig. 84). The architectural

Fig. 83   Two great artists at work on the main entrance of Selfridges department store of 1919–28 – architect J. J. Burnet and sculptor Gilbert Bayes. Courtesy of Ian Stubbs.

detailing is American Art Deco crossed with Ancient Egypt, with Burnet sending Tait to Port Tewfik under the pretence of a visit to an IWGC site to study Egyptian architecture. It was all very fashionable and employed the latest technology, including a steel frame, full mechanical ventilation, and a centralised vacuum cleaning system, with their client, businessman Richard Tilden Smith, enjoying both a penthouse apartment on the top floor and a roof garden overlooking the Thames, complete with a golf putting course, on the level above. For all its technological innovation and fashionable motifs, compared with Burnet's brilliant work in Glasgow it was rather turgid stuff. Its scale, right on the bank of the Thames, was much criticised on its completion, to which Burnet responded indirectly in his self-published monograph in 1930:

Fig. 84 Sir John Burnet and Partners' Adelaide House of 1924–25 by London Bridge – once the tallest office building in the City. Courtesy of John Stewart.

The argumentative storm which has centred around it has been considerably aggravated by the fact that the new building was perforce situated in a locality where the traditional architecture was exceptionally well represented ... it is not the architect's fault if economic circumstances of the twentieth century necessitate the erection of tall structures out of scale with neighbouring buildings still representative of a former age.(9)

The truth was that he and Tait (whose design it largely was) were quite happy to be seen as the importers of contemporary American commercial architecture to the City of London and that any general concerns that the public may have had were of little weight compared with the approval of their fellow professionals, who were already increasingly beginning to value innovation over quality.

If Adelaide House was a vast Portland stone Egyptian tomb, Vigo House – the new store for R W Forsyth on Regent Street – was a dumbed-down version of the Clyde Navigation Trust building in which Burnet's elegant corner drum, complete with doubled Ionic columns below a crowning dome, was here replaced by primitive Doric below a bizarre stone and copper carbuncle (Fig. 85). Like Adelaide House, the overall organisation is classic Burnet but the detailing, presumably by Tait, is a confusing concoction of stripped-down Classicism and stepped Mayan Art Deco. This is architecture in a state of confused transition – Classical in its organisation but Moderne in its detailing, with only the fine bronze balustrades and black Belgian marble corner entrances providing the level of sophistication that we expect of a Burnet building. It is interesting to contrast the confusion of Vigo House with Lutyens's contemporary Midland Bank Headquarters at No. 27 Poultry in the City. Here Lutyens offers us a stripped-down Classicism that is much more severe than the earlier Edwardian Baroque London bank buildings, but he never strays from the language of Classicism in plan, section, or elevation, or in his exquisite detailing. At Vigo House we have two men at work – one a committed Classicist who is attempting to respond to a changed post-war Britain and the other a frustrated Modernist who has neither the freedom nor yet a fully developed new architectural language to produce a truly Modern building. While the two men's relationship was positive, Burnet at least recognised that their shared architecture was hopelessly compromised and from around this time he began to carve out his own projects from the partnership's commissions, both in London and in his other practice in Glasgow. While he was becoming more and more limited in what he could do by his eczema, fortunately, as a distinguished member of his profession, he was able to spend time (and earn fees) assessing architectural competitions and acting as a consultant on other architects' projects.

The war memorials were to be his alone however, and his appointment by the IWGC brought him many more such commissions in England and Scotland. Lutyens's Cenotaph, which had been unveiled in 1920, was a huge influence on Burnet, as well as on most other IWGC architects, and Lutyens' and Herbert Baker's style of 'Elemental Classicism' informed almost all Burnet's designs at home and abroad. Most public memorials were organised by town and city

Fig. 85   R W Forsyth's flagship Vigo House of 1920–5 on Regent Street in London by Sir John Burnet and Partners. Courtesy of John Stewart.

Fig. 86   Dumbarton – one of Burnet's numerous
town and city war memorials from the 1920s.
Courtesy of Stephen Sweeney.

councils and funded by public subscription, and they were commissioned throughout the 1920s as decisions were finally made as to how best to commemorate their war missing and dead and the necessary funds raised. One of the first to proceed in Scotland was in Dumbarton west of Glasgow, with a beautiful site selected in Levengrove Park overlooking the River Clyde (Fig. 86). Burnet's design – a squat obelisk or pylon on a low stepped plinth with quadrant walls terminating in piers – would be used again and again. Unlike most of Lutyens's memorials (and in common with Herbert Baker's), it included a Christian cross and succeeded in striking a suitable balance between commemorating the terrible loss of life in stone and celebrating the successful outcome for Britain in a relatively modest sculpture of winged Victory. It was unveiled on 1 October 1922.

Arriving at a suitable commemoration of Glasgow's war dead followed the pattern of proposal and counter-proposal that was taking place throughout the country. John Keppie was one of many voices calling for a suitable memorial in Glasgow and, following various proposals which included a memorial bridge over the Clyde, a memorial concert hall, and the renaming of Sauchiehall Street as 'Victory Street', it was finally agreed that something like the Cenotaph in Whitehall should be erected in George Square in the very centre of the city. The Council invited architects Burnet, Lorimer, and Lutyens, and sculptor Sir George Frampton to compete for the commission, which all four declined, with one city councillor who was involved with interviewing Burnet and Lorimer later stating that they, 'did not consider there was any higher artist than themselves to whom they could submit their designs for adjudication'.(10) Lutyens offered a copy of the Cenotaph, while Burnet's friend Sir George Frampton proposed that Burnet should be give the commission as the only shortlisted Glasgow architect. The Glasgow Institute of Architects proposed an open competition and this was further developed, with a restriction that it should be open only to Scottish architects who had served in the war. In the end the Council concluded that with Sir Robert Lorimer having just been commissioned to design the national war memorial in Edinburgh Castle, and bearing in mind Burnet's father-in-law's service to the city, Burnet should be appointed.

What he produced for his hometown was his finest memorial (Fig. 87). Rather than the truncated pylon of Dumbarton (and later elsewhere), here Burnet placed a symbolic stone coffin above the simplest of tapered bases decorated only with wreaths and incised planes of stone, with an upturned sword creating a cross above the city seal, to face the square. It was located at the eastern end of George Square in front of the City Chambers, allowing the public to gather in the square and during commemoration ceremonies to look to the east, where their loved ones had fallen. His original conception was to excavate a court below ground level in front of the stone where the rolls of honour would be kept and that would provide a haven of tranquillity amid the city centre traffic, but this was vetoed by the Council and instead he created a sacred space in front of his cenotaph with parallel stone benches concluding in two sculpted guardian

Fig. 87   Burnet's Glasgow Cenotaph of 1924 in front of
William Young's City Chambers. Courtesy of David Gray.

lions. Within this space he placed his own version of Lutyens's 'War Stone', and in front of this, a large horizontal sculpted palm leaf to symbolise peace. It was unveiled in November 1924.

Like most prominent architects, he was inundated with various further memorial commissions for, amongst others, Wellington United Free Church in Glasgow, the Clyde Navigational Trust, the Clydesdale Bank in St Vincent Place, Stenhouse Parish Church Edinburgh, Merchiston Castle School and the Faculty of Accountants in Glasgow, all of which were carried out in a variety of stone and bronze plaques. His many town memorials were much more individual than the plaques and the subject of considerable care and thus variety. For Ballater and Wemyss Bay he designed free-standing stone Celtic crosses, for Grangemouth a simple stone cenotaph to which was added, rather controversially, a sculpture of a British lion devouring a German eagle (by Alexander Proudfoot [1878–1957]), while in New Cumnock he provided another elegant variant on Lutyens's 'War Stone'.

In London, he was commissioned for both the Cavalry Memorial and the Memorial to the staff of the Great Western Railway at Paddington station. The Cavalry Memorial, which was dedicated to the 4,500 cavalrymen who had died on the Western Front, was located on Park Lane, where Burnet offered a simple Doric Portland stone portico and a bronze plaque as the backdrop to a magnificent equestrian statue of St George by Adrian Jones (1845–1938). Unfortunately, due to road widening, the statue had to be moved into Hyde Park and Burnet's frame was demolished. His memorial in Paddington station has survived and his stone pylon backdrop (detailed on this occasion by Thomas Tait) also provides the base for a life-size bronze sculpture of a soldier in full kit, by perhaps the greatest of the First World War memorial sculptors, Charles Sergeant Jagger (1885–1934).

The Scottish memorials provided much-appreciated work for the Glasgow office, which was still to find its feet in a staggering economy. It was Burnet's old Scottish clients who came to their rescue – firstly R W Forsyth, who commissioned a large extension to their Edinburgh store, and then Glasgow University, who had already given Burnet the go-ahead for his memorial chapel and now commissioned a new zoology building from his Glasgow firm. After the Kodak, Adelaide and Vigo buildings, the Zoology Building was to be a welcome return to the Scots Free Style of his best work. His designs for the university had always looked backwards – firstly in the form of the Scots Renaissance and Scots Baronial buildings that recalled the Old College, but now looking back to his own earlier work in Glasgow – to the Savings Bank and his nearby Kelvinside station. His brief was to provide laboratories, a lecture theatre, and museum and he organised these around a small courtyard (where live animals were originally kept). While the interiors are competent, well-lit, and largely practical (overseen by Norman Dick, assisted by Walter Knight and James Napier) the pièce de résistance is Burnet's main elevation (Fig. 88). He placed the lecture theatre to the left of the main entrance, with the end of the laboratory wing to its right, in an asymmetrical arrangement that reflected the functions of the building, with the height of the lecture theatre matching the two-storey height of the laboratory wing. This elevation was then entirely rusticated, with deeply channelled grooves in the ashlar façade. The entrance doorway and large window over it are flanked by rusticated piers which continue through an elegant curved pediment to roof level. To the left of the door, the theatre wall is largely blank, with a series of five small, punched windows arranged symmetrically within the wall plane at low level, whereas to the right we have a large ground-floor window with keystone, below three square first-floor windows that are treated as a gallery with shared sills and cornice, above which the parapet drops down, before rising again as a single pier to turn the corner. Two functional windows to a ground-floor office are just cut through the rustication, as required. Stepping back, the ventilator to the lecture theatre provides a vertical accent and along with the vertical entrance block and corner pier, balances the overall composition against the insistent horizontals of the rustication. It is a refreshing reminder that, despite his infirmities, Burnet could still deliver architecture of the highest standard. I would even go as far as to suggest that the Zoology Building stands comparison with his Savings Bank Hall, making up for what it lacks in richness of detail and sculptural form with a restless energy produced by the well-

Fig. 88   Burnet's triumphant return to his Glasgow Free Style in his Zoology building for Glasgow University of 1922–23. Courtesy of Roger Edwards.

tooled, machine-like rustication and the beautifully judged asymmetrical balance of its various elements. The third band of rustication above ground level is pronounced and continues around the corner of the building to provide the base for the double-height windows that serve the laboratories. This elevation is treated as a colonnade, with full-height stone piers between the glazing (as at McGeogh's), but here, with its equally strong horizontal emphasis, it has a quiet dignity, particularly after the fireworks of the main elevation. There is no doubt as to this building's authorship, nor Burnet's continuing brilliance, particularly when he is working alone, far from the influence of Thomas Tait.

Burnet was back – now established as one of the leaders of his profession in London, with a busy London practice that was carrying out innovative work, and in 1922 his status was confirmed with the gold medal of the Paris *Académie d'architecture* and in 1923, he was paid the greatest compliment possible by his contemporaries when he was awarded the Royal gold medal of the RIBA. As *The Builder* reported of his presentation:

> The recipient of the Royal Gold Medal this year, Sir John J. Burnet, A.R.A., is one of our most distinguished architects, and his distinction is of quite an especial kind. We can call to mind no architect who has made a similar record of attainment and capability. His imaginative faculty, refinement, and reserve appear singularly to represent the happy combination of the Scotch and French temperaments.(11)

Burnet responded that his fellow professionals, 'could not pay him a greater compliment than to place his name on a list containing the name of his Professor and life-long friend, Jean Louis Pascal'.

CHAPTER 9: 1923–1929

The same issue of *The Builder* of 15 June 1923 that had carried news of Sir John Burnet's RIBA gold medal also included a major feature on James Miller's Kildonan with several full-page photographs and a glowing review, but there would be no gold medal for Miller. The bestowal of these honours has always been somewhat erratic and inconsistent (with fellow-Scot, the brilliant Richard Norman Shaw who was Lutyens's idol, receiving neither a knighthood nor the gold medal) and Burnet's receipt of his medal was at least as much due to his professional contributions and networking as to the brilliance of his earlier work. But Miller at least had not suffered as Burnet had done during the war and such was his bank balance in 1920 that he used the post-war slump in workload as an opportunity to extend and remodel his home at Randolphfield in Stirling, including a new stable block. Commercially, he was much more astute than Burnet (and most of his other Glasgow contemporaries) and his practice would soon be busy again.

The war brought a commemorative workload for Miller too – the conversion of a large house in Lytham St Annes into a memorial hospital and various town memorials. Of these, Barrhill and Dalrymple were simple, rough-hewn Celtic crosses (like that of Burnet for Ballater and Wemyss Bay), while Dunblane was a modest pylon with an upturned sword as a cross. Kilmarnock, had to wait until 1927 for the completion of their memorial, which was by far the grandest – a Classical sandstone tomb within which was a bronze figure, *The Victor*, by David McGill, with head bowed in silent contemplation of the cost of war, and around whom the names of the fallen are listed on bronze plaques on the walls. It was largely funded by Miller's long-term client, Alexander Walker and one has to say it is a rather insipid effort compared with the power of Lutyens', Baker's, or Burnet's much rawer Classicism. Much more successful is his Richmond Memorial Hall in Kirkoswald (1924) which was the gift to the village of John Richmond (for whom Miller had designed Blanefield). This has the strong modelling and excellent detail of Miller's best work, with its steeply pitched slate roof deeply overhanging its coursed rubble walls. The hall roof is pierced on each side by four tall, elegant hipped-roofed windows, while the main entrance gable to the road is cut back on each side to form a central gabled tower with low, flat-roofed sheltering wings on either side. It is a little gem (which was recently put up for sale by South Ayrshire Council).

Further commissions began to trickle into the office – a new hall and additional aisle for Jordanhill Church; the removal and reconstruction of the Old West Kirk in Greenock to a new site in the town; and several houses for Caledonian Railway workers at Gleneagles. Lord Forteviot instructed him to proceed with the construction of his model village, including the delightful village hall, which was clearly another development of his hall in Kirkoswald, although this time in the much lighter palette of white roughcast below a red-tiled roof. The major element of the new village was a U-shaped terrace of ten houses enclosing a village green (Fig. 89). This was focused on a large central gable with interesting, flat-roofed two-storey bay windows in each internal corner and was quite the equal of Burnet's earlier Hamilton Terrace in Lamlash. Lord Forteviot also commissioned a hostel for the homeless in Perth, Princes Street House (1923–4), (now Greyfriars House and still a hostel for the homeless a hundred years later), which Miller designed in the same red brick Georgian style with stone dressings as his Perth Infirmary buildings.

Glasgow was slowly stirring back into life and in 1922 Miller was commissioned to design a new shop, warehouse, and repository for department store owner William McLaren on a site on

Fig. 89   James Miller's Forteviot model village of 1925–27. Courtesy of Ian Gourlay.

the south side of George Square adjacent to his earlier Olympic House. It was to be built in two phases, starting with the corner to Hanover Street but, unfortunately for Miller and George Square, only the first phase was ever completed, resulting in a truncated building with its entrance on its edge rather than its centre with a massive step down from the eight-storey McLaren Warehouse and Olympic House to the three-storey office (by John Burnet Snr) that still survived between them. The contrast between these two Miller buildings is fascinating with Olympic House of twenty years earlier very much still a carved sandstone block while the McLaren Warehouse very clearly expresses its steel frame, albeit still within a Classical language of a two-storey base, five-storey body, and massive, concluding, single-storey entablature, complete with carved brackets supporting a great modillioned cornice. As far as Glasgow's commercial architecture is concerned, it is as innovative as Burnet's Kodak House in London – and just as dull.

Much richer and more interesting was his design of the Royal Automobile Club on Blythswood Square, diagonally opposite his office. The entire east side of the square had been designed by John Brash (1775–1848) in 1823 as a single palazzo with flanking wings, although, in reality,

Fig. 90   Miller created Glasgow's RAC Club within what had been a terrace of townhouses on Blytheswood Square in Glasgow. Courtesy of Tom Bastin.

it actually contained several townhouses. Miller's commission was to unite the interiors and provide a number of major new social spaces within it for the club (Fig. 90). He added a central Ionic portico to provide the main entrance and behind this an elegant, Ionic-columned, marble-floored Classical entrance hall with public rooms to right and left, overlooking the square. Ahead there was an impressive new central staircase and lift to take members to the facilities on the upper floors. The style was very much that of his ocean liners, with richly moulded ceilings, panelled walls, and chandeliers with just a dash of contemporary Art Deco. It was completed in 1926, and soon became the primary watering hole for Glasgow's business leaders, finally closing in 2002, when it was converted into a hotel and apartments, thus saving many of its exquisite interiors.

Miller's office across the square was humming once more, with Richard Gunn continuing as his highly valued lead assistant. Miller describes him as 'a brilliant and rapid draughtsman; in design he was scholarly and refined, while his knowledge of the practical side of his profession was such as is possessed by few. He loved his work and took no end of pains with any subject he had to deal with, to achieve the best result down to the minutest detail'.(1) There was no division of projects here, as with Burnet and Tait, and Miller continued to lead the work from the front, both maintaining principal contact with all his main clients and initiating and controlling the design work. Gunn is often credited with the authorship of several of Miller's projects from this period (not least because of his link with Burnet) but with his role leading and managing the work of the assistants, combined with his continuing poor health, this seems unlikely, and this expansion of Gunn's role has more to do with the views of several architectural historians who have categorised Miller as merely a commercial architect much more interested in money than art. It also constitutes a disservice to Miller's former chief assistant, James Walker who had rejoined the practice after the war and also assumed a senior role. As well as these two senior staff members, by then Miller also had a new pupil in the early 1920s – his son George – who had been educated at Fettes College in Edinburgh prior to going to St John's College in Cambridge and was now learning his trade as an architect while attending the Royal Technical College of Glasgow.

In 1924, the Union Bank of Scotland announced an architectural competition for the design of their new headquarters in Glasgow. The bank had been one of Burnet's clients previously, but in 1919, 34-year-old Norman Hird (1887–1946) – who was to go on to be one of Scotland's most prominent bankers – had taken over as their general manager, thus breaking its link to Burnet. Despite the bank's reliance on Glasgow's declining heavy industries, he wanted the new headquarters building to be seen as a sign of their confidence in the future. Miller entered and won the competition, with a design that owed much to several recently completed American banks. This American influence was attributed to Gunn, who unlike Miller, had visited the United States before the war, but the reality was that firstly, Norman Hird, their prospective client, had travelled extensively in the United States himself during his studies of their banking systems; secondly, the latest American bank buildings were generally viewed as being state of the art by the British banking profession; and thirdly, they had been well covered in the architectural press, including specifically, McKim, Mead and White's National City Bank in New York (1904–10) where they had added four floors on top of an earlier colonnaded base. No-one equalled Miller's

Fig. 91   Miller's magnificent Union Bank of Scotland of 1924–7. Courtesy of Ian Stubbs.

competition record, which was based both on the quality of his submissions and the care that he took in accurately identifying what his prospective client was looking for and then tailoring his submission to press all the right buttons. He read Norman Hird like a book and delivered exactly what was required.

Miller's design (which was beautifully presented) – which is so often dismissed as simply a provincial version of a typical New York bank – is actually a piece of particularly well-resolved architecture (Fig. 91). The first three floors provide a massive banking hall, the like of which had never been seen before in Glasgow, above which was a floor of offices and the boardroom for the bank, below three more floors of speculative offices, which were topped off with a pierced frieze sheltered by a huge, overhanging cornice below a final attic floor. A raised basement (containing armour-plated vaults) provided the plinth for the mighty Ionic colonnade and this was infilled at ground level with a rusticated ground-floor wall that screened the interior from passers-by (handling money and drinking in public houses then both being regarded as semi-private activities in Glasgow). A fine double-height, central entrance doorway gave access to what was, and still is, one of the grandest and most dignified interior spaces in the city. Above ground level, the windows to the banking hall are in a distinctly Greek bronze grid, with the bank's first floor offices, which look out below the frieze of the colonnade, in clear glass. The upper floor provides a solid stone band, with square punched windows echoing the giant colonnade below and this supports the palistrade, which shoots up to the fifth floor below another punched stone frieze and the massive overhanging cornice.

Even acknowledging its debt to McKim, Mead and White, this is a particularly fine composition through which the building's functions are clearly expressed with no resort to industrial styling. Miller's handling of the massive block is extremely skilful and its reading oscillates between a street-level classical temple of finance, a city-centre office block, and a mighty, carved stone treasure chest with an overhanging lid (Fig. 92). The top-lit interior is equally fine – calm

Fig. 92   The main banking hall of Miller's Union Bank – one of Glasgow's greatest commercial interiors. Courtesy of Kim Traynor.

and extremely dignified – with the central public area of the banking hall defined by full-height marble Doric columns, the walls lined with *forêt de brousse* marble and the glazed screen of the skylight repeating the Greek grid of the exterior windows. It is now a branch of Lloyds Bank, who maintain the building beautifully but, having lost the tellers' marble counters during recent times, the space now lacks a level of detail at the human scale, which makes it much colder and austere than it originally felt. Inside and out, Miller's detailing is beautifully proportioned and as sharp as in his best work. Construction was delayed by industrial action including the General Strike of May 1926, with the building finally being opened by the Prince of Wales in November 1927, the *Architectural Review* of the following April describing it as 'one of the finest buildings of the kind erected in this country in recent years.'(2)

In London, Burnet's office was now a hive of activity. Selfridges was a banker for Burnet, just as the Royal Infirmary had been for Miller for so many years, providing a base workload for the office until its eventual completion in 1928. Tait and Raeside between them were now effectively managing the practice and the commission for the Second Church of Christ Scientist in Notting Hill Gate which Burnet had secured before the war, became Tait's first solo effort. As prescribed by their client, the building was to be in Romanesque style (which was the style of the Mother Church in Boston and similar to Sir Herbert Baker's contemporary Ninth Church of Christ Scientist in Westminster) and Tait provided them with a rather spartan series of external courtyards and vaulted interior spaces in slim red brick. The next few major commissions were now to be Tait's alone, including the mighty Art Deco, Daily Telegraph building on Fleet Street and Carliol House in Newcastle, both of which continued the earlier Egyptian themes of Adelaide House (Fig. 93). While both buildings contained elements of Burnet's style, including the use of a proscenium feature to frame the giant colonnade of the Daily Telegraph building and the entrance of Carliol House, Burnet's contribution was minimal. George Eastman, Burnet's client for Kodak House, donated £200,000 to the London Royal Free Hospital to fund the establishment of a dental clinic in London and Burnet was given the design commission, producing a rather insipid, watered-down, Classical brick building on Gray's Inn Road. This proved to be Burnet's last London building and he left his partners to manage it and the rest of the London office work so that he could concentrate on his war memorials for the IWGC.

While most of these were in the Mediterranean and Middle East, one of the first to be completed was a memorial in Brussels that was funded by the IWGC in gratitude to the people of Belgium for the assistance they had given to British prisoners of war. Burnet produced a long, low stone backdrop that was carved with a frieze depicting scenes from the war, in front of which was another superb sculpture by Charles Sargeant Jagger depicting a British and Belgian soldier standing side by side. It was unveiled in 1923 by the Prince of Wales.

His work on what had been the Eastern Front during the First World War soon absorbed him and, as it was more remote from the commemorations in France and Belgium, afforded him considerable latitude in terms of both design and site selection. In Egypt he designed the Heliopolis memorial at Port Tewfik on a promontory on the banks of the Suez Canal. This commemorated the 4,000 men of the Indian Army who had died in Egypt and Palestine during the war with no known grave, and took the form of a waterside pylon flanked by two magnificent crouching tigers,

Fig. 93   Sir John Burnet and Partners Art Deco *Daily Telegraph* building on Fleet Street of 1928. Courtesy of John Stewart.

sculpted by Jagger. Unveiled in May 1926, it was destroyed during the Six-Day War in 1967. In Jerusalem he designed both the cemetery, which included over 2,500 graves, and a memorial to the 3,300 servicemen of the Empire missing in operations in Egypt and Palestine. Like most of Burnet's memorials, it continues the theme of stepped planes of stone, here enclosing the cemetery and rising up to a central stone chapel, flanked by two sturdy stone pylons. The chapel itself is a rather strange concoction of Egyptian and Art Deco architecture that culminates in a shallow dome with more than a hint of the strange eruption on Vigo House. While it is beautifully detailed, it adopts the stripped-down Classicism of Lutyens, Baker, and by then, Charles Holden, but looks ponderous in comparison with their designs and is far from Burnet's best work.

Most of his work, however, was on the Gallipoli peninsula where allied forces had attempted to open up a new eastern front against Germany's ally, Turkey. The campaign, which lasted almost a year, was a disastrous failure, resulting in approximately 250,000 casualties on both sides, and while the overwhelming majority of those killed were British, the losses among Australians, New Zealanders, and Indians were considerable too. Burnet designed three memorials and thirty-one war cemeteries on Gallipoli, the largest of which was the Helles memorial, which stands on a site on the very tip of the peninsula, where its 30-metre-high coursed rubble obelisk can be seen from passing ships as well as from the land (Fig. 94). It is a memorial both to the battle at Cape Helles and to the whole Gallipoli campaign, and bears the names of the 20,000 men who died with no known grave. This is by far Burnet's simplest and finest work in the east and it was unveiled in May 1924.

Fig. 94   Burnet's finest war memorial for the Imperial War Graves Commission – the Helles Memorial on the Gallipoli Peninsula of 1924. Courtesy of Hans de Regt.

In addition to his work for the IWGC, Burnet had two more significant commissions at this time, both of which were in Glasgow. For these he returned to the styles of his best earlier work and to something of that quality as well. The first of these had been brewing for some time; namely, the new chapel for Glasgow University, which had started with his original commission in 1913 but gained momentum in 1919 when it was identified as a war memorial to the 755 men connected to the university who had lost their lives in the war. The plan was to complete George Gilbert Scott's quadrangle by adding the chapel in the centre of the west wing of his main university building. For Burnet, both Scott's buildings and the history of the university dictated a return to the Gothic, in which he had excelled with his early Barony Church. Indeed, there were to be many similarities between the two projects, despite a gap of forty years. Dunblane Cathedral was the model, with the chancel, lit by three great lancet windows, now projecting into Scott's western courtyard (Fig. 95). As at Dunblane, carved choir stalls (here by Archibald Dawson [1892–1938]) mark the transition from the nave to the great chancel arch, but here the contrast between the darker nave (between the existing buildings) and the brightly lit chancel (which is lit on three sides in the quadrangle) is even more dramatic. While Gomme and Walker rate Barony Church the better, there are few Scottish Gothic interiors that beat Burnet's university chapel for intimacy and atmosphere. Unlike Barony and Dunblane, its structure was reinforced concrete, though few worshippers would ever guess it, and Burnet also managed to accommodate the famed stone Lion and Unicorn stair that had been salvaged from the Old College in his plan, as well as adding an elegant fleche on the chapel roof in which was rehung the bell from the Old Blackfriars Church which had stood next door to the College buildings on the High Street. After considerable delays, it was consecrated on 4 October 1929 and with the exception of its reinforced concrete structure, the whole chapel complex was a long and fruitful look backwards for both architect and client.

Burnet's other final Glasgow commission was a new Glasgow office for the North British and Mercantile Insurance Company (1926–9) right back in the heart of the city centre, slightly up the hill from Miller's Union Bank, at 200 St Vincent Street. It was to be the last significant building that the great John James Burnet was ever to design and fortunately, he went out on a high note. There was no attempt to express the buildings steel-framed structure – no hint of Egyptian styling or American Art Deco. This was to be one final, great Classical Glasgow office building in carved sandstone (Fig. 96). Like Miller's bank, it can be read as a single block, but here its broad dentiled cornice is pierced by two great rocketing chimneys that flank the main elevation to St Vincent Street. It stands on a grey granite plinth from which the sandstone rises, with five arched bays to St Vincent Street providing an obvious central entrance, and four to West Campbell Street around the corner. The bays to St Vincent Street are divided by double Doric columns within the plane of the wall and the central doorway is marked by taller, free-standing columns with figurative sculptures by Archibald Dawson. Each arch is then further subdivided with aedicules topped by massive keystones below Diocletian windows, while within the two great entrance columns are two smaller columns supporting a carved panel that once read 'North British and Mercantile Building'. Above this, within the arch, almost as if Burnet knew that he was signing off – was one last segmental pediment. High above on axis, between the third and fourth

Fig. 95   A return to his earlier Gothic of Barony Church for Burnet's graceful
Memorial Chapel for Glasgow University of 1913–29. Courtesy of Tom Bastin.

Fig. 96   Burnet's last major building represented a return to the
Classicism of his greatest work – his North British and Mercantile
Insurance Company building of 1926–9. Courtesy of Tom Bastin.

floors is a sculpture of Saint Andrew and higher still on the very corner of the building, a last sculpted cartouche. Above the arches, nothing could be plainer, with the great ashlar wall rising sheer to the massive cornice, the office windows cut sharply into the stonework with a single band of stone forming a sill to the third-floor windows and gracefully dropping to every third window below, to form a keystone. There is a hint of Charles Holden's British Medical Association building on the Strand (1906), but it is no more than a hint, and frankly, Burnet's solution is the finer. It is an exercise in precision and restraint and a triumphant return to Classicism by one of its masters, which proved to be an entirely appropriate swansong.

Unfortunately, its construction proved to be long, difficult, and extremely stressful for all involved, with many of the difficulties arising from Burnet's absence in London. An assistant in Glasgow interpreted Burnet's elevational drawings to show the jointing of the granite plinth as channelled, and when Burnet saw it he demanded that the completed stone be recut, which had to be done at his firm's expense. There was also an error in the design of the steelwork, which would have affected the main staircase window, and this had to be dismantled, redesigned, and reconstructed with Burnet, Son & Dick footing the bill for this as well. The cost of Burnet's corrections finally totalled over £10,000 and this proved to be the final straw for Norman Dick, who was already frustrated at trying to run a practice with a partner who was either 400 miles away in London or 2,000 miles away in the Middle East most of the time. Burnet's Glasgow practice was thus dissolved.

In London, Burnet now played the role of the elder statesman. His knighthood and gold medal were followed in 1925 by his election to the Royal Academy. He was a regular judge of architectural competitions, acting on behalf of the RIBA, and was engaged as consultant on projects to review their design and suggest improvements. Dundee City Council, for example, invited him to advise them on the planning of a new civic centre in the heart of the city. James Thomson, the city architect (1852–1927) who had designed the muscular neo-Classical *Caird Hall*, had retired on its completion in 1924 and Burnet (having now completely abandoned his brief role as a pioneer of Modernism) advised that a Beaux-Arts square surrounded by Classical buildings should be created in front of Thomson's sturdy colonnade. In 1927, he was paid the considerable honour of being appointed to the international jury to select the new building for the League of Nations headquarters in Geneva as one of nine architects from nine of the fifty-five countries in the League. He was in elevated company, along with Hendrik Berlage, Koloman Moser, Josef Hoffmann, and Ivar Tengbom, under the Presidency of Victor Horta. Unfortunately, the competition collapsed into chaos when the judges, despite meeting sixty-four times, were unable to select a winner from the 377 entries, most of which either exceeded the competition budget or broke its rules. After declaring twenty-seven entries to be winners, it was finally agreed that five architects should collaborate on a design, including Burnet's good friend Henri-Paul Nénot from Paris, who was later accused of plagiarism by Le Corbusier and died before the building's eventual completion in 1936.

Burnet's London practice was now being managed by David Raeside and led by Thomas Tait, and Tait was finally finding his feet as a Modernist. His office buildings of the 1920s represented an architecture in transition – steel framed but stone clad; classically planned and organised but with Moderne styling, which were apparently the work of Sir John James Burnet but were actually by Thomas Tait. But in the latter part of the decade Tait produced a series of new houses that were among the first in Britain that could genuinely be described as Modern architecture. These included *Le Chateau* in Briantree and four streets of modern houses at Silver End in Essex for W. F. Crittal, the steel window manufacturer, Crowsteps in Newbury, Berkshire for Dr Alan Simmons and West Leaze, in Aldbourne, Wiltshire for Dr Hugh Dalton (who would go on to be chancellor of the exchequer). These were all flat-roofed, white rendered, horizontally glazed, cubist compositions artistically on a par with contemporary designs by the early heroes of Modernism – Walter Gropius, Robert Mallet Stevens, Bijvoet and Duiker, and Le Corbusier himself. This was truly radical architecture and Tait rebuilt the practice's London team to deliver it, hiring Clifford Strange (who would go on to design Wembley Town Hall), Franz Strengelhofen, (who had trained and worked in Germany), and Frederick McManus (who had just returned from New York). Sir John Burnet and Partners was now largely Burnet's practice in name only, but it was thriving once more with an energetic young team, and with a regular income once more Burnet was confident enough to move out of London and lease Killermont, a large Arts and Crafts house with extensive grounds near Rowledge in Surrey, from where he occasionally commuted to London by chauffeur-driven Rolls Royce.

The name Sir John Burnet and Partners was now well established in London, and despite little actual input from Sir John Burnet, the brand and his contacts were quite enough to keep pulling in work for the practice. In 1927 they were commissioned by Lloyds Bank to build their new headquarters near the Bank of England in Lombard Street in the heart of the City. As with several of their contemporary buildings, Burnet's influence on the design was largely in providing Tait with tried and tested architectural precedents and solutions. Lloyds was a conservative client and had little interest in Tait's Art Deco and even less in his Modernism – as far as they were concerned, they had hired the architect who had extended the British Museum and it was exactly that brand of Classicism to which they aspired for their headquarters (Fig. 97). The triangular site for the building stretched from Cornhill on the north (where the main entrance and principal elevation were located, thus emphasising its proximity to the Bank of England) through to Lombard Street to the south and a double-height banking hall was provided in the centre of the building, accessible from both streets. The design is very similar to Miller's Union Bank, though it used a much fussier Ionic. Externally, a two-storey arcaded base below an entablature at mezzanine level supports a twelve-bay Corinthian colonnade with deep cornice and several stepped attic floors above. The elevation to Lombard Street is similar, but with flat pilasters in lieu of the Corinthian colonnade. It would appear to be everything their client desired – dignified, restrained, correct and now very conservative, verging on dull. It was a massive project and with the design complete, Campbell, Jones, Sons & Smithers were appointed as executive architects to carry out the bulk of the detailed design work and to oversee construction.

At this stage in his career Thomas Tait proved to be just as flexible in terms of style as Burnet had originally been, designing a new church for the Christian Brethren in Hendon, north London as (to quote Pevsner), 'a severe well-proportioned Tuscan barn',(3) while his Slipstream Parade in Burnt Oak, north London, was another exercise in flat-roofed, streamlined Modernism.

He designed the stone abutments of several steel bridges around the world, including the famous Sydney Harbour Bridge and the bridges over both the Limpopo and Chao Phraya rivers in a stepped Art Deco style that drew on Burnet's IWGC memorials. In 1928, he entered the international competition for the Centrosoyuz building in Moscow, losing to Le Corbusier, and in 1929, the competition for the new Masonic Hospital in Hammersmith, which he won with a flat-roofed brick design, which, like so many public buildings in Britain of this period, owed a huge debt to Willem Dudok's (1884–1974) ground-breaking Hilversum Town Hall, which was then under construction. Burnet had little to do with any of this work and following the termination of

Fig. 97   John Burnet and Partners' Lloyds headquarters in Lombard Street in the City of London of 1927–30. Courtesy of John Stewart.

his appointment with the IWGC in September 1928 had no work of his own until his appointment at the end of the year as consultant for the design of the enormous Unilever House, overlooking the Thames by Blackfriars Bridge, the principal architect being James Lomax-Simpson (1882–1977). Like Lloyds Bank in the City, Unilever House has numerous typically Burnet features. The addition of magnificent equestrian statues on tall plinths at either gable end (by Burnet's friend, Sir William Reid Dick), help to raise this rather sumptuous, curving office block well above the average of the period. Sir John Burnet and Partners were purring along nicely and there was certainly no work on this scale being built north of the border.

Glasgow's economy was still struggling and compounded by further industrial unrest. While James Miller could still beat most other practices for work, there were few significant projects

Fig. 98   One of the entrances to Wyggeston Grammar School
in Miller's Utility Classical style. Courtesy of John Stewart.

around for him to fight for. With the Union Bank largely designed and under construction, he once more began to look further afield for new work. After the disappointment of not winning the competition for new buildings for his alma mater, Perth Academy in 1927 (losing out to Thomas Aitken Swan [1883–1945] of Edinburgh) he entered and won the competition for Wyggeston Grammar School in Leicester later the same year, with a design that can perhaps best be called Utility Classicism (Fig. 98). His proposal was symmetrical in plan, with a central entrance and school hall, parallel to which were two wings of two-storey teaching accommodation linked by single-storey glazed corridors (which created a series of sheltered external courtyards between the buildings). Each of the three long blocks also had their own separate entrance at the end of the wing. It was a very practical solution that offered excellent daylighting to all the teaching spaces and through subtly advancing and receding the brick wall planes and parapet levels around the entrances, along with the use of tall arched windows to the hall and entrance doorways and the sparing use of stone dressings to parapets and entrances, gave his client an educational complex of considerable dignity and architectural quality at relatively little expense, indeed, his proposal had been selected from among the other twenty-three entries because, in the view of the judges, it was the, 'most simple, economical and straightforward design.'(4) As usual, Miller appears to have given his prospective clients exactly what they were looking for. Wyggeston School's buildings, with their stepped massing in red brick with stone dressings, was very fashionable at the time and it was typical of much of the best 1920s and 1930s British architecture with the budget and grandeur of his Union Bank in Glasgow very much the exception rather than the rule, much as he had foretold in his lecture to the Glasgow Institute of Architects shortly after the end of the First World War.

Just before the completion of the Union Bank, Miller landed another major commission in England for the Cadbury family in Bourneville in Birmingham, where he was instructed to design both a major new extension to their factory – the Cocoa Block – and a new dining hall and tea garden for their staff. Both buildings were something of a return to Classicism for Miller (Fig. 99). Like Wyggeston, they had symmetrical plans and were constructed in brick with stone dressings, but there the similarities ended. The Bourneville buildings were organised with very clearly expressed ground floors (with stone banding to the dining hall) topped by a stone string course below either two (in the case of the dining hall) or three storeys (in the case of the Cocoa block) of glazing within brick piers below a familiar Miller, sharply dentiled projecting stone cornice topped with a tall brick parapet. Both buildings had corner pavilions. That of the dining hall had canted stone-mullioned bay windows that enclosed a largely glazed elevation facing the tea garden. This cascaded down from a modest balcony on the second floor to a broad one in the first floor, and so to an almost entirely glazed ground floor with doors opening onto a generous, south-facing terrace, from which broad steps once led on down to a lawn with a fountain below. While the interiors had nothing of the grandeur of Miller's great railway hotels, this sequence of rest spaces and terraces nevertheless provided Cadbury's workers with a very elegant and civilised environment, with at least a modicum of the glamour of Turnberry or Gleneagles. Although it was far from Miller's best work it kept his team in Blythswood Square busy until late in 1929.

Fig. 99   Miller's dining hall for Cadbury's at Bournville of 1927–9 provided exceptional staff facilities by the standards of the period. Courtesy of Gerard Higgins.

Authorship of architectural design is fraught with claims, counterclaims, self-delusion, and misrepresentation, and even with documentary evidence such as signed drawings it is often impossible to assign responsibility for the design of a building accurately to an individual. In Miller's case we know that by the late 1920s he had been producing architecture of a very high standard for almost forty years, with an ever-changing series of assistants supporting him. He was now in his late sixties but (unlike Burnet) was fit and healthy, still riding and playing golf regularly and very much in charge of his office, but around this time, like Burnet (another Classicist at heart) he began to focus his still considerable energies on the projects where this style was most appropriate, leaving Richard Gunn and James Walker to experiment with something more radical.

Other work trickled in and was assigned accordingly – a fire at Dupplin Castle resulted in a commission to repair it from Miller's friend, Lord Forteviot, who also commissioned a row of cottages in Perth. After specifying numerous Crittal windows at Wyggeston and Bourneville, Miller managed to relieve Thomas Tait of any further work at Crittal's own Silver End development and Miller's team built a street of flat-roofed, white-rendered houses of their own there. He reworked Wyggeston in brick with stone dressings and arched windows, with a rather spartan interior lit by a shallow glazed dome, for a small synagogue in Salisbury Road in Edinburgh. Then in 1928, came a major new commission for a furniture showroom and warehouse for Henry Levitt on Renfield Street in the centre of Glasgow, diagonally opposite Miller's Union

Fig. 100   By the late 1920s James Miller was dominant within the central
Glasgow grid, with his Woodhouse Warehouse of 1928–9 bringing some
suave sophistication to Renfield Street. Courtesy of Tom Bastin.

Bank. This was an opportunity to roll back the years and provide Glasgow with one of its last commercial palazzos.

Originally known as the Woodhouse Warehouse (1928–9) and latterly as the Prudential Building, it has none of the strength or muscularity of the bank, but it more than makes up for it in its cool sophistication (Fig. 100). It is suave and debonair, and almost too posh for Glasgow. Giant, fluted Ionic pilasters rise from ground level past first-floor balconies to a second-floor frieze and stone balustraded running balcony. The second floor is rusticated, with punched square windows below the next four floors, which are in smooth ashlar. On the fifth floor are two great windows spanning two floors below richly-decorated oval windows, and a typically sharp concluding modillioned cornice. Every detail has a machine-like precision, much enhanced by the contrast between the beautifully tooled stonework and the great Joseph Armitage's (1880–1945) swags and sculpted panels. This is a very, very elegant composition and it is a shame that Renfield Street is so narrow here that few people appreciate the delights above the dominant second-floor balcony.

Unlike Burnet, whose brilliant North British and Mercantile Building was nearing completion at the same time just further up Blythswood Hill, Miller was far from finished in the Glasgow grid, but both architects and their teams would now have to contend with a new and entirely unexpected challenge, in the shape of a catastrophic economic correction that took place across the Atlantic in October 1929.

CHAPTER 10: 1929–1947

Architectural practices are particularly sensitive to economic cycles. They often struggle to find experienced staff to carry out their commissions during the good times and battle just as hard to find work for their staff during the bad. In economic downturns usually the first thing that clients cancel is their planned building project and in even the best-managed practices, such as James Miller's, existing projects can be delayed and new opportunities hard to find. In the 1920s, when Glasgow was particularly badly affected by the end of wartime production, he was able to look elsewhere, but in October 1929 when the New York Stock Exchange crashed, it signalled the start of an economic crisis that reverberated around the globe. Britain hadn't experienced the boom in the 1920s that had led to bust in the United States, and in fact the immediate reaction of British economist John Maynard Keynes was that '[t]here will be no serious direct consequences in London. We find the look ahead decidedly encouraging'(1) – but within days, world trade began to contract and the impact on British manufacturing, in particular, was devastating. Within a year, British exports had reduced by half and unemployment had more than doubled from one million to two and a half, at a time when there was little or no unemployment benefit. Miller and his practice had survived the impact of the First World War better than most, and though he was now sixty-nine years old, he proved to be still quite capable of battening down the hatches and steering his crew through this latest storm, albeit with far fewer options available on this occasion than before.

For Burnet, the impact was much more dramatic. Tait's Masonic Hospital project was put on hold early in 1930 and with no new commissions, the practice's finances were soon under strain. David Raeside had been taken seriously ill and was soon confined to a nursing home in Southend-on-Sea, where he died in March 1930, leaving Tait, who had as little interest in business matters as Burnet, in sole charge of the practice. Burnet's own health had declined to the point where his chronic eczema meant he could no longer do any work and, with Tait unable to afford to buy him out, he found himself unable to retire. It was Burnet's secretary, Helen Lorne, who came to their rescue with the suggestion that her brother, Francis Lorne, who was then an associate of the major New York practice of Bertram Goodhue Associates, should invest in the partnership. She suggested that with his knowledge of the business of architecture, he would be an ideal replacement for David Raeside (Lorne had already published *Architectural Office Administration* in 1921) and although Bertram Goodhue was also suffering from the downturn, Lorne personally was still quite capable of purchasing a partnership. The deal was soon done, allowing Burnet effectively to retire while retaining the nominal role of senior partner and a continuing share of the firm's profits. His practice was renamed Sir John Burnet, Tait & Lorne, and Burnet celebrated his rescue in typical style, with the purchase of a new Rolls Royce. At seventy-three-years old, his architectural career was effectively over.

James Miller, three years younger and still fit, was far from done. The railway architect was now a member of the Royal Scottish Academy, a commissioner of the Royal Fine Art Commission for Scotland and a member of the Scottish Architectural Advisory Committee of the Department of Health for Scotland and, as happened during the First World War, his regular clients came up with the goods to sustain his team. Lord Forteviot, who after the Caledonian Railway Company had been one of Miller's friends and most loyal clients, had died a month after the Wall Street Crash in November 1929, but his son John commissioned Miller to design a new bottle and case-making workshop for Dewar's Whisky in Perth in 1930. The new municipal buildings in Troon, which Sir Alexander Walker had been promoting since 1915 when he had gifted the town the land on which they were to be built, were also finally given the go-ahead, after one more gift from Sir Alexander, this time to finance the building.

The contrast between the Troon municipal buildings and Miller's earlier civic buildings in Clydebank in 1900 is interesting. In 1900, Clydebank's shipyards were booming and their Free Style town hall was built in intricately carved sandstone with copious sculpture and a tall stone

Fig. 101 It was a return to Classicism for Miller as well, in his Troon municipal buildings of 1930–2. Courtesy of Gordon Thomson.

clocktower, whereas by 1930 the still relatively wealthy town of Troon could afford only brick with stone dressings (Fig. 101). Nevertheless, Miller and his team made the most of this limited palette and captured something of the spirit of this rather genteel seaside town in the new civic buildings. The main elevation to South Beach is dominated by a Palladian central bay, complete with stone pilasters and a balustraded parapet above a sturdy Doric porch at ground level. The semi-basement is also in stone, from which rise stone-dressed arched windows and this pattern, with rectangular windows above, is continued around the building. This is another return to straight Classicism for Miller and a very accomplished one at that, with the Roman tiles and first-floor Juliet balconies to the side elevations giving the building a particularly Italianate feel as well as something of a seaside summer holiday mood. To the rear of the building the concert hall steps forward with five bays of giant fluted pilasters enclosing double-height windows to light the hall. The concert hall itself, which seats 888 people, is very much a re-run of Clydebank, with a three-sided balcony below an elegant shallow vaulted ceiling. It is a delightful little public building and its neighbouring extension is a painful reminder both of how little we now spend on our civic buildings and how astonishingly low the standard of building design has sunk (it really could not be described as architecture).

With Miller's business development in overdrive, within the first year of what became the Great Depression he added several further new commissions, including the architectural design for the Kincardine Bridge (for which his team produced two beautifully detailed Art Deco arched stone pylons) and two major new buildings in central Glasgow.

The first of these was a new head office for thread-makers, J. & P. Coats, on St Vincent Street (currently Sutherland House) (Fig. 102). Their site was no more than a slot, about ten metres wide, into which Miller shoe-horned an eight-storey building of considerable elegance. The main entrance is flanked by rather stylish, low walls in polished black marble that contrast with the buff of the main elevation. Two central pilasters are Ionic, while the outer two are plain, giving the first two floors something of the feeling of a Burnet proscenium. Above this level, the building shoots up to its final eighth floor where, rather than providing a traditionally squat attic, Miller designed tall glazed French windows that opened out from the panelled boardroom to a balcony, thus offering the directors a spectacular view across the rooftops of the city. On its completion in 1931 it made a very sleek addition to what is perhaps Glasgow's most architecturally interesting street.

The other commission was a bank. If Miller had once been pigeon-holed as the railway architect, then the 'hospital architect' and then the 'hotel architect', he was now the first name on the lips of Glasgow bankers when they came to considering an architectural appointment and his Union Bank had set a new high bar for the building type in the city. On this occasion it was the directors of the Commercial Bank of Scotland who invited Miller and his team to provide them with a monumental treasure chest. He did not disappoint with a highly original treatment that distilled his Union Bank format into an almost abstract white block on the corner of West Nile Street and West George Street (Fig. 103). His usual model of banking hall, office frieze, and speculative offices above was here given a new purity, being carried out not in red Glasgow sandstone but in gleaming white Portland stone, above a polished black granite base. Here, the

Fig. 102   Such is the architectural quality of Glasgow's St Vincent Street that Miller's
elegant J. & P. Coats building of 1930–1 goes almost unnoticed. Courtesy of Roger Edwards.

Left: Fig. 103   Another mighty Glasgow bank by Miller – the Commercial Bank of Scotland on West George Street of 1930–1. Courtesy of Tom Bastin.

Right: Fig. 104   Black marble and Portland stone give Miller's Commercial Bank a sleek nobility. Courtesy of David Gray.

granite also sweeps up to form a surround to the main entrance door, which was topped with stylised acroteria, while the capitols of the fluted pilasters are a new Industrialised Ionic order (all carved by Gilbert Bayes) (Fig. 104). Like his nearby Coats building, it is cool, stylish, and an utterly convincing piece of architecture.

While Miller somehow still managed to keep his team busy, most other practices were struggling, and the competition for the design of a new Norwich city hall caused quite a stir, attracting 143 entries from across Britain. Miller was among the many unsuccessful competitors and Thomas Tait came very close to winning it, being placed second. Fortunately, Tait's design for the Masonic Hospital at Hammersmith was given the go-ahead, both keeping the wolf from the door and allowing Francis Lorne to find his feet. To his frustration, Tait soon discovered that Lorne had no intention of simply assuming Raeside's supporting role as practice manager, nor of adopting Burnet's former methods of developing the business, such as offering potential clients dinner at his home or at one of his clubs. Lorne's experience in the United States had moulded a very different type of architect. He was dapper, always perfectly groomed, and continued to wear the latest American clothes. He shocked Tait by greeting clients in the office in his silk shirt sleeves and was often sharp-tongued with their staff, overseeing a massive clear-out of what was left of Burnet's old guard shortly after his arrival. He unashamedly promoted the practice, courted publicity and even ferreted out undeveloped sites himself and then set out to find potential clients for them. Despite his years in the United States, he quickly developed a considerable social network in Britain, with his friend, Freda Dudley Ward, the Prince of Wales's mistress, providing him with introductions to their set. Among the new staff that he brought in was Gordon Farquhar, his brother-in-law, who had worked for Raymond Hood in the United States and soon it was Farquhar and Helen Lorne who were administering the practice and together undertaking the Americanisation of its systems and processes. The office and their clients were soon split between Lorne and Tait and, with the Glasgow practice of John Burnet, Son & Partners no longer active, Tait began to pursue work in Scotland as well. Sir John's only involvement by this stage was as a major shareholder, and as such, he attended the biannual board meetings, to which he was driven up from Surrey by his chauffeur. Through good luck more than judgement, he and Jean were now enjoying a financial security during his retirement that they could not have envisaged for much of his career.

The Masonic Hospital was opened by King George V in 1933, when he also conferred the title of 'Royal' upon it. It was greeted with rave reviews in the architectural press, even earning the RIBA's 'Building of the Year' award in 1934. With Scotland now open to Sir John Burnet, Tait & Lorne, Thomas Tait now set his sights on the commission for St Andrew's House in Edinburgh, which was to be the new home of the devolved Scottish Office. Its procurement had been rumbling on for many years with several competitions and much controversy(2) when, among much lobbying, a long list of twelve architects was finally selected. 'Lord Weir, in a well-argued letter, pressed for the inclusion of James Miller who was now seventy-three',(3) but without success. A shortlist of three emerged, and with Thomas Tait the only Scot among them, and in deference to local sentiment, he was awarded the commission. His design, which included many familiar elements of Burnet's architecture, was a finely judged, modern stone building that responded superbly to its dramatic site and on its completion in 1939 it confirmed that it was now Tait, and not Burnet, who was Scotland's most influential architect.

Despite missing out on St Andrew's House, Miller's practice was still busier than any other in the country, with new buildings for the Perth Infirmary, a small weights and measures office in Stirling, new wards for Stirling Infirmary, various speculative housing developments, extensions to a paper mill in Bridge of Allan and a new stand for the sports ground of George Watson's School in Edinburgh. However, concerned that his son George was missing out on major project experience, Miller arranged for him to join the London office of Sir Herbert Baker. Baker's partner Alex Scott had worked for Miller in his London office before the war and was happy to repay the favour. With the Bank of England, South Africa House on Trafalgar Square, a stand at Lords, two further banks in London and two in South Africa on his books, Baker's was the busiest practice in the country and George Miller gained invaluable experience there during the next few years.

In October 1933, tragedy struck with the sudden death of Richard Gunn, aged only forty-four years. As Miller wrote in his obituary, 'For some time he had been in somewhat indifferent health, which caused considerable anxiety to his friends, but the end came more suddenly than expected'.(4) With George now in London, James Walker again took over, after a gap of twenty years, as chief assistant to Miller.

Then, Miller won another major Glasgow bank commission – and it would be Miller's last and best – for the Commercial Bank of Scotland, on a site on the corner of Bothwell Street and Wellington Street in the city centre. Miller had shown in his previous bank buildings that he was quite capable of reflecting function in three-dimensional form without abandoning Classicism, with the bank's own facilities clearly expressed at the lower levels of the building and the speculative offices treated differently above. In Bothwell Street this was to be a purely bank building and is expressed as such, with the Commercial Bank's customers being offered a secure home for their cash in a mighty white stone vault (Fig. 105). The ordering of colonnade, frieze, and attic is repeated from the previous buildings but here also varied with dramatic effect. Once more the first floor of offices is included within the colonnade to increase its height and, while the elevation to Wellington Street repeats the pilasters of his previous Commercial Bank on West George Street, on Bothwell Street two mighty Corinthian columns support the mass of stone above. Like the J. & P. Coats building slightly further up the hill on St Vincent Street, the elevation is decidedly vertical, but the overall feeling of the building is of mass, accentuated by an attic floor that is significantly taller than the frieze floor below it and almost entirely solid, with just three modest windows punched into its Bothwell Street elevation and five to Wellington Street. While many of Miller's contemporaries were toying with Egyptian motifs, his design for the Commercial Bank was a primitive temple that looked as if it would endure as long as the pyramids. It might well be steel framed and centrally heated, but through its ancient architectural language it provoked an abundance of powerful metaphorical responses. This is architecture of a high order.

It is built in pure white Portland stone above a polished black marble base, but here the top of the marble base is set at the back of the building on Wellington Street, from where the ground level falls away sharply towards Bothwell Street, so that the base is almost as high as the entrance doors by the time it reaches the front of the building, adding considerably to the overall feeling of monumentality. The sculpture (by Gilbert Bayes), which is mainly confined to the panels between the frieze windows and is also incised, rather than being proud of the plane of stone, again reinforcing this feeling that the entire building was carved from a single block like some vast Michelangelesque sculpture.

In distilling the architecture of his previous bank buildings to such a degree, Miller and his team were no doubt influenced by younger architects such as Charles Holden, who was taking Baker and Lutyens's elemental classicism to a new level, and also George Valentine Meyer (1883–1959) whose Broadcasting House in London (with relief sculpture by Eric Gill 1882–1940), had just been completed in 1932; but this bank is purer, more severe, and even more powerful. Again, its authorship within Miller's office is unclear: did Gunn design it before his death, is it James Walker's or the work of John Wellwood Manson (1902–1952), who had joined

Fig. 105   Miller's last and finest bank design – his Commercial Bank of
Scotland on Bothwell Street of 1934–5. Courtesy of Rhiasiart Hinks.

the office in 1931? Despite his age, Miller was fit and still quite capable of operating effectively
as an architect (by comparison, the great Frank Lloyd Wright was still designing buildings at
the time of his death aged ninety-two – albeit fairly whacky ones) so at the very least, Miller
deserves credit for leading the design team of the Commercial Bank, although it was completed
in his seventh-fifth year.

As the economic recession deepened, Miller still managed to somehow maintain a flow of new commissions. Many were extensions to his previous buildings, such as at Stirling and Perth Royal infirmaries, but there were also new buildings, some of which were substantial, including a new nurses home and maternity building for Edinburgh Royal Infirmary, a sports pavilion for Marr College in Troon and two houses – Barstobrick near Castle Douglas and Balkissock House at Ballantrae (the latter is now nearly derelict). Both of these are in white render below slate roofs with unusual, flat-capped chimneys. There were also several major new public buildings; the Glasgow and West of Scotland College of Commerce, Canniesburn Hospital and Convalescent Home and the Royal Scottish National Institute, Larbert Colony, all of which were executed in a similar style.

These three latter buildings represent a significant departure for Miller and may indeed, at last, indicate that responsibility for design was passing to the next generation. At first glance they might all be taken for the work of Thomas Tait – classically planned, symmetrical, and yet with flat roofs and horizontally proportioned steel Crittal windows. The College of Commerce (part of Strathclyde Police Headquarters until its demolition in 2019) was in brick, while Canniesburn and the Larbert Colony (demolished 2015) were in white render and all enjoyed a central entrance block that stepped up a storey or so above the general roofline. Architecturally, they were not without merit, being well-proportioned and typical of much British architecture of the period, but beneath its Moderne styling, Canniesburn Hospital (which has survived) actually represents something much more radical.

Since his appointment to design the Royal Infirmary in Glasgow in 1900, Miller had established himself as something of an expert in hospital design. This had led to numerous more hospital commissions, but he was also regularly consulted on the latest practice and developments. In 1916, for example, he was invited to review a new book on hospital construction for the *RIBA Journal*, while in 1933, he was appointed as lead assessor for the architectural competition to design a new infectious diseases hospital in Hawkshead (which, coincidentally, he awarded to Thomas Tait), and he was a member of several committees of the Department of Health. Canniesburn was built as an auxiliary hospital for the Royal Infirmary on a site donated by James MacFarlane, the chairman of the Hospital Board, and discussions with Miller had started as early as 1930 over what would be a radically different approach to hospital design.

The 20-hectare site was in (what was then) a semi-rural area between Glasgow and Bearsden to the north-west of the city and the new facility was intended to act as a private hospital with 120 beds for 'the wealthy of moderate means', whose fees would help to support thirty convalescent patients from the Royal Infirmary (Fig. 106). Though it was not as innovative as Bijvoet and Duiker's Zonnestraal Sanatorium of 1925–31 in Hilversum , for example, in its architecture, it was to be an open-air hospital, along these lines. Its central entrance with double-height hall served long wings of wards and private rooms (utilising the horizontal planning approach that Miller had introduced to Scotland in his Stirling Infirmary of 1928), which opened out via French windows to terraces and balconies, allowing the convalescent patients to recover in fresh air, far beyond the smoke and grime of the city centre, while the private patients (who were eventually replaced by more convalescents) simply enjoyed their delightful parkland surroundings. It is

Fig. 106   Miller's 'open-air' Canniesburn Hospital of 1935 represented a further
innovative development in Scottish healthcare. Courtesy of Colin MacKenzie.

a testament to the quality and thoughtfulness of Miller's hospital designs that, despite the
extraordinary changes that have taken place in healthcare in the intervening decades, almost all
his hospital buildings remain in use today.

By this time, John Burnet was experiencing hospital architecture from a very different
perspective and the travel from Killermont up to London to see his physician was proving more
and more of a challenge. In 1935 he and Jean decided to return home and purchased a cottage,
55 Woodhall Road in Colinton, a southern suburb of Edinburgh (which, along with others in the
road, had been designed by Sir Robert Lorimer). His niece Edith oversaw a number of alterations
to the property in advance of their move north and by the end of the year they were back in
Scotland. There they welcomed a constant stream of former assistants, and it would appear did
little else, one of Burnet's visitors later recalling that 'he had no profession and no recreation –
nothing of interest for him to turn to, no hobbies of any kind. He passed through life with one
all-absorbing interest which burned him dry.'(5)

The following year George Miller also returned from England and was made a partner in
his father's firm, which was renamed (no doubt with considerable pride on his father's behalf),
'James Miller & Son'. With George now back and James Walker continuing as chief assistant,
Miller finally began to transfer the day-to-day management of his practice to his son and, barring
specific clients' requests for his own personal involvement, focused on continuing to generate
new business for the team.

By the mid-1930s, Britain's architecture was in a state of considerable confusion, as it
fluctuated between traditional and modern styles. On the Continent, the battle lines were more
strictly drawn, and the giants of the heroic period of Modernism, such as Gropius and Le Corbusier,
had already appeared to have abandoned the past entirely. Even British architects, such as

Thomas Tait who were regarded as Modernists, still produced classically planned buildings and most British architects who aspired to Modernism still looked both forward to the future with excitement, and backwards towards the past with a yearning for the architecture in which they had been trained. The British public generally showed little interest in the new continental style and it was regularly the subject of newspaper and magazine cartoons lampooning the avant-garde clients who lived in flat-roofed modern houses. Like so many of their contemporaries, James Miller & Son's architecture occupied this middle ground, veering towards Classicism either when a client requested it or it was felt to be appropriate, and towards Modernism when they were free to do so. In either case, the result was a rather dreary architecture for a rather dreary decade. Unfortunately, for Miller's practice and their future reputation, their fine white stone bank in Bothwell Street, just down the hill from Burnet's swan-song at 200 St Vincent Street, would prove to be their last great work.

At least they had plenty of work. In 1935 they entered and won the competition for a new head office (known as Braehead House) for the linoleum manufacturers Michael Nairn and Company in Kirkcaldy (Fig. 107). This was a significant commission for a new corporate building in a parkland setting across the road from the factory itself. Miller's design was a compact, two-storey building arranged around a central courtyard. Its pitched roofs were behind a long horizontal frieze and parapet, using the now ubiquitous metal Crittal windows throughout. There were hints of the stepped planes of Wyggeston in the main elevation, but here they were in stone, with a central section stepping forward and upwards to provide the main entrance, and its stone arch echoed in a round-headed first-floor window. To the rear, the building took on something of a palatial feel where it faced the park, with a long central section stepping forward

Fig. 107   With Miller's reducing involvement, the work of James Miller and Son became increasingly formulaic, such as in his headquarters for Michael Nairn and Company in Kirkcaldy of 1935–9. Courtesy of Ian Gourlay.

to create a nine-bay, double-height, palistrade from where the directors could look out across their terraced gardens and on to the Firth of Forth, with their boardroom, which was treated as a single-storey garden pavilion, enjoying the same view. Having been finally completed in 1939, the whole building has recently been converted into apartments and many of the interiors have fortunately survived, including the galleried entrance hall, panelled ground-floor rooms with carved fireplaces and door-heads and the beautiful panelled boardroom with its decorated plaster ceiling.

From the same period is St Nicholas' Church in Cardonald completed in 1937, which is a low, rather gloomy, brown brick design in the south-west suburbs of Glasgow. It is lit with a series of round-headed lancet windows to the narthex, nave, and sanctuary, and its interior is in exposed brick with half-round arches to the nave. The interior is interesting in terms of its similarity to many of the small churches of Sir Herbert Baker, for whom George Miller had so recently worked. Veering towards genuine Modernism and building on the practice's earlier experience at Silver End, are two flat-roofed, white-rendered, steel-window framed little houses – 30 Old Kirk Road in Corstorphine and Balnagarrow in Cramond, both with horizontal corner glazing to suggest a framed structure. There were also three further minor hospital commissions – a nurses' home for the Royal Infirmary, a small 20 bed ear, nose and throat hospital in Greenock and buildings for the Gilbert Bain Hospital in Lerwick, all of which have since been demolished.

More significant were new offices for Stirling County Council in a brown brick similar to St Nicholas, but here lifted somewhat by light sandstone dressings. This was very much a reworking of the Nairn building, with brick pilasters enclosing tall, metal-framed windows divided by herringbone brick panels. The main entrance has a three-bay stone portico with an exquisite bronze doorway, complete with acroteria and flanked by figurative sculptures. Interestingly, this building is still used by the Council, while their later sprawling reinforced concrete-framed offices having recently been demolished (with one councillor describing their demise as 'the end of this unloved and much derided 1960's building that has blighted the Stirling skyline for too long').(6)

Miller's last big win was the new BBC Broadcasting House in Belfast – an extraordinary achievement, considering that he had been one of the finalists in the competition for Belfast City Hall some forty years previously. The new building was to replace their earlier premises on Linenhall Street that had been established in the 1920s and that they had now outgrown. The model for the design was Broadcasting House in London, which used its offices to provide wrap-around sound insulation for the wholly internal recording studios. The site occupied the curving corner of Bedford Street and Ormeau Avenue, which Miller tracked exactly with his main elevation (Fig. 108). It was originally intended to be built in white Portland stone, like the version in London, but unfortunately Miller & Son's budget would not stretch that far and so it was carried out in a buff yellow brick above a stone base that rose up to provide a stone surround to the main entrance, which was topped with a long stone balcony on which 'British Broadcasting Corporation' was carved. Above this level, the rows of windows are organised vertically within giant pilasters that join above the fourth floor to form a frieze. It is a well-resolved solution and, combined with the gentle curve of the façade, gives the building a considerable dignity despite

Fig. 108   Originally planned to be built in Portland stone, nevertheless Miller and Son's Broadcasting House in Belfast still exhibits a certain dignity. Courtesy of Tom Bastin.

Fig. 109   One of Miller's final projects – the painstaking restoration of the Church of the Holy
Rood in Stirling of 1936–40, where his ashes were later interred. Courtesy of Tom Bastin.

the lack of Portland stone. It is not a great building, but it does have a rather understated elegance and is vastly superior to its later extension on Ormeau Avenue. As far as the business of James Miller & Son was concerned, it represented three years of solid work during the Depression, and after numerous delays construction commenced in 1938, eventually leading to an official opening on 5 May 1941. Miller's personal contribution to the design of the project is unclear but we do know that as far as one of the practice's projects of the late 1930s was concerned, it was Miller's alone and it was very close to his heart.

Miller had worshipped at the Church of the Holy Rude in Stirling, the city's medieval parish church, since moving to Randolphfield in 1911. Founded in 1129, its adjacency to Stirling Castle, a long-favoured residence of the Scottish monarchs, had brought it numerous royal baptisms and the coronation of James VI in July 1567. The oldest surviving parts of the present church dated from 1456 and over the following centuries it had been divided firstly into two and then into three, to serve first two and then three different congregations with the three interior spaces all decorated differently. In 1936, Miller was invited to carry out a major restoration of the church with the aim of removing the internal walls, reunifying the building, and exposing once more its fine oak medieval timber roof structure (Fig. 109). He was well aware of the church's importance and its place in the history of Scotland, and viewed the commission as an honour, for which he accepted no fee. Unlike many nineteenth and twentieth-century church restorations, he carried his out with sensitivity and due respect for the original fabric, thus re-unifying and restoring one of the country's most important ecclesiastic buildings.

In 1936, it was proposed that another Empire Exhibition should be held in Glasgow in 1938 to mark the fiftieth anniversary of the original 1888 Glasgow exhibition. Thomas Tait was selected without competition as the unanimous choice of the organisers for the role of architect-in chief, his commission for St Andrews House in Edinburgh combined with his partnership with Burnet being more than enough to satisfy them. The contrasts between 1930s and 1880s Glasgow could not have been sharper or harsher. From having been the industrial powerhouse of the Empire the city had declined to a point where only rearmament was lifting its heavy industries off their knees. The Exhibition was to be another glorification of the Empire on which the city had grown prosperous and yet the Independent Labour Party that now controlled the City Corporation unsuccessfully proposed that it should be a celebration of international brotherhood instead. It was again funded by bankers and industrialists together with a substantial guarantee from the public sector in the form of both central government and several Scottish local authorities. It was to be located in Bellahouston Park in the poor south-west of the city, rather than in Kelvingrove Park in the city's wealthy west end and, with Thomas Tait as its lead architect, it was to be a Modern utilitarian vision of the future rather than an escapist fantasy. Unsurprisingly, rather than making a substantial profit (which in the case of the 1888 Exhibition had largely funded the building of the art gallery and museum), it never achieved its planned visitor numbers and its backers lost three shillings and five pence in every pound invested.

To justify his preferred architectural style, Tait employed the same Orwellian double-speak that would soon be used to promote the comprehensive redevelopment of the entire city centre and the replacement of the city's sandstone tenements (once they had all been successfully recategorised as 'slums') with 'streets in the air', saying, 'We cannot try to erect buildings in the old, medieval style of architecture where there are certain structural features which necessitate modern treatment and modern requirements with big spacing which the old medieval architecture would not allow us to carry out.'(7) He denied that the style of the exhibition buildings was to be Modern, a word he apparently disliked (and certainly knew would be unpopular with the public), insisting that his proposals were based entirely on a rational analysis of the challenge facing him. After this half-baked theorising, he then proceeded to produce a Beaux-Arts plan with formal water gardens for the exhibition ground, within which he, his team of young Scottish architects, and the architects of most of the pavilions, designed Modern buildings.

His model was the earlier Stockholm Exhibition of 1930, overseen by the brilliant Gunnar Asplund, which had introduced Modernism to Scandinavia, and he replicated their highly glazed white buildings, complete with coloured banners, flags, advertising graphics, floodlights, and a great observation tower on the summit of the small hill on the site.

Almost all the exhibitors and countries of the Empire played ball, producing a series of white, flat-roofed buildings, which at least gave the complex a certain consistency, and Tait made the most of the few natural features of the site, with his composition building to a crescendo with a restaurant and tower on the hill. At night there were floodlights, dancing fountains, and fireworks. It was bright, clean, fresh, forward-looking, and extremely popular with Glaswegians, many of whom paid their one shilling entrance fee several times, but a particularly wet and windy summer put a dampener on Tait's vision of a bright new dawn.(8)

The only building that did not conform to Tait's guidelines was the South African pavilion by James Miller & Son, which took the form of an elegant (white) traditional Cape Dutch farmhouse. It was actually the work of George Miller, and it seems almost certain that he drew on the previous experience of his former employer, Herbert Baker, in developing its design. Having somehow managed to evade Tait's 'thought police', he produced one of the most popular buildings on the site, as *The Glasgow Herald* confirmed: 'With its white walls, brown roof, solid wooden doors and stepped gable this pavilion stands out among the utilitarian architecture of the other buildings in the park and most visitors to the Exhibition have been impressed by its design.'(9) Miller had given his client exactly what he wanted once more and done so to the best of his firm's ability. As one would anticipate of someone who was so well connected in the city, his firm also carried out numerous further exhibits for the Royal Scottish Automobile Club, the Automobile Association and Beattie's Bakery, among others. The exhibition was opened by the King and Queen on the 3 May 1938 and closed on 29 October.

It was unfortunate that Tait's senior partner was unable to experience his protégé's tour de force. Since his move to Edinburgh his health had continued to decline, now mentally as well as physically, and on 2 July 1938, while visitors were flocking to Bellahouston Park for a glimpse of what the future might hold for Glasgow, John James Burnet died peacefully at home, aged eighty-one. Thomas Tait had replaced him as Scotland's architectural innovator and it would be Tait's Modernism that would now hold sway, with Burnet's many masterpieces increasingly dismissed as irrelevant anachronisms by the next generation of young Scottish architects. His death was suitably mourned both in the popular and architectural press, and in an obituary running to nine pages in the *RIBA Journal*, with personal contributions from Alexander Paterson, Thomas Tait, and Theodore Fyfe, and with Paterson expressing the view of his numerous assistants, friends, and clients: 'As a friend he was wise in Council, fair in judgement, confirmed in his faiths and in his outlook buoyant. It follows that for my part, "take him all in all, I shall not look upon his like again"'.(10)

James Miller was one of the last survivors of that last generation of Glasgow architects who had together used the wealth of the mighty British Empire to create a great sandstone city by the River Clyde. The Adam brothers, William Stark, David Hamilton, Charles Wilson, John Honeyman, Alexander Thomson, James Sellars, John Burnet Snr, John Campbell, Charles Rennie Mackintosh, James Salmon, Burnet and Boston, and JJ Burnet had all made their various contributions, grappled with the challenges of the grid, celebrated the corners of the blocks, moulded the façades and crafted roofscapes, incorporated sculpture, fine metalwork, and carved timber into their works of art, led the expansion to the west and given their clients city churches, offices, banks, apartments, hospitals, railway stations, schools, and shops, all of which would soon be under threat of demolition.

Miller had more than played his part and was content to let his son now find the way forward. In 1938, his old client, Henry J. Levitt, who had commissioned Miller to design the elegant Woodhouse Warehouse in Renfield Street, now needed a retirement home of his own and wanted Mr Miller Snr. to provide him with another Classical design. He had purchased a site overlooking the Royal Burgess Golf Course in Cramond in Edinburgh and for him there, Miller designed Almond Lodge in 1939 – his last work. It is almost as if Miller had come full circle, returning to the English Queen Anne style of his first domestic projects with a perfectly symmetrical two-storey, brick H-plan house with tall chimneys, hipped roofs, dentiled eaves and, in lieu of his firm's now almost ubiquitous Crittal windows, twelve-pane timber sash windows to front and rear. There is nothing original whatsoever about it – it is just a fine, large, beautifully proportioned private house, and one with which his client was no doubt delighted. Unfortunately, his delight was short-lived as it was requisitioned by the government immediately on its completion as an emergency medical stand-by hospital for troops stationed nearby. The country was now on a war footing once more and years of growing international tensions finally led to Britain declaring war on Germany in September 1939.

Miller was now seventy-nine years old and he and his practice had already survived one war (which had all but ruined Burnet). He was determined that he and George would survive this one. Within months of war being declared, they had been commissioned both to convert Gleneagles Hotel into an emergency hospital and to design and construct Killearn Emergency Hospital for military casualties, fifteen miles northwest of Glasgow. Miller's factory-produced timber buildings were completed in 1940 (and were still in use in 1972). George who was now thirty-seven years' old, was too old for the first wave of conscription and was continuing to manage the practice and their various projects of war work when in the spring of 1940, he was taken ill with a fever that was soon diagnosed as typhoid. There had been a number of localised outbreaks in the city throughout the 1930s and with limited available treatments, it was still a potentially deadly disease. It quickly became only too clear that George's case was severe and he declined rapidly, dying on 14 May 1940.

The family was devastated. With his son and heir gone, Miller retired fully from practice. What had been the family firm was sold to John Manson, one of the assistants, at which point it was renamed Miller, Son & Manson, with James Walker continuing as chief assistant for a short time before himself retiring. James Miller lived on at Randolphfield with Emelina for seven more years, finally dying of stomach cancer aged eighty-seven on 28 November 1947. He had never sought or won Burnet's professional accolades and the notices and obituaries after his death were therefore relatively modest. John Manson and James Walker penned his obituary for the Journal of the *RIAS* journal:

> In practice for close on half a century, he devoted his whole life to architecture, each achievement acting as a stepping-stone to some further success.... All his buildings served their particular function, and much of his success might be attributed to his ability to look at the problem from his client's point of view as well as from that of the architect.... Very reserved by nature, he did not enter much into public life and was well content to let others talk architecture while he was doing the job.(11)

He was a fine architect whose work has rarely received the credit it deserves, but he would have been content to know that from humble beginnings, he had become the most prolific architect that Scotland had ever produced.

EPILOGUE

By 1947, Glasgow was on its knees. It had been left with all the problems arising from its rapid industrialisation a century before and little of the wealth that it had generated. Just as after the First World War, when war production stopped, although Britain was victorious, the economic costs of the conflict for the country were devastating. Two-thirds of her export trade was gone, the country was saddled with massive war loans to service, rationing continued and in August 1947, just three months before James Miller's death, mighty India, 'the Jewel in the Imperial Crown', was lost, together with four-fifths of the Empire's entire population.

Social progress however, was now rapid, driven by Clement Attlee's Labour Government, which had won a landslide victory in the 1945 General Election. In 1946 the National Health Service was established, providing free healthcare to every citizen of Glasgow for the first time. Scotland's coal industry was nationalised that year, too, and in 1947 the electricity companies followed, with the railway companies entering the public sector in 1948, including the Caledonian Railway's vast network. As a staunch conservative, Miller would have been appalled.

Both JJ Burnet's and James Miller's practices continued after their deaths. In Miller's case, John Manson led the practice, even opening a London office in 1950, before his own death in 1952. At that time the practice was taken over by Frank, Burnet, Bell & Partners, who completed the work then in progress. Burnet, Tait & Lorne continued very successfully in London and opened an Edinburgh office while St Andrew's House was underway as well as winning international work in South Africa and elsewhere. Gordon Farquhar, who had been made a partner in 1937, died in December 1945, following his release from a Japanese prisoner of war camp. At around that time, Lorne moved to Scotland and took charge of the Edinburgh branch, where he continued until the late 1940s before moving to South Africa, where he had briefly worked before. Unfortunately, he withdrew his capital from the partnership, which necessitated Tait taking on new partners to refinance the practice, including his son, Gordon. Tait himself died aged seventy-two in 1954, with the practice continuing as Sir John Burnet, Tait & Partners for many years, with Gordon becoming senior partner and his son Gavin eventually succeeding him. By the 1960s, their practice was largely commercial, operating in both the UK and the Middle

East, with the quality of their work having declined with each new generation. By the 1980s, much of their output was an insult to the name of Sir John Burnet under which they were still trading, with one of their projects, America House in the City of London, described by Pevsner's *Guide* as 'a shockingly tawdry exercise in Postmodern pattern-making.'(1) At around this time they were acquired by another large commercial practice and Sir John's name was finally laid to rest.

Since their deaths, the reputations of both Burnet and Miller have faded, and there was a time after the Second World War when almost everything that they had built was threatened with demolition. Glasgow Corporation's Chief Engineer Robert Bruce proposed in 1945 that the entire city centre, 'the inner core of the city', should be demolished (yes – everything) and rebuilt as a Soviet-style civic centre along the lines of Tait's Empire Exhibition. Many would have thought his insensitivity, arrogance and apparent utter contempt for the past and the quality of the city's architecture was breath-taking, and even exceeded that of the other engineers who thought it would be a good idea to route the M8 through the city centre, rather than around it. Bruce produced a vast model of this 'Glasgograd', along with a professionally produced film entitled *Glasgow Today and Tomorrow* to promote the vision, but fortunately, Glasgow Corporation rejected the plan and probably thought that perhaps his power had rather gone to his head. While the central grid (where most of Burnet and Miller's buildings are located) survived, many of the city's suburbs were simply wiped from the map. Miller's North British Locomotive Company Headquarters is one of the few buildings to have survived in Springburn, for example, where many of the modern blocks that replaced the sandstone tenements are now unfit for human habitation. Of course, many tenements were no better, but they needed bathrooms and toilets as the survivors were given in the 1970s and 1980s – not total annihilation. A war was being waged against the past and propaganda was the weapon of choice. 'Progress' – 'slum clearance' – 'overspill', and 'the future' were the watchwords as the wrecking balls swung. Engineers, architects, and planners believed that they were building a brave new world in which the architecture of the old world had no relevance and offered no lessons. By the 1970s views began slowly to change. This happened much too late to save much of the city's architecture, so we must be very grateful that most of Burnet's and Miller's buildings survived the destruction and are now almost all listed, and hopefully protected.

So just how good were Burnet and Miller? Burnet was the stronger designer without a doubt. He had neither the ability of Mackintosh or Thomson to develop a new language of architecture, but his application of the Classical language to the offices, houses, and apartments of Glasgow was highly creative and inventive, and just as importantly, was carried out to an exceptionally high architectural standard. He (and the many sculptors who assisted him) also worked brilliantly in more than one style, happily shifting to Gothic for ecclesiastic work or Baronial for domestic, whereas Mackintosh and Thomson maintained stylistic consistency – a trait that is greatly valued by Modernists. Within his Classical output, he was responsible for developing the Glasgow Free Style which was taken up by numerous other architects and widely applied, to the great benefit of the city, whereas both Mackintosh and Thomson were individual artists with few followers. His 'low churches' were the only hint of an Arts and Crafts influence on his work, but they are also a significant and further successful group of buildings within his extensive portfolio. His contribution towards the development of Modernism in his Kodak House and Tailoring Institute buildings has been much lauded, but at a century's distance, they are both deadly dull compared with his best work, and after a while he seemed to have been more than content to let Tait pursue this tributary, while he returned both to Classicism in the Zoology Building and Gothic in the Memorial Chapel for Glasgow University. To this extent, in many ways, he can thus be regarded as one of the best and last great Victorian architects. The standard of Burnet's best work, such as the Savings Bank and the Athenaeum, place him among the greatest Scottish architects of all time, along with the likes of Thomson, Mackintosh, the Adam Brothers, Sir William Bruce, James Gibbs, and Richard Norman Shaw.

Miller was a very different man, who largely had to educate himself in the art of architecture. His is an extraordinary tale of self-improvement and success. His early buildings, while always competent, were unremarkable, but as he developed his business, he also grew in confidence as a designer and was soon producing work of an extremely high quality, if not in all, then at least in parts of his buildings. Wemyss Bay station is an outstanding Victorian engineering structure and is now recognised as one of Britain's finest stations, Caledonian Mansions and St Andrew's East Church show him to be at least the equal of most of his peers in Glasgow, while 8 Lowther Terrace, Dunholme and Kildonan, while not reaching the level of Lutyens or Voysey, were certainly on a par with much of the best English Arts and Crafts work. His sheer volume of work has had more impact on Scotland, particularly the west of Scotland, than any other architect, and when one considers that he was responsible for everything from St Enoch's underground station to Gleneagles Hotel, via Hampden Park, Turnberry and Peebles Hydropathic hotels, the Institute of Civil Engineers in London; Glasgow, Stirling, and Perth Royal infirmaries, the interiors of the *Lusitania* and the *Aquitania*, the Glasgow Exhibition of 1901, Glasgow Central Station, numerous office buildings, including the Anchor Line and the Union and two Commercial Bank of Scotland buildings in the centre of Glasgow, it seems extraordinary that he is not a household name, at least north of the border. But perhaps his quiet nature, his focus on satisfying his clients and looking for the next one, rather than seeking professional approbation, not to mention the relative lack of contemporary interest in this period of Scottish architecture, have played their part. If Burnet deserves to be placed among the greats, then Miller at the very least deserves to be widely known as Scotland's most prolific architect.

What might have happened if Miller had accepted Burnet's proposal of partnership is an interesting speculation, but as Burnet was by then committed to London and Miller to Glasgow, perhaps little more than what they achieved separately. With two such different characters from such diverse backgrounds, it is certainly hard to imagine them collaborating on a project. If they had worked together earlier in their careers, Miller would have been Burnet's assistant or practice manager, and by the time Burnet approached him, Miller was then in a stronger position.

What we do know is that both architects rode the wave of Glasgow's extraordinary late nineteenth and early twentieth-century economic success at a time when it was one of the

Fig. 110   The rich sculptural detail that characterised Burnet and Miller's best work here on the offices of the General Accident, Fire and Life Insurance Company of 1909. Courtesy of John Stewart.

wealthiest cities in the world. They put that wealth to good use, creating art of the highest standard in sandstone and granite, and their masterpieces from this period should be treasured accordingly, just as much as any of the finest paintings or sculpture in the Kelvingrove Art Galleries or the Burrell Collection (Fig. 110)

NOTES

Introduction

1. Andor Gomme and David Walker, *Architecture of Glasgow*, 2nd revised edition (London, Lund Humphries, 1987) p. 205.
2. Ibid., p. 210.
3. Ibid., p. 56.
4. Ibid., p. 61.
5. Audrey Sloan with Gordon Murray, *James Miller 1860–1947* (Royal Incorporation of Scottish Architects, 1993) p. 35.

Chapter 1

1. Michael Anderson and Corinne Roughley, *Scotland's Populations from 1850 to Today* (Oxford, Oxford University Press, 2018).
2. Robert Jeffrey, Giants of the Clyde: The Great Ships and the Great Yards (Black and White, Edinburgh, 2017).
3. Stana Nenadic, 'The Glasgow Story: 1830s to 1914: Everyday Life' https://www.theglasgowstory.com/story/?id=TGSDA, accessed 8 August 2021.
4. Andor Gomme and David Walker, *Architecture of Glasgow*, 2nd revised edition (London, Lund Humphries, 1987) p. 161.
5. Converted to a night club in 1982, it was gutted by fire and finally demolished in 2004.
6. Blair Lodge School was closed in 1904 following financial difficulties and a disastrous outbreak of infectious disease, reopening as Scotland's first Borstal in 1908, which went on to become HMP Polmont Young Offenders Institution.
7. *The Glasgow Herald*, 27 December 1844.
8. *RIBA Journal*, 26 June 1920 p. 40.
9. Giacomo Barozzi da Vignola, *The Five Orders of Architecture*, 1562
10. Thomas Tait, *RIBA Journal*, 18 July 1938, p. 893.

Chapter 2

1. The Glasgow Herald, 4 April, 1879.
2. As the profession was unregulated at this time, Miller could have done much worse. As he later recalled, 'I have a vivid recollection during my apprenticeship of having to pass morning and evening a shop the sign board of which bore the words 'John Blank, Family Grocer and Wine Merchant', and on a plate on the door jamb, 'John Blank, Architect and Surveyor'. If my memory serves me right, John was more at home with his tea, sugar and spirits than with his architecture.' *RIBA Journal* 25 June, 1921.

3. J. M. Reid, *Glasgow* (London, Batsford, 1956) p. 120. Mr John Stewart, the only director without an overdraft with the bank at the time of closure, was freed on £15,000 bail, before being found guilty along with his fellow directors in January 1879 by a unanimous verdict.

4. Elizabeth Williamson, Anne Riches and Malcolm Higgs, *The Buildings of Scotland: Glasgow* (London, Penguin, 1990) p. 259.

5. Andor Gomme and David Walker, *Architecture of Glasgow* 2nd revised edition (London, Lund Humphries, 1987) p. 177.

6. Thomas Tait, *RIBA Journal*, 18 July 1938.

7. *Dictionary of Scottish Architects*, Sir John Burnet. www.scottisharchitects.org.uk, accessed 8 August 2021.

8. The École had much less appeal in London where the quality of the local architectural education available at the Royal Academy and Architectural Association schools of architecture was much higher than in contemporary Glasgow or Edinburgh.

9. Perilla Kinchin and Juliet Kinchin, *Glasgow's Great Exhibitions* (White Cockade Publishers, Wendlebury, 1988) p. 52.

10. This was Queen Victoria's second visit to Glasgow. She had first visited in 1849, when she was appalled by the slums, hated the weather, and resolved never to return.

Chapter 3

1. Elizabeth Williamson, Anne Riches and Malcolm Higgs, *The Buildings of Scotland: Glasgow* (London, Penguin, 1990), p. 387.

2. As noted by Gomme and Walker in *Architecture of Glasgow*, 2nd revised edition (London, Lund Humphries, 1987), p. 202, the great clock of Charing Cross Mansions, was long 'neglected and handless', but now restored, while the dreadful shopfronts still make 'an irritating and irrelevant distraction'. Like so many fine stone Glasgow buildings, Charing Cross Mansions has been cut off at the knees, with its ground floor almost entirely eradicated and replaced by either continuous sheet glass or modern shopfronts of staggering banality below cheap plastic signs. 'Gallus' is a colloquial term most often used in the west of Scotland, and especially Glasgow, to describe an act of boldness or daring.

3. Gomme and Walker, *Architecture of Glasgow*, p. 204.

4. The Glasgow Free Style, with its rich sculpture and Scottish Renaissance details was adopted in many of the later Glasgow tenements.

5. This same motif, a soaring bay concluding in an arch, was reworked very successfully further down Buchanan Street in the North British Rubber Building by Robert Thomson in 1898.

6. Rob Close and Anne Riches, The Buildings of Scotland: Ayrshire and Arran, Yale University Press, 2012, p. 686.

7. *RIBA Journal*, 15 August 1938.

8. Williamson et al., The Buildings of Scotland, p. 195.

9. Fortunately, the original shop fronts have recently been reinstated; an example that I hope will be followed in all the city's category 'A' listed buildings, at the very least.

10. Williamson et al., The Buildings of Scotland, p. 307.

11. *The Builder,* 9 July 1898.

12. Roger H. Harper, Victorian Architectural Competitions: An Index to British and Irish Architectural Competitions (London, Mansell, 1983).

Chapter 4

1. Even if Mackintosh's buildings had been selected and built they were always intended to be temporary.

2. Bessie Louise Pierce, *As Others See Chicago: Impressions of Visitors 1673–1933* (Chicago, University of Chicago Press, 1933), p. 351.

3. James Miller, 'The Business Side of Architecture'. A paper originally read before the Glasgow Institute of Architects, 29 November 1920.

4. Thomas Tait, *RIBA Journal*, 18 July 1938

5. Theodore Fyfe, *RIBA Journal,* 15 August 1938.
6. Elizabeth Williamson, Anne Riches and Malcolm Higgs, *The Buildings of Scotland: Glasgow* (London, Penguin, 1990) p. 209.
7. Simon Jenkins, *Britain's 100 Best Railway Stations* (London, Penguin Random House, 2017).
8. The Exhibition Illustrated, 4 May 1901, p. 7.
9. *RIAS Journal*, Spring 1948.
10. Thomas Tait, *RIBA Journal,* 18 July 1938 (And so, the myth of the disorganised but creative architectural genius also bites the dust).
11. Burnet's beautiful columns were removed when the building had an Art Deco makeover in 1936 (traces of which can still be seen) and though something approximating to Burnet's originals have now been reinstated in fibreglass, this caused permanent damage to an exceptional work of art.

Chapter 5

1. Simon Jenkins, *Britain's 100 Best Railway Stations* (London, Penguin Random House, 2017) p. 299.
2. Rob Close, John Gifford and Frank Arneil Walker, *The Buildings of Scotland: Lanarkshire and Renfrewshire* (London, Yale University Press, 2016) p. 782.
3. Jenkins, Britain's 100 Best Railway Stations, p. 309.
4. In response to any accusation that I have lamented the demolition or loss of either Burnet's or Miller's buildings while condoning the demolition of the original historical Fairnilee House, the charge is easily answered. Burnet replaced the old tower house with architecture that was vastly superior.
5. Andor Gomme and David Walker, *Architecture of Glasgow* 2ⁿᵈ revised edition *(*London, Lund Humphries, 1987) pp. 205–6.
6. Alastair A. Jackson and Alastair A. Jackson, 'The Development of Steel Framed Buildings in Britain, 1880–1905', Construction *History*, vol. 14, 1998, pp. 21–40; p. 32.
7. If you think my criticism of most modern commercial architecture is too harsh, simply look at McGeoch's replacement on the corner of West Campbell Street.
8. John Wellwood Manson and James Carruthers Walker, *RIBA Journal,* January 1948.

Chapter 6

1. Martin Bellamy and Bill Spalding, *The Golden Years of the Anchor Line* (Stenlake, Catrine, 2011) p. 7.
2. *Dictionary of Scottish Architects*, David M. Walker, scottisharchitects.org.uk,
3. Theodore Fyfe, *RIBA Journal*, 15 August 1938.
4. McKim's masterpiece, which was one of the finest railway stations in the world, was demolished in 1963; the wealthiest country in the world apparently being unable to pay for its maintenance.
5. The North British Locomotive Company exported their trains to Canada, Argentina, France, Spain, South Africa, the *then* Rhodesia, Kenya, Uganda, Tanzania, Malawi, Egypt, Palestine, India, Sri Lanka, Australia, and New Zealand, as well as serving their UK domestic market. A film entitled *North British,* featuring the company's activities, including their buildings, is available at movingimage.nls.uk at the National Library of Scotland.
6. Simon Bradley and Nikolaus Pevsner, *The Buildings of England, London 6* (London, Yale University Press, 2003) p. 332.
7. Nikolaus Pevsner, 'Nine Swallows – No Summer', pp. 203–4, in '*The Anti-Rationalists'*, edited by Nikolaus Pevsner and J. M. Richards (London, Architectural Press, 1976).
8. historicengland.org.uk
9. Alexander Stuart Gray, *Edwardian Architecture: A Biographical Dictionary* (Ware, Wordsworth Editions, 1988) p. 260.
10. Bradley and Pevsner, The Buildings of England, London 6, p. 274.
11. 'A School Board survey of 1906 revealed that a 14 year-old boy living in a poor area of Glasgow was, on average, 4 inches shorter than a similar-aged child from the city's West End' (Stana Nenadic, 'The Glasgow Story: Second City of The Empire: 1830s to 1914: 'Everyday Life', https://www.theglasgowstory.com/story/?id=TGSDA). Nevertheless, no-one was safe from the regular epidemics of cholera and typhoid that struck the city – Alexander Thomson having lost four children to cholera in the previous century.

Chapter 7

1. Interestingly, Alexander Scott also worked on the designs for the *Aquitania*, suggesting that there was little further work for the London team as the Institution of Civil Engineers reached completion.
2. Andor Gomme and David Walker, *Architecture of Glasgow* (London, Lund Humphries, 1987) p. 61.
3. It is extraordinary how long these architectural grudges are held. Historic Scotland's current 'Statement of Interest' for the Infirmary still refers to the controversy surrounding the architectural competition.
4. Nikolaus Pevsner and J. M. Richards, *The Anti-Rationalists – Art Nouveau Architecture and Design* (Architectural Press, London, 1976) p. 206.
5. Simon Heffer, *The Age of Decadence: Britain 1880 to 1914* (London, Windmill Books, 2017) pp. 677–8.
6. Catherine Bailey, Black Diamonds: The Rise and Fall of an English Dynasty (London, Penguin).
7. '*The Times*', 18th February, 1914 pp 10
8. '*The Architectural Review*', Vol 35, 1914 pp 150-154

Chapter 8

1. Audrey Sloan with Gordon Murray, *James Miller 1860–1947* (Royal Incorporation of Scottish Architects, 1993) p. 35.
2. Kildonan House. http://portal.historicenvironment.scot LB1052, accessed 8 August 2021.
3. Rob Close and Anne Riches, *The Buildings of Scotland: Ayrshire and Arran.* (Yale University Press, London, 2012) p. 407.
4. *Architectural Review*, April 1928, pp.124–9.
5. Royal Ordnance Environmental Services Group, 'NFF.4 Georgetown History', Royal Ordnance Archives.
6. Throughout the war only three women died at the Houston factories (or Georgetown, after Lloyd George, as they became known). They were Agnes Ferguson, Agnes Heffernan, and Lizzie Walker. Much of Filling Factory No. 6 at Chilwell was destroyed on 1 July 1918, when eight tons of TNT exploded, killing 134 people. Production resumed there on the following day.
7. E. H. Carter and R. A. F. Mears, '*A History of Britain: Liberal England, World War and Slump* (Stacey International, London, 2011) p. 154.
8. James Miller, 'The Business Side of Architecture', *RIBA Journal* 25 June 1921. A paper originally read before the Glasgow Institute of Architects on 29 November 1920.
9. A. Trystan Edwards, *Sir John Burnet and Partners Architects*, Preface (Masters of Architecture, Geneva, 1930) p. x.
10. Glasgow City Archive G3 (1).
11. *The Builder*', 29 June 1923, p. 1038.

Chapter 9

1. RIAS Quarterly Illustrated Journal, Autumn, No. 44, 1933.
2. *Architectural Review*, April 1928, p. 124.
3. Bridget Cherry and Nikolaus Pevsner, *Buildings of England: London 4: North* (London, Yale University Press, 2002) p. 160.
4. The Architect and Building News, 2 May 1929, p. 562.

Chapter 10

1. Richard Overy, The Twilight Years: The Paradox of Britain Between the Wars (London, Penguin, 2010) p. 96.
2. The entire saga is documented in detail in David Walker, *St Andrew's House: An Edinburgh Controversy, 1912–1939* (Historic Buildings and Monuments, Scottish Development Department, 1989).
3. Ibid., p. 27.
4. RIAS Quarterly Illustrated Journal, Autumn, No. 44, 1933.
5. Dictionary of Scottish Architects, scottisharchitects.org.uk.
6. *Stirling News*, 20 January 2014.

7. Thomas Tait was offered a knighthood for his efforts, but unfortunately his wife Constance broke confidentiality at a bridge party, an indiscretion that was reported by a gossip columnist, and the offer was withdrawn.
8. *The Glasgow Herald*, 26 February 1937, p. 7.
9. *The Glasgow Herald*, Empire Exhibition Special Number.
10. Thomas Tait, *RIBA Journal*, 18 July1938, p. 894.
11. RIAS Quarterly Illustrated Journal, May No. 72, 1948.

Epilogue

1. Simon Bradley and Nikolaus Pevsner, *The Buildings of England, London 1: The City of London* (London, Penguin, 1997) p. 419.

GLOSSARY

The Orders of Classical Architecture

Doric	plain column capital with no base to column
Ionic	voluted capital usually with a fluted column
Corinthian	bell-shaped capital composed of acanthus leaves
Tuscan Doric	particularly simple Roman version of the Greek Doric

Architectural Terms

acroteria	decorations on the top or lower corners of a pediment
aedicule	small, temple-like shrine
analytique rendu	fully rendered and coloured architectural drawing
ancien regime	pre-revolutionary France
armorial panel	setting for a coat of arms
ashlar dressings	smooth stones adjacent to doors or windows
balustrade	row of small columns topped by a rail
bartizan turrets	circular, overhanging wall-mounted turret
Baroque	late Renaissance architecture (1600–1760 in Italy)
bull-faced	projecting rough-faced stone
Byzantine	the architecture of the Byzantine Empire
canted bay	angled bay
cartouche	carved tablet representing a scroll
caryatid	sculpted female figures serving as columns
cat-slide roof	steep roof reaching almost to ground level
colonnade	row of evenly spaced columns
console	bracket or corbel – often scroll-shaped
corbel	projecting block of stone, often supporting beams
crow-stepped gable	gable wall projecting above roof level and stepping up to the ridge
cupola	spherical roof like an inverted cup
dentiled cornice	tooth-like blocks supporting a projecting cornice
eaves gallery	recessed covered gallery at the top of a building

Eclecticism	mixing of architectural styles
engaged column	column embedded within a wall that projects only partially
entablature	the upper part of a classical building, above the columns
esquisse	early sketch that encompasses the main elements of a design
finial	ornamental termination to a gable or dome
frieze	decorative band below the cornice of a Classical building
Gothic	pointed style of medieval architecture
hammer-beam roof	stepped timber roof structure without a central tie
half-timbered	combination of exposed frame and infill
harled whinstone	dense roughcast stone
incised decoration	decoration cut into the face of a building, rather than projecting
keystone	central stone in an arch – often sculpted
lancet window	tall, pointed window
lychgate	covered gateway
Mannerist	distorted or exaggerated Renaissance architecture
modillioned cornice	tooth-like blocks supporting a projecting cornice
Moghul	the pointed arched architecture of the Middle East
ogee roof	roof with an S-shaped profile
parapet	portion of a wall rising above the roof gutter
pediment	triangular piece of wall above columns in Classical architecture
piano nobile	principle and most important (usually first) floor of a building
piano rustico	ground floor of a building
plasticity	exhibiting a sculptural presence
porte-cochère	projecting covered entrance for cars or coaches
Prairie style	in the horizontal style of Frank Lloyd Wright's early houses
Queen Anne	Victorian architecture inspired by the period of Queen Anne
rustication	recessed joints in stonework
scissor-trussed	crossing diagonal timber truss members
Scots Baronial	based on the architecture of the Late Middle Ages in Scotland
Scottish Renaissance	Scottish Classical architecture of the sixteenth and seventeenth centuries
scrolled shield	armorial shield decorated with curved elements
segmental pediment	pediment with the triangle replaced with a segment of a circle
Serlian window	tripartite window with arched central section
Shavian	reminiscent of the work of architect Richard Norman Shaw
snecked sandstone	regular blocks of stone with smaller stones in the joints
tenement	generally four-floor, multiple occupancy apartment building
tourette	small circular tower that projects from the wall of a building
wainscoting	panelling to the lower portion of a wall

BIBLIOGRAPHY

Anderson, Michael and Roughley, Corinne. *Scotland's Populations from 1850 to Today* Oxford: Oxford University Press, 2018.

Author. *Modern Architectural Art: Sir John J. Burnet & Partners*. Cheltenham: J Burrow, 1924.

Bailey, Catherine. *Black Diamonds: The Rise and Fall of an English Dynasty*. London: Penguin, 2007.

Bellamy, Martin and Spalding, Bill. *The Golden Years of the Anchor Line*. Catrine: Stenlake, 2011.

Biddle, Gordon. *Britain's Historic Railway Buildings*. 2nd edn. Shepperton: Ian Allan, 2011.

Biddle, Gordon and Nock, O. S. *The Railway Heritage of Britain*. London: Michael Joseph, 1983.

Bradley Simon and Pevsner Nikolaus. *The Buildings of England, London 1: The City of London*. Penguin, London, 1997.

Bradley, Simon and Pevsner, Nikolaus. *The Buildings of England, London 6*. London: Yale University Press, 2003.

Carter, E. H. and Mears, R. A. F. *A History of Britain: Liberal England, World War and Slump: 1901–1939*. London: Stacey International, 2011.

Cherry, Bridget and Pevsner, Nikolaus. *Buildings of England: London 4: North*. London: Yale University Press, 2002.

Close, Rob, Gifford John and Walker, Frank Arneil. *The Buildings of Scotland: Lanarkshire and Renfrewshire*. London: Yale University Press, 2016.

Close, Rob and Riches, Anne. *The Buildings of Scotland: Ayrshire and Arran*. London: Yale University Press, 2012.

Country Life, December 26 1985 ('The Grand Hotel Afloat: Cunard's Maritime Masterpieces')

Dictionary of Scottish Architects. David M. Walker, scottisharchitects.org.uk, accessed 8 August 2021.

Edwards, A. Trystan. *Sir John Burnet and Partners Architects*. Masters of Architecture, Geneva, 1930.

Fyfe, Theodore. *RIBA Journal*, 15 August 1938.

Gifford, John. *The Buildings of Scotland: Perth and Kinross*. London: Yale University Press, 2007.

Gifford, John, McWilliam, Colin and Walker, David. *The Buildings of Scotland: Edinburgh*. London: Penguin, 1984.

Glasgow City Archive G3 (1).

Glendinning, Miles, MacInnes, Ranald and MacKechnie, Aonghus. *A History of Scottish Architecture, from the Renaissance to the Present Day*. Edinburgh: Edinburgh University Press, 1996

Gomme, Andor and Walker, David. *Architecture of Glasgow*. 2nd revised edn. London: Lund Humphries, 1987.

Gray, Alexander Stuart, *Edwardian Architecture: A Biographical Dictionary*. Ware: Wordsworth Editions, 1988.

Harbeson, John F. *The Study of Architectural Design*. New York: WW Norton, 2008.

Harper, Roger H. *Victorian Architectural Competitions: An Index to British and Irish Architectural Competitions.* London: Mansell, 1983.

Heffer, Simon. *The Age of Decadence: Britain 1880 to 1914.* London: Windmill Books, 2017.

historicengland.org.uk

Howarth, Thomas. *Charles Rennie Mackintosh and the Modern Movement.* 2ⁿᵈ edn. London: Routledge and Keegan Paul, 1977.

Jackson, Alastair A. and Jackson, Alastair A. 'The Development of Steel Framed Buildings in Britain 1880– 1905'.*Construction History*, vol. 14, 1998, pp. 21–40.

Jeffrey, Robert. *Giants of the Clyde: The Great Ships and the Great Yards.* Edinburgh: Black and White, 2017.

Jenkins, Simon. *Britain's 100 Best Railway Stations.* London: Penguin Random House, 2017.

Kildonan House. http://portal.historicenvironment.scot LB1052, accessed 8 August 2021.

Kinchin, Perilla and Kinchin, Juliet. *Glasgow's Great Exhibitions.* Wendlebury: White Cockade, 1988.

MacGibbon, David and Ross, Thomas. *The Castellated and Domestic Architecture of Scotland from the Twelfth to the Eighteenth Century.* Edinburgh: Mercat Press, 1971.

Manson, John Wellwood and Walker, James Carruthers. *RIBA Journal*, January 1948.

Miller, James. 'The Business Side of Architecture'. *RIBA Journal*, 25 June 1921. A paper originally read before the Glasgow Institute of Architects on 29 November 1920.

National Library of Scotland *North British.* Available at movingimage.nls.uk.

Nenadic, Stana. 'The Glasgow Story: Second City of The Empire: 1830s to 1914: 'Everyday Life', https:// www.theglasgowstory.com/story/?id=TGSDA, accessed 8 August 2021

Overy, Richard. *The Twilight Years: The Paradox of Britain Between the Wars.* London: Penguin, 2010.

Pevsner, Nikolaus and Richards, J. M. *The Anti-Rationalists – Art Nouveau Architecture and Design.* London: Architectural Press, 1976.

Pevsner, Nikolaus. 'Nine Swallows – No Summer'. In *The Anti-Rationalists*, edited by Nikolaus Pevsner and J. M. Richards London: Architectural Press, 1976.

Pierce, Bessie Louise. *As Others See Chicago: Impressions of Visitors 1673–1933.* Chicago: University of Chicago Press, 1933.

Reid, J. M. *Glasgow.* London: Batsford, 1956

RIAS Journal, Spring, 1948.

RIAS Quarterly Illustrated Journal, Autumn, no. 44, 1933.

RIAS Quarterly Illustrated Journal, May No. 72, 1948.

RIBA Journal 25 June, 1921.

Royal Ordnance Environmental Services Group. 'NFF.4 Georgetown History'. Royal Ordnance Archives.

Sloan, Audrey with Murray, Gordon. *James Miller 1860–1947.* Royal Incorporation of Scottish Architects, 1993.

Stirling News. 'Stirling Council's New Viewforth Building All Set for Demolition'. 20 January 2014.

Tait, Thomas. *RIBA Journal*, 18 July 1938 (Burnet obituary)

The Architect and Building News. 2 May 1929, p. 562.

The Architectural Review, vol. 34, 1913 pp 137–41 (Institute of Civil Engineers Building)

The Architectural Review, vol 35, 1914 pp. 150–4 (British Museum Extension)

The Architectural Review. April 1928, pp. 124–9.

The Architecture of the Ecole des Beaux Arts. [Catalogue] 29 October 1975–4 January 1976. New York: Museum of Modern Art, www.moma.org/calendar/exhibitions/2483, accessed 8 August 2021.

The Builder, vol. 109, 9 July 1915, p. 30 (*The Lusitania*)

The Builder, 29 June 1923, p. 1038.

The Builder, 12 December,1947 (Miller obituary).

The Builder, 1989.

The Exhibition Illustrated, 4 May 1901, p. 7.

The Glasgow Herald, 27 December, 1844.

The Glasgow Herald, 26 February 1937.

The Glasgow Herald, Empire Exhibition Special Number.

Walker, David. *St Andrew's House: An Edinburgh Controversy, 1912–1939*. Historic Buildings and Monuments, Scottish Development Department, 1989.

Wall, Robert. *Ocean Liners*. London: New Burlington Books, 1977.

Whiffen, Marcus and Koeper, Frederick. *American Architecture 1607–1976*. London: Routledge and Keegan Paul, 1981.

Williamson, Elizabeth, Riches, Anne and Higgs, Malcolm. *The Buildings of Scotland, Glasgow,* London: Penguin, 1990.

INDEX

(page numbers in italics refer to illustrations)